THE ENGLISH TRIBE

The English Tribe

Identity, Nation and Europe

Stephen Haseler
Professor of Government
London Guildhall University

First published in Great Britain 1996 by
MACMILLAN PRESS LTD
Houndmills, Basingstoke, Hampshire RG21 6XS
and London
Companies and representatives
throughout the world

A catalogue record for this book is available
from the British Library.

ISBN 0–333–65838–8 hardcover
ISBN 0–333–65839–6 paperback

First published in the United States of America 1996 by
ST. MARTIN'S PRESS, INC.,
Scholarly and Reference Division,
175 Fifth Avenue,
New York, N.Y. 10010

ISBN 0–312–16004–6

Library of Congress Cataloging-in-Publication Data
Haseler, Stephen, 1942–
The English tribe: identity, nation and Europe / Stephen
Haseler.
p.   cm.
Includes bibliographical references and index.
ISBN 0–312–16004–6
1. National characteristics, English.   2. Group identity—England–
–History—20th century.   3. Nationalism—England—History—20th
century.   4. England—Civilization—20th century.   5. England–
–Relations—Europe.   6. Europe—Relations—England.   I. Title.
DA566.4.H39   1996
305.8 ' 00941 ' 09045—dc20   95–51722
                                                                                    CIP

---

10   9   8   7   6   5   4   3   2   1
05   04   03   02   01   00   99   98   97   96

Printed in Great Britain by
Ipswich Book Co Ltd, Ipswich, Suffolk

Contents

Preface

Only a few years ago the idea that the nation-state of the United Kingdom
– the 'sovereign' political structure which has governed the people of
the British Isles for almost 300 years – was facing dissolution would
have been more than contentious. So, too, would have been the notion
that 'Englishness' – one of the world's strongest and most enduring
stereotypes and self-images, the identity and culture which I argue had
been created and sustained by this nation-state – was also facing a
potentially terminal crisis.

Yet, since then (as I attempt to outline in the Introduction) the twin
pressures of global capitalism and European union have intensified –
to the point where the unthinkable is now simply the controversial.
Although I share the view that the Single European Act and the Treaty
of Maastricht represented a quantum leap in the creation of a super-
state, there were many who believed that the European currency crises
of 1992–3 had set back the European project, possibly fatally. These
events are now proving to have been something of a false dusk; for
the new century will certainly see the emergence – in one form or
another – of a new European political and economic order.

Whether this new Europe will ultimately cohere into a federal, or a
confederal, union – and whether Britain's absorption into the union
will be slow or swift, positive or grudging – are side issues compared
to the historic content of what is happening to the British as, in the
aftermath of empire, war and cold war, we re-order our relationships
with our close neighbours. These changes which Europe is forcing on
the British are the most profound since the Civil War and the settlement of 1688–9, when the basic contours of the modern British state
and its nationhood were constructed.

Yet, instead of these dramatic events representing a time of sorrow
and nostalgia (always a tempting possibility for a culture unused to
adapting to change), they could instead become an occasion for hope.
As I attempt to outline in Chapter 6, 'Goodbye to All That', it is through
this new European dimension that we might finally achieve the elusive culture of citizenship, a written constitution and an entrenched Bill
of Rights; and we might also be induced to refashion the class structures which still inform a 'them and us' industrial culture. Also, as under
the impact of Europe we begin to witness the emergence of regional

'provinces' (including city-states), then this, too, will be a positive development – for it will allow the kind of local self-government and democracy which the centralised United Kingdom (what I call throughout this book 'the UK-state') has, up until now, refused to countenance.

Yet for many, although the loss of the nation-state is troublesome, the prospective loss of 'national identity' is traumatic. It is this anxiety which fuels not only the nationalists, Europhobes and Eurosceptics, but many more besides. Yet, as I suggest in Chapter 4, 'True Brits, Real England', for the British true 'national identities' (representing the nations, even the regions, of the British Isles) have rarely over the last 300 years been able to express themselves. For what is often meant by 'national identity' is really 'state identity' (identification not with the nations of the British Isles but with the over-arching nation-state of the United Kingdom).

We have had another problem with our 'national identity'. Are we English or are we British? And are those of us who live in England both English and British? There is little question that ever since 1707 the English have dominated the Union, and that the idea of 'English-ness' has determined British 'national identity' and 'national culture'. Yet, as I attempt to outline in Chapter 1 – in a short survey of 'the making of Englishness' – this identity was essentially contrived, and it had little to do with the lives of real English and British people. (Hence, although I use the term Englishness without quotation marks, there is a strong case for using them throughout the text.) Joel Kotkin in his influential book on race and the new global economy has described the English as a tribe. Yet this 'English tribe', supposedly possessing a 'strong sense of common origin and shared values' was not really a tribe at all (see Joel Kotkin, *Tribes*, New York, 1992, p. 4). 'English-ness' was the identity of a small caste which ran the 'tribe' and, more importantly, the state, and it became – partly by imposition, partly by acceptance – the uniform identity. Thus, the end of the UK, and the demise of this uniform identity, provides a chance to express finally the diversity of the peoples of the British Isles. This book is dedicated to a rediscovery of that diversity.

The need to modernise has been a theme of radicals and reformers for most of the twentieth century. Yet, their endeavours have largely been in vain. The culture of Englishness has been too strong for them. Although both Labour's socialism and social democracy and Thatcher's 'enterprise revolution' possessed radical modernising elements, they were all too timid, foundering on the rocks of the traditionalism of the state and its culture.

Yet, the European project is different, because it is total. It challenges, in a way in which domestic radicalism was never able to, the core institutions and values of the British state. A real 'cultural revolution' is coming from outside the shores, from beyond the water's edge – from a civilisation of which the British are certainly a part, but only a part.

As an Englishman, born when the country still – just – had an empire, and schooled when 'Empire day' was still celebrated, I too probably believed in the maxim that to be born English was to 'have drawn the top card in life'. I was certainly proud to belong to 'the English tribe'. Nationalism historically was a progressive force as it broke down feudal bonds and hierarchies. Yet, as the postwar decades rolled by and the country's power waned, I began to witness a defensiveness about national culture, a growth in provincialism, even in xenophobia. And the country's famed cultural content also began to exhibit a narrowness, a degeneration into what I describe as theme-park Englishness, or 'Englishness for export'.

Amongst those who accept much of this analysis, some will still find it difficult to contemplate life without the United Kingdom and its associated national identity – without, as some would have it, 'being British'. Long-held loyalties and affections may be involved here. Yet the state, and even the nation, have not for some time been adequate, or desirable, objects of loyalty and affection – emotions more properly directed at family, friends and locality. And, 'being British' has always been a plural phenomenon, involving a variety of identities, and a variety of nations. It is my hope that we can express this new plural and diverse reality and welcome the new European future.

London   STEPHEN HASELER

Introduction: Globalism, Europe and Identity

It seems only a few years ago that, as the self-regarding maxim had it, to be born English was to have drawn 'the top card in life'. And, reflecting this assessment, 'Englishness' had indeed become one of the world's strongest and most enduring stereotypes and self-images. As late as 1990 a literary critic-cum-travel writer, himself English, could write:

> of all nations we have perhaps the most strongly defined sense of national identity – so developed and so stylised, in fact, that we are frequently conscious of it as a burden or restraint. Willy-nilly, we take abroad with us a sense of England and our own Englishness like a precious family heirloom or, worse, like a sort of virginity to be preserved intact from all the dangers which threaten it.[1]

Yet, as the twentieth century has progressed, and the cards dealt the English have formed increasingly 'lower hands', the English (as well as the wider British) have seemingly lost their erstwhile self-confidence, have become defensive about their nationality (about 'preserving their virginity') and suspicious of forces which would threaten it: they are (we are), in fact, experiencing a serious crisis of national identity. How this crisis arose, and how it can be resolved, is the subject of this book.

To some extent the crisis is artificial, for, as I argue (in Chapter 1), 'Englishness' itself is contrived and manufactured, hardly a true reflection of the plurality and diversity of life of the English. Rather, I argue that Englishness has few popular roots, and was little more than the highly self-conscious identity of the country's aristocratic leadership as it developed and survived during the eighteenth, nineteenth and twentieth centuries. Yet as the British state (the kingdom formed in 1707 on the basis of the 1688–9 settlement) triumphed, so too did Englishness. So much so that Englishness became a national, quasi-official (almost received) identity, self-image and stereotype not just for the English but also for all the peoples of the British Isles.

And, later, as the kingdom (the United Kingdom) expanded abroad

1

into an empire, Englishness became more than an 'official' identity – it assumed the role of a cultural ideology (with a view of human nature, a basic social analysis, and codes and rules for living). However, this identity, and ideology, created during the emergence into empire, and refined during the height of empire, was – as I develop in Chapter 2, 'An Audit of Englishness' – utterly unsuitable for the British in the more egalitarian, democratic, commercial and less Anglicised world of the late twentieth century.

Incidentally, I am more than aware that throughout the chapters on Englishness I have concentrated upon what amount to male images and identities of Englishness. It would have been difficult to do otherwise. For, as Jane Mackay and Pat Thane have argued in discussing the Englishness of the English woman, English nationality was overwhelmingly a male concern. 'The Englishwoman remains a more shadowy figure than the Englishman', they argue, and not simply because the women were often seen by men as the appendages of their husbands, but also 'because ... women were believed to possess trans-national qualities ... women indeed had no fixed nationality ... had no role in the intense contemporary debate about nationhood'.[2]

With the collapse of British power (and the end of empire) Englishness, its fortunes seemingly linked to the standing of what had by then become the *United Kingdom*, lost its anchorage; and is still (on the verge of the twenty-first century) unable to come to terms with the country's reduced standing and importance in the world. Chapter 3 attempts to get to grips with this problem of identity, and outlines how the political culture of the United Kingdom, and particularly of its political elites, still imbued with ideas of 'sovereignty', 'independence', even 'national identity' itself, is utterly incongruent with the age of interdependence and globalisation. I argue that the idea of 'British independence' or 'sovereignty' became progressively redundant during the twentieth century, and fully so during the decades since the Second World War, as the country underwent a massive cultural invasion from the United States as well as witnessing its own ability to defend itself becoming dependent upon the Americans.

I also argue that as the power of Britain declined, so 'Englishness', as it had done so often before, re-touched its image and images. Whilst carrying forward some of the characteristics of its eighteenth- and nineteenth-century antecedents, it became decidedly softer. A list of the literary contributors and symbols tells the tale. Robin Hood, Dick Whittington, John Bull, Britannia, the explorers and military heroes (like Wellington and Nelson), the strong, colourful, 'hearts of oak', 'free-born Englishman' image – all gave way to a more moderate, domestic, misty, rustic, even twee, image. English liberty and English conquest made way for the English countryside – a transformation from the builders of Englishness to its inheritors.

It was, as I argued earlier, the beginning of the creation of contemporary theme-park Englishness – or, 'Englishness for export' – the cultural form of the increasingly important heritage industry. The novelist and journalist Sebastian Faulks has summed up the English theme-park as 'a place in which Dorothea Brooke gives instructions to Mrs. Bridges while Kenneth Branagh in a deerstalker is barking his shin on the bootscraper in the fog outside' – themes and images counter-poised by Sebastian Faulks to the realities of modern British loutishness: 'Whatever their [French] faults, you would normally feel you could risk sitting next to a Frenchman in a restaurant without expecting he might at any moment throw up on you.'³

This new image of Englishness was to be massively reinforced by the two great new industries of the late twentieth century – the mass media (movies, television, glossy magazines) and the travel business. The postwar movie industry set the tone with the stage Englishness of the stiff upper lip, wartime grit, twee country cottages, grand country-house shooting parties, and the upstairs–downstairs world of Lords, Ladies, butlers and chamber-maids. It was the era of Hollywood Englishness (which many within the English cultural elite contributed to even as they mocked its product). Thus the 'English' image was sent abroad – and then reflected back as the world's image of Englishness.

The new theme-park Englishness was even less representative than older forms of Englishness. Earlier constructions of national culture had possessed some kind of tangential relationship to the life and values of the old upper classes. In the real world of the very late twentieth century, with the traditional upper-class lifestyle virtually extinct, the ideal of Englishness was no longer to be found – except, perhaps, in parts of the rural horse country of Virginia.

Yet, to compound this problem of English (and British) national self-image, the UK-state has not only declined comparatively, it has, during the five post-Second World War decades, had to contemplate its erosion; and now, at the very end of the twentieth century, its effective extinction within a wider European Union. And it is this stark political transformation which is tipping an identity problem over into an identity crisis.

I argue in this book that there seems little doubt that we are now coming to the end of the British story. A thousand years of separate development (in which the last 300 years or so have seen a strong, self-conscious and highly successful nation-state) is finally drawing to its close – under the twin forces of globalisation and the dynamic of European unity.

The global capitalist system has been building by fits and starts for well over a hundred years – making its most spectacular progress since 1945, and again, after the fall of communism during the 1990s. Even the most cursory glance at the picture of this global economy shows a world in which the old-fashioned nation-state (of which the United Kingdom is a near perfect example) has lost its ability to control events. The UK can no longer manage the business cycle, fix its interest rates without regard to global and regional factors, control capital movements (and even labour movements), run a deficit without regard to other nations' deficits, and fix its own tax levels without regard to foreign tax conditions. Nor, crucially, could it defend itself during the cold war or settle alone regional conflicts. And, in order to prosecute even a small war (like the Falklands in the early 1980s) it needed the support of powerful allies.

The fateful process of global capitalism has already made redundant the old 'national sovereignty' model (to which the UK political establishment remained attached well into the 1990s). Economic globalisation means that a multiplicity of foreigners – foreign speculators, foreign companies, foreign governments, and, crucially, foreign consumers – may have a bigger long-term impact on the economic well-being of the peoples of the British Isles than do decision-makers (including consumers) within the UK's domestic boundaries. It also means that the UK-state authorities, or any individual state authority, remain relatively powerless in the face of the demands and decisions of transnational corporations (who owe loyalty to no state or nation). The global flow of trade is now more important to the future well-being of the lives of Britons than the character of the politics at Westminster; and the trade in currencies (spot trades, forward contracts, futures or options and swaps), amounting to $1000 billion in 1994, is of greater import *domestically* in the British Isles than any decision emanating from the UK Treasury (International Monetary Fund figures reported in *The Washington Post*, 17 July 1994). Such is the defeat suffered by the nation-state at the hands of global capitalism.

Globalisation's reach is cultural as well as economic. The growth in travel and tourism, the emergence of global media, and, crucially, of world-wide information network, is truly creating the famous 'global village'. And nation-states – even should they wish to – remain incapable of turning back the tide. Amongst the nation-states which would seemingly most resist the internationalisation (indeed the Americanisation) of culture is France. Yet, so powerful is the tide of global democratic culture that Coca-Cola is sold in French cafes, McDonald's thrives in Paris, 'Le Drugstore' appears on the Boulevard St Germain. And globalisation leads to cultural swaps, as a French touch appears in the fashion of young Americans: 'it has become chic to wear Vernet sunglasses and Dior ready-made clothes, to ski with Rossignol equipment, and to drink Evian water. If anything we have learned that modern culture is eclectic and porous.'[4]

Amidst this blitzkrieg of global capitalism and its culture, politics, inevitably, fights back. Political authority over global economics will be difficult to achieve; yet, it will attempt to re-assert itself in new guises (other, that is, than the nation-state) and in forms which can properly negotiate with, and regulate, the transnational corporations and the global financial players. One such form will be the worldwide supra-national institution – such as the World Trade Organisation (WTO) created by the latest GATT treaty to enforce its provisions. American nationalists are already finding this new organisation a dangerous harbinger of things to come: as an advertisement sponsored by the Citizens Trade Campaign, sponsored by the consumer-rights activist Ralph Nader, argued: 'this deal [creating the WTO] could cancel out US laws – laws that protect our environment . . . defend family farms and protect workers' rights'.[5]

Yet, the primary political response to globalisation is unlikely to reside in world bodies like the WTO or the UN. Rather, it will more probably emerge out of the regional, 'trading bloc', groupings – a dynamic which the late twentieth-century British experience in Europe can testify to. And, in Europe's case (though not yet in those of the North American, Pacific and South-East Asian blocs), even formal, legal, political control over economics no longer resides exclusively, and sometimes even *primarily*, with the old nation-state governments. The UK-state formally surrendered its legal sovereignty when, in 1972, the British 'sovereign' Parliament acquiesced in the legal requirement of the European Community that where European and British law conflicted then European law would prevail.

Whatever form European union ultimately takes, it will inevitably – as I attempt to outline in Chapter 5 – supplant the United Kingdom as the dominant political forum in which the shape and character of the lives of the peoples of the British Isles are determined. For a time in the early 1990s – under the twin pressures of German reunification and recession – it seemed that further European unity might come to a shuddering halt. Yet this proved to be a false dusk, and by the mid-1990s it appeared that the Union (including the British) were on the verge of a further bout of integration – the road to a single currency and the reality, if not the title, of fully fledged federalism.

Difficult though it was for the UK establishment to accept, the key dynamic forcing the precise arrangements within their European home in the 1990s was the Franco-German political alliance. On top of the global pressures for union, there was a fateful congruence of interests between the old-style national leaderships in Paris and Bonn. The French, seriously worried about the emergence of a strong, independent Germany in the heart of Europe, and in the interest of anchoring Germany to the West, were prepared to abandon their own 'national sovereignty' in what, no matter the protestations to the contrary, would amount to a federal Europe. And the German leadership, who were seeking a larger political role for themselves – and a mechanism for constraining their own nationalists for all time – were seeking to subsume the whole German state (including the prized Bundesbank) within a federal Europe. It was a further measure of how empty the idea of 'the sovereignty of the United Kingdom' had become, that the political class in Britain had, on an issue which would decide its fate, become essentially a by-stander.

Yet – as I argue in Chapter 6, 'Goodbye to All That' – as a radical agent for change, the European dynamic, working its will upon the traditional structures and values of the UK-state, may succeed where generations of declaratory radicals – Liberals, Radical–Liberals, Labourists, Social Democrats, Socialists, Socialist intellectuals, trade unionists – have failed. Britain's social establishment, and most of its *ancien régime* class institutions, were, to some extent or another, legitimised and sanctified by the power and resonance of a UK-state which, at the very end of the twentieth century, was no longer in control of its erstwhile territory. Europe, by widening horizons and boundaries, marginalises all the major English class institutions – the monarchy, the Lords, the established church, the public schools, the Oxbridge colleges, the BBC, the Whitehall establishment – and by widening the field upon which they play, opens them up to competition from other centres of influence.

Thus, after the false dawns of Labourism in 1945 and Thatcherism in the 1980s, the real 'cultural revolution' is coming from outside the shores, from beyond the water's edge. And, as the British people are released from the exclusive political control of the UK-state, they will be enabled constitutionally – as the European Union, over time, provides the long sought-after radical demand of a written constitution enforced by a constitutional court.

Yet perhaps the most profound of all the changes driven by Europe is the contribution it makes to the breaking asunder of the unitary character of the United Kingdom. By weakening the nation-state (the UK) from above, Europe has helped unleash the growth of sub-state nationalism from below – particularly in Scotland.

During its time as a strong and successful state, the UK (like other multi-ethnic and multi-cultural states) encouraged the idea that the 'nation-state' and 'nation' were interchangeable. As Mathew Horsman and Andrew Marshall have argued, 'the nation-state was . . . required to create a myth of "nation" to attract each succeeding generation to its bosom. In this way, a shared history, a mythisised past, a series of rituals, common attitudes and invented traditions are created and disseminated in relentless fashion.'[6] And now that this myth is exploded the contrived political construct which is the unitary state of the UK – which over the last 300 years has imposed itself over and above the various 'national' and cultural diversities in the British isles – stands exposed.

The end of the British nation-state (the United Kingdom of Great Britain and Northern Ireland), and the 'national' identity it fostered, is, for many contemporary English writers and commentators, a time for regret and sorrow. I must confess that I look at the end of 'the island story' from the opposite vantage-point. The state was in many aspects undemocratic and stubbornly pre-modern; and as I have already argued (and develop in Chapter 4) the national identity of 'Englishness' was not only seriously unrepresentative but also damaging.

I used to agree with the antecedents of today's Eurosceptics that a European super-state was an unreal proposition. Yet, since the early 1970s the reach of the global capitalism has been breathtaking, and the collapse of communism, and the consequent disengagement of the Americans from Europe, has fundamentally altered the geo-political map. Britain is no longer able to keep its distance from Europe now that the presence of its powerful patron on the other side of the Atlantic is nowhere near what it used to be. And it is disengaging with an injunction to Britain to be 'at the heart of Europe'. As the departing US ambassador to Britain argued in 1994 'There is a simple observation that if Britain's voice is less influential in Paris or Bonn, it is likely to be less influential in Washington.'[7]

The transition of the peoples of the British Isles from their bounding by the UK-state – and into a global economy and a European fate –

will, however, not be without its difficulties (as I also outline in Chapter 5). Those who find it hardest to adjust are the old (the generation who measure Europe by their experiences in the Second World War) and some specific elites – those who have done very well out of the old nation-state together with contemporary Westminster politicians whose careers are invested in it. And domestic resistance to Europe can still lead to a nationalist resurgence and even the re-alignment of the political parties.

Yet, ultimately, there are limits to the viability of UK nationalism. The alternative vision it presents – of an off-shore island, outside of the European Union, attempting, with a population of over fifty million, to compete in the world rather like the 'Asian Tigers' – is hardly convincing. Nor, ultimately, is an appeal to 'the island mentality', 'the British way of life', to British separateness. The fact is that life in post-Second World War Britain – where millions enjoyed hitherto unknown prosperity and stability – has been tolerable not *because* of our sovereign independence and separateness, but, on the contrary, because of our 'integration' into the Western trading and financial system and its economic co-prosperity sphere. Nationalists tend to forget that their audience is the children of the Marshall Plan as much as the Maypole.

1 The Making of Englishness

In the mid-fifth century three small ships – carrying no more than a few hundred barbarian soldiers – embarked from the sand-dunes and pine-woods of Germany, crossed the North Sea, and fetched up on the pebble ridge of Pegwell Bay. The English had arrived in Britain.[1]

The English are, of course, German: Germans from Jutland, Germans from the 'Anglen' in Denmark (the origin of 'Anglo'), Germans from Lower Saxony. In an early display of good manners these German tribes came to Britain in the fifth century AD not by conquest but rather by invitation – issued by their Celtic host, the British leader Vortigern, after the Romans had left. Yet these same English, brought in as mercenaries to help stabilise the civilised parts of the island, soon developed ambitions of their own, and when the British attempted to cut their rations, they seized land on which to raise their own food. 'These ferocious Saxons', wrote the monk Gilda, were like wolves brought into the fold, 'pretending that they were going to fight for our country, but really to fight against it'.[2]

In the resulting struggle this 'Battle of Britain' was won by the English. The rebellious English mercenaries called upon their Germanic kinspeople across the North Sea to help them, and soon a German-derived English community of warriors was established in Britain. In an early sign of superior ruthlessness the English massacred a large part of the British leadership class after having invited them to a peace conference.

England was born as the English established a beachhead in the eastern part of the island (in East Anglia and Kent). After the British leader Arturius ('King Arthur') died, and the British (the Celts) dissolved in warring factions and warlordism, the English – reinforced by a wave of English immigrants – mopped up most of the rest of the island south of Scotland and east of Wales. And as England took hold, the British retreated to the 'celtic' regions of the island and across the sea to Brittany.

For four hundred years these Germanic tribes which called themselves English, and spoke dialects of what they called *Englisc*, spread out into the new polity of England, the Saxons into south-east England

9

and Wessex ('West Saxons') and the Angles into the rest.

The English were really Germans. They were also provincial and heathen; until, that is, Christianity came to the German tribes during the sixth and seventh centuries, bringing with it a continental influence – primarily through the increased use of Latin. These Germans, now the early English, were also rather stand-offish. They did not intermarry with the local Celts, nor did they adopt or inherit any of the local institutions (either Roman or Celtic) of the lands they occupied.

Yet they increasingly consolidated their hold on the lands south of Scotland and east of Wales. They also managed to accommodate, and finally incorporate, a major new tribe (again of Germanic origin), the Vikings (or Danes), following the series of Viking raids which ended in the eleventh century with a Danish king on the throne of a more or less united English polity. Thus, on the eve of the Norman invasion, the answer to the question 'who were the English?' remains fairly straightforward. Essentially, by today's standards, they were hardly much of an ethnic mix – basically Germans of one form or another, with more than a touch of Germanic Danish thrown in!

In the first decade of the eleventh century another continental tribe (the Frenchified Normans – like the Germans, also of Indo-European descent) was to add itself into the mix (if not, yet, the melting pot) that was England. Unlike the Germans, the Normans came to the island – in 1066 – uninvited, and by superior technology and organisation clearly established an ascendancy. Thus, some eight hundred and seventy-eight years before another cross-channel invasion (D-Day), German tribes (calling themselves English) were fighting Frenchified Normans (another highly mobile Germanic tribe) on English soil for the soul of England and Englishness. And 'the French' won, though not in the same way that the original Germans had prevailed over the British (who either left or were expelled).

The old Germanic tribes took some time to accommodate themselves to England's new rulers. A powerful myth developed in which the true English (the Germans) were portrayed as living under an oppressive regime – the 'Norman Yoke'. Yet, the Norman addition to Englishness gave it a more literate dimension (as well as giving the English language many hundreds of new, French and Latin, words). And, politically, England's new ruling class united the peoples in a way that the Germanic tribes (including their famous leader King Alfred) were unable to do.

England's ethnic mix settled down somewhat after 1066. So the country (England could just about be called 'a country' by then) entered the

second millennium not only as a decided part of the European continent (as it had been under the Romans) but primarily populated, as
were large swathes of the continent itself, by the descendants of an
identifiable Germanic culture and ethnicity. As the English developed
and evolved during the twentieth century there were to be no further
major continental additions to the population to compare with the events
of the fifth and sixth centuries and 1066. Neither the threatened French
invasions of the early nineteenth century, nor operation 'Sea Lion',
the 1940 invasion plan of a new wave of Germans, came to anything.
Nor were there to be any new mutations of the basic character of the
language (English retained its fundamental Germanic structure even
though the country was dominated by French-speaking Normans for
several centuries).

Some centuries later, Flemish, Huguenots, Jews, Welsh, Scots, Irish,
West Indians, Indians and Pakistanis, and other immigrants to England, would join the ranks of the English – an enriching of Englishness which the putative mid-twentieth-century German military invasion
would, had it succeeded, have both unravelled and stopped.

ORIGINS

A serious idea of Englishness – a self-awareness of England and its
people as a sharply separate and distinctive cultural entity – did not
begin to cohere until the eighteenth century, alongside the emergence
of nationalism.

Yet, some historians locate a self-conscious Englishness much, much
earlier. Some point to the Normans as England's nation-builders, the
creators of a united people, and thus as the founders of Englishness.
They point to the fragmentary quality of life before the Normans, of
disparate tribal loyalties, of divisions between chieftains. Norman Cantor,
perhaps the premier American medievalist, even calls the administration of Anglo-Saxon England 'the government of the absurd', agree-
ing with F. W. Maitland that England only got under way through the
centralising political genius of the Normans.[3]

The historian Geoffrey Elton, on the other hand, locates 'the effective creation of the Kingdom of England' some hundred and forty years
before the Norman Conquest, in AD 927 – the year the King of Wessex
established control over the Danish and English parts of Northumbria.
Indeed it was these same Northumbrian English who produced that

'decisive maker of the English people' the Venerable Bede. It was the
Bede who suggested, even as early as the late ninth century, before a
single country of England had a single English king, that there was 'a
remarkably precocious sense of common "Englishness", and not just
in politically interested circles.'[4]

Elton comes down firmly in favour of a pre-Norman view of the
origins of Englishness. He argues that what the Normans inherited,
following their decisive victory in 1066, was an 'English kingdom peopled
by an English nation' which was 'united to a degree unknown at this
time in either France or Germany'.[5]

Part of Elton's argument is that the early English kings and the English
Catholic church were both unifying factors. However, monarchy and
religion as agents for the founding of England are two-edged swords.
The early English kings (like Offa of Mercia or Ine of Wessex) certainly established some laws of rulership which would later serve to
impose a state upon the peoples of England, but these early kings remained, in reality, chieftains of regions, contributing to the political
fragmentation of the islands. Also, there is considerable evidence that
the most famous of all the early English kings, Alfred the Great (reigning
in the late ninth century) attempted to re-unite the English and the
continent through a a flowering of learning and scholarship (specifically, by translating Latin scripts into English). And, although the church
could also be viewed as an agency 'turning the settled bands of peasant
warriors into a people', it was also, until the late sixteenth century, a
decidedly anti-national force – the 'one universal church' limiting the
development of separatist Englishness by its transnational character and
loyalties.[6]

So some argue that it was the thirteenth century, almost two hundred years into Norman-controlled England, that saw a decisive step
towards an identifiable sense of Englishness. The baronial revolts against
royalist Norman power that peppered the thirteenth century finally gave
forth, during the reign of Henry III, to what Elton has described as a
'communitas Angliae' – a real English community, embodying an English
nation, which increasingly spoke for that nation, or collectivity of peoples,
(often against kings more interested in military conflicts in France)
through parliamentary meetings. Certainly, by the time Henry III's son
Edward I took over he was recognising this new reality, and playing
to a new national gallery when he stirred up patriotic feelings against
the French king: 'it is his detestable purpose, which God forbid, to
wipe out the English tongue'.[7]

Others believe that the Hundred Years War between England and

France (which broke out in 1337) created an English national consciousness. Indeed, so successful were the English – they seemed to
win most every battle they entered, against a much larger military force
(at Crécy they were outnumbered by three to one, at Poitiers by five
to one) – that 'perhaps for the first time, though certainly not for the
last, the English began to suspect that God was an Englishman'.[8]

Even more than war, however, the physical separation of an island
people from the continent was always a powerful factor separating the
Germanic tribes in England from those in the rest of northern Europe.
And language, too, was also beginning to play a vital role; indeed the
story of the development of the English language – and its battle with
French and Latin after the Conquest – may present us with a key to
unlocking the mystery of the emergence of this early phase of English
identity.

Although, following the Norman invasion, French became the official
language of government – of court, society and the educated classes –
it always remained a minority language. Georges Bourcier argues that
'the peasantry were barely touched by any cultural revolution' although
French remained 'a badge of good social standing'.[9] And Robert Claiborne
reports that 'by 1300, in fact, nearly everyone in England spoke English', what today we describe as 'Old English'.[10] And for most of the
people English was their only language. As a poet in the reign of
Edward I wrote:

> Common men know no French
> Among a hundred scarcely one.

And these 'common people' – as some historians have continued to
call them – increasingly saw French as a mark of foreignness.[11]

There was certainly an English consciousness alive in the heartfelt
words of the thirteenth-century introduction to the famous biblical poem
'Cursor Mundi', a book 'translated into English for the love of the
English people, English people of England, and for the common man
to understand'.[12] Yet, as late as the fourteenth century, the universities
and the upper classes were still resisting English – preferring French
and Latin – and thus the English peoples remained linguistically divided, a major limitation on the growth of national consciousness.

The English language made its great breakthrough in the late fourteenth
century. English was adopted as the official language of government
(Henry V was the first king to use English in the court documents)
and the great storyteller–poet of the English language, Geoffrey Chaucer,

appeared on the scene. The communications revolution in printing and publishing (led by William Caxton) which took hold in the fifteenth-century established the hegemony of English amongst the English and within England; and Caxton chose English (in fact, London-English – the brand of English prevalent in London – there being several English's) as his published language. In an intriguing sign of the times the association of London brewers decided in 1422 to make English the 'official' language of their written documents.

And then there was William Shakespeare. When his chronicle plays appeared English was transformed from a primitive form of communication into the language of a new learning, a process helped forward too by the publication and wide dissemination in 1604 of the King James Bible – published in English! Some one hundred and fifty years later, by the time of the publication of Dr Johnson's seminal English Dictionary (1755), the English language was fast becoming not only a major language but the primary cultural agency for the spread of English manners and ideas – of Englishness.

Of course, this emergence of an increasingly popular and standardised English was crucial to consciousness of being English. Yet, even whilst this standardised English was destroying French and Latin in Britain it remained seriously fragmented by dialect, a diversity which, intriguingly, has lasted well into the television age of the late twentieth century.

In fact the age of Shakespeare (and Marlowe), the late sixteenth century, saw not only a flowering of the popularity and usage of the English language (what is now called Medieval English) but also a confluence of great events. It was the age of the Reformation, arguably a seminal event in the building of the English nation-state. The Reformation (guided by Thomas Cromwell) saw an increment in the growth of English national sensibility, caused by an increasing sense of separateness resulting from the religious differences between the English state and the continental religious system led by Rome. This debate concerning the authority of the English king and common law over that of the Pope and canon law was tailor-made for incipient nationalists.

It was also the age of the Renaissance – which added thousands of new words to the English language, thus further enhancing its unifying potential. And, at the same time, England and the English were becoming a serious maritime power and people, a process which, by bringing a warrior people into contact with 'foreigners', enhanced their sense of identity and separateness, and also their sense of exceptionalism. No wonder Shakespeare could talk of a 'sceptr'd isle set in a silver sea' which was 'the envy of less fortunate lands' – the Shake-spearian braggadocio which, without a hint of irony, was, incredibly, recycled as late as 1994 as part of a television advertisement for tea.

Some decades later, the second (Oliver) Cromwell would add to the work of the first (Thomas) Cromwell. Ideologically, the parliamentary forces in England's Civil War were suffused with nationalist senti-ment. The idea of a 'chosen people' – albeit possessed by a liberal, anti-authoritarian, rationalist mentality – runs through much parliamentary proselytising. The militant protestantism of the Parliamentary forces had, after all, tended to advance the idea of the English as 'chosen'. Bishop Aylmer had declared 'God is an Englishman' as early as 1558! And the Stuarts, by enlisting Irish and Scots on the side of the King, only served to reinforce this growing English sensibility not only amongst the victors of the Civil War, but amongst the broader English radical tradition.

However, there remained strict limits to the growth of English self-consciousness. Even as late as the early eighteenth century, life in England was still very cosmopolitan – specifically in its higher reaches. In his seminal work *The Rise of English Nationalism*, Gerald Newman provides an intriguing insight into how aristocratic supremacy in Brit-ain in the eighteenth century was a source of cosmopolitanism. His argument is, basically, that landed aristocrats consolidated and enhanced their position during this period – with huge profits – but also cul-turally differentiated themselves from the rest of the population by a cosmopolitanism (particularly an affectation of Frenchism in manners). They were a confident, international elite, in Newman's words, 'Fine Fellows travelling in the age of cosmopolitanism'.

But the French-speaking English aristocracy also contributed to the emergence, below the surface of the landed elite, of a reaction, amongst the 'common people' – as the 'lower orders' began using their com-mon use of English to assert what was beginning to amount to a somewhat aggressive underground national patriotism. This patriotic sensibility clustered around the English language was not, though, to burst forth until some time after the revolutionary events in France at the very end of the eighteenth century. (Although, for a time, the aristocracy was beginning to look somewhat politically isolated, after the French Revolution and the French revolutionary wars they too adopted, in-deed led, the cause of national patriotism.)

In the meantime, during the early part of the eighteenth century there developed something of a contest between aristocrats and bourgeois as to who was the purest cosmopolitan:

The aristocrat defended his superiority by ridiculing the upstart, and by exaggerating the purity of his own cosmopolitan tastes. In travel as in dress he was driven to devise 'modes more exclusive'. The unmistakeable sign of this was the founding in the late 1760s of the Macaroni Club, whose members distinguished themselves by gulping pasta from their butter plates. While thousands were now rattling across the channel for their 'brief round of travel', the Beau Monde, brandishing spaghetti, showed that they had gone all the way to Italy.[13]

Cosmopolitanism was more, though, than 'gulping pasta'. It had a decidedly cerebral dimension. Eighteenth-century England saw England's elites (many largely traceable to the Normans) still seriously imbued with French cultural and intellectual influences. Anglo-French intercourse was routine. The rationalism of Voltaire – which was a powerful intellectual force amongst some English elites – empowering the growth of universalist notions and thus limiting English (and, just as important, French) consciousness.

Also, during the previous century, north-western Europe (and not least the British Isles) had witnessed a veritable scientific revolution which respected no national boundaries or emerging national cultures. And this new respect for science, together with the growing penchant for global exploration, served to secure the idea of the underlying unity of mankind – and thus inhibit the developing sense of national identity.

Thus, in the early decades of the eighteenth century, it was by no means certain that what was later to become a strong (indeed fierce) national consciousness would indeed emerge. The British Isles was still a decidedly plural place. Although all the trends pointed towards unification and commonality, the sheer diversity of the country was still evident: peasants co-existed uneasily with aristocrats and a growing bourgeoisie (both of which possessed serious cultural links to the continent); identities were fragmented, linked to a thousand locales, and perhaps a few regions, there was a wide diversity of ethnicity (including fragmented Celts, Huguenots, Jews, as well as varieties of English); and there were two, sometimes three languages spoken in the land. None of this augured well for the development of a unified national consciousness. The only unifying element – potentially working against all this diversity – was the English landed aristocracy. Yet, as we have seen, they were, because of their cosmopolitan interests, to discourage a unified national sensibility – at least for a while!

THE INCUBATION: 'LAND, CLASS AND RACE'

Yet all of this was soon to change. In the space of a few short decades in the latter part of the eighteenth century the idea of England began to form, contributing one of the world's strongest national identities to the age of nationalism.

Some historians are quite precise about this birth of national consciousness. Newman argues that 'the English quest for National Identity began around 1750 and was subsequently complete by 1830'.[14] And Linda Colley, in her weighty and comprehensive account of the birth of the nation, also suggests that it was during the eighteenth-century that a sense of British national identity was 'forged'.[15] Geoffrey Elton also locates the pivotal period as what he describes as 'the long eighteenth century'.

Yet, the eighteenth century saw more than the emergence of a national sensibility. It also witnessed the making of the form – or character – that such an English identity would possess. It was, thus, the incubation in which the *culture* of Englishness – its very DNA – was born. And the culture nurtured in this incubation was to last for well over 200 years. It was to dominate the islands in which it was born, determining not only their cultural development but their politics, economics and social development as well. And it was to expand overseas and provide the culture and ideology of rule for one-third of the globe.

This Englishness, born in the eighteenth century, was, therefore, premodern, certainly pre-industrial. The industrial revolution was getting under way some time *after* the idea of Englishness had been formed, and thus 'the English idea', although it used and managed industrialism, *and also survived it*, was, remarkably, hardly touched by what was perhaps the most significant contribution the English people made to modern civilisation. Instead of coming to represent commerce and democracy (as did the American idea a century or so later) Englishness was built upon a pre-industrial trinity of 'land', 'class' and 'race'.

The English idea, formed in an era of landed power, before middle- and working-class males and women even achieved the vote, was also pre-democratic. Englishness was an exclusive affair. During its formation, the peoples of the islands were no part of the idea of Englishness; they were, in fact, excluded from contributing to it. Rather, Englishness was the property, and reflection, of the caste that solidified its hold on the country at the time when England (by then called Britain, and, later still, to be called the United Kingdom) was about to take off as the world's leading power.

During this crucial era land was power – economically, politically and, through private control of the emerging literary world, culturally too. And it was owned by a very small group indeed. Setting the tone for the later development of Englishness, these landowners were decidedly non-entrepreneurial – most of their ancestors had either stolen land or acquired it by nefarious practices in the politics of the court. In fact, 'these men of noble and gentle status', who 'owned virtually all the land', 'exploited it in the main by offering it on long leases to farmers who employed a paid and landless labour force'.[16] Yet, they went unchallenged by the slow and uneven development of English radicalism, and consolidated themselves into what amounted to 'a new unitary ruling class'. 'Nobles and notables closed ranks and became more homogeneous in terms of wealth, marriage patterns, lifestyles and ambition.'[17]

This historic formation of a new class was preceded by a major demographic upheaval in which a large portion of the country's elite in effect disappeared because of their inability to produce male heirs.[18] Thus distant male cousins, and sometimes even women, were to become part of this fateful landed interest. These founders of Englishness had also admitted to the fold some landed families from the Celtic peripheries, many of them, of course, originally English. During the eighteenth century Scots, Welsh and Irish landed folk moved south, some of them to be closer to the heart of the developing global trading system; and some English landowners, anticipating a profit during a period in which land prices and profitability were rising, moved into estates on the Celtic fringes.

Colley argues that this mixing of English and Celts amounted to the arrival of a new *British* landed establishment.[19] Yet, although this newly forged ethnic mix of a class was real enough (even though there were a number of supposed 'Scots' and 'Welsh' who were really English) it hardly matters. For the fact was that the English dominated this class, with most of the arriviste Celts being more than willing to become 'honorary Englishmen'.

Thus did English culture, manners and politics, somewhat invigorated from outside, continue undisturbed. Like a dress-rehearsal for so many who were to follow them – nineteenth-century businessmen, twentieth-century professionals and the lower middle classes – these upper-class Celts (if that was what they were) were simply assimilated into the mould of Englishness.

This eighteenth-century landed elite was to fuse land and class in a manner which would create the peculiar character of the English class system – and become such a pronounced part of the cult of English-ness – for the next two hundred years. Englishness not only became virtually synonymous with a culture of class distinction, it also still stands starkly apart from other types of class systems. Whereas most of the industrialised world formed their modern classes – and thus their contemporary class sense – during the age of industrialism, pro-ducing the hierarchies of capitalism (a large middle class of business entrepreneurs and professionals, and a 'blue-collar' working class), the English social hierarchy was forged by land: the ownership of it, the relationship to it. And this, essentially feudal, perspective of social hierarchy – infused with, overlaying, and underlying the more normal capitalist classes of the nineteenth century – is what has made the English class system seem both so intriguing and so perverse.

At the heart of this newly-created Englishness was the remarkable and resilient English social idea of the 'Gentleman'. So powerful was this new social form that two centuries later it was a recognised social type for the twentieth century's world-wide media audience. 'The English gentleman' had established itself in the global culture in a manner which simply cannot apply to a 'French gentleman' or an 'American gentleman' (or, for the contemporary English, 'Indian gentleman', which still has a patronising tone about it!).

'I was by birth a gentleman' said Oliver Cromwell in a speech to Parliament in 1654, 'living neither in any considerable height, nor yet in obscurity.' Yet, this idea of 'the gentleman' as a middling kind of middle-class person did not last. In eighteenth-century England the notion of 'the gentleman' emerged from the idea that civilised life and man-ners were the product of a propertied, landed existence. This idea de-rived from the lifestyle of 'the gentry' – the property-owning medieval middle class of thegns and knights who, in return for enjoying the property of their social betters, paid off their feudal lords and kings – as it developed in earlier centuries. The gentry, and gentlemen, though, were essentially an officer class existing under the nobility, but acting as another layer of authority placed above the rest of the, non-landed, population.

Conceptions of race, and racial superiority, also make their appear-ance in this formative period for Englishness. The eighteenth century saw a dramatic expansion of research by the English into the origins of the English, and the growing understanding of common ethnic ori-gins led to an interest in the racial background of the people of the islands, racial classification, and inevitably, in racial braggadocio and ranking. This was the time when the first 'stirrings' of an idea of distinction between 'French' and 'Gallic' on the one hand, and 'Anglo-Saxon' on the other, took root.

Much literary sentiment in the late eighteenth century was decidedly racist. Not only was the white man superior to the black, brown and yellow (an unshakeable assumption at this formative time in British colonial life) but the English – or Anglo-Saxon – was also considered to be superior (in particular, more honest and trustworthy) to the white 'foreigner' from the continent. 'It was no accident... that John Bull himself, largely an invention of the 1750s (though with roots earlier), was already by the sixties acquiring definition in English periodical literature as a "very worthy, plain, honest old gentleman, of Saxon descent".'[20]

These racist ideas were relatively tame compared with the scientific racism to come later in Victorian times; however, they formed part of a more general belief in the superiority of the English. God became an Englishman (intriguingly he was never a Briton) not by revelation but rather by stages. In Plantagenet England the elite had developed a good line in propaganda in which anti-foreign sentiment was mixed with a view of the English as 'God's elect', an idea which was still alive and well as it infused much of the puritanism and parliamentarianism of the seventeenth century. Indeed, Oliver Cromwell saw the English he led as almost divine – putting this awesome thought in a declaration in 1654: 'the dispensations of the Lord have been as if he has said, thou art my first born, my delight amongst the nations'.

Much other literary rhetoric, if not exactly seeing the English as divine, none the less saw them as inherently exceptional and superior. In the fifteenth century, in the grandly titled *The Governance of England*, Sir John Fortescue had given '*lasting currency* ... to two English convictions: that every other realm groaned under despots and that everywhere else the peasantry had to live on mere vegetables, while in England Kings governed with the active consent of their subjects and people ate good red meat'.[21] This 'currency' certainly lasted into the eighteenth century and beyond. But the eighteenth century was to focus and legitimise this innate notion of exceptionalism – in a nation-building anti-French consensus.

This eighteenth-century ideology of Englishness had as its unifying feature – paradoxically – a very non-ideological notion: a disdain for general ideas and theories. 'Land, class and race' meant familiarity and tradition. Reason, by contrast, became suspect. It undermined the social order, which was the primary concern of the new landed class.

Subversive ideas of universal rights had appeared during the Civil

War amongst some of the more extreme supporters of the Parliament. Closer to home, eighteenth-century radicals were beginning to set their demands for change to the existing order in terms of abstract principles, such as 'liberty'. Eighteenth-century England's most prominent radical, John Wilkes, was developing a potentially combustible mix of patriotism and universal rights – 'O sweet liberty! Wilkes and Liberty! Old English Liberty!' went the refrain.

Englishness defined in these terms would have taken a very different course. It would have become an essentially revolutionary ideology – rather in the manner of 'Americanness': which had set out on its own separate journey during the eighteenth century, and was indeed revolutionary, being based upon abstract ideas of political equality and freedom, principles which would cohere into the powerful twentieth-century ideology of democracy.

Englishness, though, fell under the guiding hand of an establishment which, viscerally hostile to both the French and American revolutionary traditions, remained sceptical not only about reason, and about first principles, but about intellectuals too. Thus, Englishness came to embrace an anti-intellectualism, and intellectuals were perceived as being hostile to established order, essentially creatures of the city – proselytising their urban values and seeking to undermine the settled culture of the rural swathes of landed England.

Thus did Englishness – as it echoed down the centuries to the present time – come to elevate the traditional, the familiar and the practical (indeed 'the practical man' assumed a special place in the national roll-call of honour). And in the process, Englishness subtly, and not so subtly, devalued the intellect, the imagination, indeed creativity itself. In England, though nowhere else, you could even be 'too clever by half' – a term of mild derision.

Englishness's theorists have always denied that their conservative ideas amount to anything as 'crude' as an 'ideology'. Instead, they are described as 'instincts', 'views', or, as High-Tory theorist Ian Gilmour suggests in one of the most comprehensive accounts of English conservatism, 'themes'.[22] Indeed, many adherents of Englishness would hardly dissent from Keith Thomas's half tongue-in-cheek depiction of its guiding idea: as 'Parliament, Magna Carta, roast beef, and plum pudding' (as against, as he puts it, 'the wooden-shoes of the downtrodden, ragout-eating, Catholic French').[23]

The ideology of Englishness was not, like many other ideologies, based upon universal rules. It was, in fact, like all nationalisms, particularist rather than universal. But it was an ideology none the less

– as powerful and influential in its time (and its time is still, just, with us) as Liberalism, Socialism or Fascism. And it has held the British in its sway as much as Democracy has held the Americans – and longer and more completely than Communism has held the Russians.

BUILDING THE NATION

This 'non-ideological' ideology of Englishness – the mix of 'land, class and race' – was to become the official ideology of a new nation-state. As the eighteenth century progressed, the idea of the nation-state (of nationalism) progressed with it. If, as Peter Fortudo suggests, 'the later seventeenth century was the time when the language of patriotism became firmly established in the repertoire of English political rhetoric' then the middle to late 1770s was the time when this patriotic sentiment became national, and nationalistic, in tone.[24] It was during this eighteenth century that the patriotic anti-French hero Jack Tar appeared on the scene, as did the pugnacious cartoon character John Bull (who was to remain a symbol of England even as late as the Second World War). Also, an early version of 'God Save the King' was first performed in 1745, and the nationalistic sea-song 'Hearts of Oak' (written in 1759) was widely performed.

This new nation-state was, of course, not England, but rather Britain – created by the Act of Union of 1707 – a Union which, in itself, probably gave something of a boost to nationalist sentiment, as there was now a political institution, as well as a well-defined landmass surrounded by sea, to rally around.

Yet even more important was the role played by the aristocratic leadership of the new nation-state. This landed aristocracy, no matter its changing character, was the one great over-arching, or truly 'national', social force in the England and Britain of the eighteenth century – thus always potentially able to impose its ideas upon the rest of the population. However, as we have seen, the cosmopolitan fancies of many aristocrats and 'gentlemen' were somewhat at odds with the 'stirrings' of eighteenth-century nationalism. And cosmopolitanism – or pretensions to it – died hard. After all, French manners and Latin words had helped set these elites apart from 'the common people' in the first place; and ideas of national identity (and national exceptionalism) were, ultimately, socially unifying and even democratic (as they applied to all, not just to the few).

So, with much of the anti-aristocratic dissent, protest and radicalism of the period taking on a very distinctive patriotic tinge, the English nobility faced a choice: between embracing patriotism and nationalism (and siding with the lower orders and the burgeoning bourgoisie) or, by keeping themselves distinct, allowing radicals to stir up nationalist sentiment against them.

In what amounted to one of the most momentous social developments in British history, the landed leaders of England chose patriotism, and, inevitably, nationalism. And not surprisingly so. For, as the eighteenth century came to its close, Britain was becoming a home for aristocrats – a stable island of privilege in a world of revolutionary upheaval. French revolutionary ideas were seen as posing a direct threat to the social order – to the aristocracy – in Britain. The fear was growing that the British aristocracy might go the same way as the French. So, many aristocrats stopped flaunting French clothes and speech, and instead placed themselves at the head of what amounted to a nationalist cultural revolution – the effects of which are still with us well into the latter part of the twentieth century. (Intriguingly, the landed English were never again to return to cosmopolitan ways, to a trans-national lifestyle or sympathy, not even in the late twentieth century when many of their heirs and imitators became ostentatiously provincial!)

By compromising with the new age of nationalism, the English aristocracy's ideology of Englishness was not only preserved, it expanded – embraced by many amongst the broader population. Thus, the growth of national sentiment in this crucial eighteenth century acted as a transmission belt for these landed-class ideas of Englishness – carrying them not only to the lower orders but also through to the next century and beyond. Every ratchet upwards in national consciousness reinforced the ideas of land, class and race formed in this period of incubation.

The threat of revolution which turned the aristocracy to nationalism was part of a more general awareness of 'foreignness'. A sense of being English (and political support for England, or Britain) was induced not so much by militant domesticity as, with all nationalisms, by an emerging rejection of 'alien' *otherness* – in this case the twin 'othernesses' of Catholicism and Frenchness.

Ever since Henry VIII the idea of a Protestant England set against a Catholic continent had been a subtle, though powerful, image in the forging of national identity. Yet these religious roots of Englishness have rarely been given the recognition they deserve. Perhaps one of the reasons is that, until recently, historians have tended to concentrate less upon the divisions between Protestants and Catholics and more upon the conflicts within Protestantism (see Colley, Ch. 1). Also, the role of religion in creating an English national identity – which centred around the idea that England's Protestantism separated her from Catholic Europe – was increasingly mixed up with a more political hostility towards France. France, and Frenchness, perhaps even more than Catholicism – which was often seen as France's agent – became the primary symbol of the alien 'other'.

It is hardly surprising that France and the French should figure prominently in the building of English nationalism. For the nationalist English this gnawing fear of the French was always understandable. The turbulent events of revolutionary England in the seventeenth century had led to the exile of the Stuarts, and for the next sixty years or so the country was faced with a series of invasion scares and insurrections orchestrated from France by the ousted dynasty. They tried an invasion of Scotland in 1708, and in 1715 there was a serious uprising throughout Scotland and parts of northern England in favour of James Edward Stuart (seeking to become James III), who some thirty years later was still at it, launching an invasion which came close to capturing the capital. Of course, the ideological battles and political loyalties which swirled around the Hanover–Stuart feud will have fed a growth in hostility to France, but by far the most significant reaction came from those – not least the traders and merchants – whose life would have been severely disrupted by the upheavals of a Stuart revolution and restoration.

Also, the events of 1789 in France – that 'other' identity by which Englishness could be measured, encouraged, and honed – posed both a revolutionary and, later, a geo-political threat to the British state. 'More than twice as long as the First and Second World Wars added together, the wars against Revolutionary and Napoleonic France were almost as geographically extensive as far as British involvement was concerned.'[25] And in order to prosecute this bitter world-wide conflict, the London government employed the kind of patriotic propaganda and ceremonial which could only intensify the already growing sense of Englishness, a conscious identity which was even further enhanced by the taking up of arms, and the spilling of blood, by the English masses in the anti-French cause.

And, of course, the sea helped. In these conflagrations with the French, in which real threats existed on the other side of the water, 'England' became an island, a splendid, isolated island, cut off from continental troubles, an image which could only but reinforce the critically important idea of English separateness.

In this very conducive political environment the idea of Englishness was given a huge shot in the arm – certainly among the literary classes – by the Irish High-Tory Whig Edmund Burke. He flattered to instruct. For Burke, English politics was indeed distinctive: unlike that of France, English stability was based upon a superior understanding of the importance of unbroken organic national development. The English, a practical people, quite properly resisted theorising, and did not proceed from first principles. By comparison, Burke's great intellectual opponent, the English radical Tom Paine, set – by his own example – a completely different notion of Englishness. For Paine, an active participant in the two great revolutions of his time, the American and the French, the English were not special or exceptional; they were governed by the same – universal – rules as anyone else. If anything, the English, during their seventeenth-century revolution, had been amongst the pioneers of this universalist liberal thinking.

Yet, with the defeat of France, Tom Paine was to lose his battle with Edmund Burke. Paine was burnt in effigy in his homeland, and died abroad. For almost two centuries his works (and, as importantly, his political activities) have been devalued and marginalised by the dominant literary forces in the kingdom which he tried to overthrow. (Only recently has a statue to the great man been erected in his native Thetford – and has his own, decidedly *outré*, universalism begun to become somewhat appreciated.) Burke's ascendancy was a prelude to two centuries in which the English world of letters would exhibit, somewhat perversely, an innate suspicion of 'French' reason and universalism together with an unswerving belief in English exceptionalism.

In the building of the nation-state, these cultural and ideological clashes – between Catholicism and Protestantism, between France and England, between the universalism of Paine and the nationalism of Burke – were central. Yet so too was the changing economic and technological environment of the eighteenth-century British Isles.

In pre-industrial times, with most of the British people linked to the land and existing in isolated village communities, there was, obviously, a limit to the development of a national consciousness, and thus a popular underpinning for a nation-state. It was the revolution in industry, technology and communications which changed all this. Just as three centuries later the technology of globalism broke down existing political boundaries, so, too, in the eighteenth-century British Isles, did the industrial revolution. The communications and travel revolution of the eighteenth century – allowing the development and spread of commerce into a new national single market – was the real radicalising, nation-state building, agent. It opened up the frontiers, breaking down the barriers of locale (of village and community) as it established a national mass market for goods and services.

Caxton had introduced the printing press into England around 1476, and the printed word (he published the works of Chaucer) became both a boundary breaker and socal unifier. And, in the eighteenth century, with the quantum leap in the technology of communications, not only was London able to reinforce its political ascendancy, but the ideas and images, the manners and codes which were to serve as the common culture of the new nation-state were transmitted from one end of the islands to the other. This was the age when 'John Bull' and 'Britannia' were being honed for a national audience, when the rules of cricket (1744) and whist (1745) were drawn up and printed, when Samuel Johnson, Jonathan Swift, David Garrick, and cartoonists James Gilray and Robert Newton, as well as an array of pamphleteers were at work.[26]

Industrialisation was a terrific boon for the literary classes, the writers, artists and clerics. Early capitalism may indeed have been too materialistic for some of the intellectuals of the day, but the technology it carried in its baggage allowed their messages to be carried to an ever wider public. And their message was increasingly nationalistic.

There had indeed been a scholarly and literary revolution during the latter half of the eighteenth century, in which a nationalist historiography and literature had emerged. It was hardly surprising. After all, writers communicated by language and increasingly, now almost totally, the language – the 'tool of the trade' – was English. The ever-increasing consciousness of the English language, and its history as separate and distinct from French and Latin, was bound to fuel a wider literary political and cultural separatism.

Yet, these new literary classes were not helpless, simply corks on the water drifting with a growing nationalism. They were to play their part, too, in the building of a nation-state. In fact, the role of the writing and arguing classes was crucial: for they performed no less a role than that of creating and producing the images – what Gerald Newman has called the 'artistic projections' – that helped define and describe the new national identity – the idea of Englishness. Indeed, as Newman argues provocatively, they may have created it.

For the concept of national identity, though presented as a finished product to der Volk as if it were a single distillation of characteristics deeply embedded in all true countrymen, is originally simply an artistic projection, an image deliberately fashioned by a single group in the age of 'stirrings' and national awakening. Qualities *chosen* by frustrated intellectuals and projected as *national* traits.[27]

And, of course, these 'artistic projections', these 'national traits', were then copied and, over time, became established.

It is always difficult to allocate the exact responsibility for intellectual change, like that of ideas and images of identity: how much is caused by the creative writer, by the use of his or her media, or by broader forces including the resonance the image and idea receives amongst elites and the generality of the public? Yet, whatever the exact hierarchy of influences, the fact was that the character of Englishness put into words and cartoons during this crucial period formed a mould that has only changed at the margins since.

The defining characteristic of this invented Englishman was his moral elevation. This moral aspect of the ideal Englishman was drawn from the earlier notion of the honour and uprightness of 'nobility', but it also reflected a morally pretentious period in the country's history. Great literary figures were praised as much for their moral as for their technical and dramatic achievements. Politicians – even in the afterglow of the age of Newcastle – were to be respected, not only for their statecraft but also for their moral worth. 'Honour' was a serious idea taken extremely seriously. Above all, always important in England, morality supposedly set you above the common folk – who were morally lax and without civilisation. Thus, any Englishness constructed during this time was bound to be ladled in goodness.

Sincerity emerged as a key moral attribute of the new Englishman. And by 'sincerity' was meant an amalgam of innocence, honesty, originality, frankness, above all truthfulness and moral independence. 'This was the "sincerity" that became the legendary characteristic of that English–Virginian gentleman, the first President of the United States, who would "never tell a lie".'[28] And these characteristics came to be known, over time, as 'character': a man of 'character' was *assumed* to be of *good* character. The character given to this new Englishman has lasted down the centuries, and can even help explain the unique forms (and pomposities) of British public life in the late twentieth century – exhibited by the extravagances of 'honourable gentleman', the 'honourable and noble gentleman', the 'honourable and noble lady', your 'majesty' and 'with all due respect'.

'Character' ('sincerity' and 'truthfulness') was not, though, quite enough for the ideal, and idealised, Englishman. He also needed to possess social position and a modicum of power – and, inevitably, to be linked to the life of the land. It was here that the figure of 'the gentleman' emerges. Fashioned by the literati in the eighteenth century (from the raw material of the gentry), 'the gentleman' arrived centre-stage during Victorian times and was still going strong in inter-war Britain, although by the late twentieth century he, alongside other national stereotypes, had degenerated into a stage Englishman for the tourist trade.

'GREAT BRITAIN' OR 'GREATER ENGLAND'?

During the fateful era when English national identity was born there emerged a new dimension to the new nationalism. England – and Englishness – was expanding to cover more and more of its adjacent territory. By the end of the eighteenth century not only had a new, and enlarged, nation-state – of *Great Britain* – taken hold on the islands, but the ideology of Englishness held sway within it. And through the agency of this new state (*Great Britain* was later to become the *United Kingdom* and further expand its political authority through imperial expansion) the English idea would be transmitted to the world.

The idea of Britain had never died out. The early modern English memory had carried within it notions and images of Celtic Ancient Britons, who, long before the English arrived, had probably given the islands the name of Britain. Celtic leaders, such as the fierce anti-Roman warrior Boudicca, and Arturius (King Arthur of Colchester, or 'Camelot'), were probably also becoming legendary.

These Celts spoke a tongue – called British – named after the island, and they occupied the land until the first serious Roman invasion in the first century AD. As the wars with the English dragged on, the British people were divided: some left the country altogether, to settle in Brittany, and others formed a *British* resistance to the English, based in the west and north of the country. Over the next few centuries the British became a conquered people, and, although Britishness continued to exist in the outlying areas of the islands, mainly through Celtic tongues, it formed a peripheral existence. It was to stay that way, even after the English re-invented themselves by reviving the terms Britain and British in the early eighteenth century.

Peter Scott has called Britain an 'invented nation', 'not so much older than the United States'.[29] It was, to be precise, only 70 years older. Britain was born in 1707 – by the Act of Union between England and Wales (England had annexed Wales in 1536) and Scotland. The idea of a British nation-state had been mooted for some time, and as early as 1603 James VI of Scotland (James I of England) had adopted, for the purpose of diplomacy only, the title 'King of Great Britain'. After the union the term 'Britain' caught on. By the 1770s the new country had its martial music – Rule *Britannia* (1740) and God Save the King (1745) – its *British* Museum (1753) and its Encyclopaedia *Britannica*.

The expansion and reconstruction of the English nation-state, its transformation from England to Britain, was a series of essentially political, and military, acts – starting with the 1707 Act of Union and ending with the defeat of the Jacobites at Culloden in 1746. Yet, as the eighteenth century progressed, the islands were indeed becoming more culturally and ethnically homogeneous. English aristocrats had moved north of the border to take possession of new estates which they reckoned, in this era of rising land prices, would bring them serious profits. More importantly, Scottish landowners (and some Welsh and Irish too) had moved south to be nearer to the capital with its financial acumen and trading links to the world.[30]

The English ruling landed elite, their confidence badly shaken by the loss of the American colonies and by what they saw as the humiliating defeat of 1782, were, in consequence, quite keen to revivify the country by 'growing the nation' and absorbing the Scottish aristocracy. They used the Scots to somewhat reform their patrician style, turning themselves into 'a less frivolous, harder-working and publicly more responsible class'.[31] They also wanted help, both military and financial, with their increasing world role.

Even so, many English people feared this transmutation into Britishness. One such, and the leader of the English resistance to the British idea, was John Wilkes. Wilkes, and his Wilkesites, represented the true canon of the newly-minted ideology of Englishness which sprang upon the scene as the self-confidence of the English elites grew apace during the late seventeenth and early eighteenth centuries. They believed the English were uniquely free and uniquely prosperous. The Scots, on the other hand, were divided between a nobility who were 'tyrants' and 'the common people who are slaves'.[32] And union with these people would pauperise the English.

It is Wilkes's rhetoric of freedom and liberty, linked to his political support for the out-groups of his day – the middle-class businessmen and professionals, the gentlemen manqués who were using patriotism to improve their social position – which has placed him amongst the country's foremost radicals, indeed as a founder of English radicalism. Yet his message, like so much of English 'leftism' before and after, was essentially reactionary. Unlike Paine, his passion for liberty was not universal or based upon principles; rather, it stopped at the Straits of Dover and Hadrian's Wall. Englishness, not freedom, was his ultimate belief-system.

Yet, as it turned out, Wilkes had nothing to fear from the British idea. 'Great Britain' was always a misnomer; 'Greater England' would have been better. After all, the English aristocracy had built the new state. They forged its constitution and ideology in 1688 at the time of the Glorious Revolution, and in 1707 – there was, intriguingly, no written constitution (except the Act of Union itself) – all they did was extend the whole 1688 settlement north of the border. London, not Edinburgh (nor, as in a new federal system, some small town or city in a border area) became the capital. Furthermore, their ideology of Englishness was the only serious contender to be the governing culture. It had no competitors.

English landowners – and their supporters – dominated the new super-state's aristocracy, not least by the sheer power of numbers and financial resources. And the Celtic landowners who joined this new British aristocracy added little in the way of cultural pluralism: they were simply absorbed into the ruling group as they adopted – like millions who would come later – the lifestyle and manners of official Englishness. (This was the new British ruling class, a group whose heirs, inheriting an empire as well as land, would – literally – rule the world. It was also the group who, by mixing land with industry and finance (primarily finance), came to form the ruling class of the United Kingdom – exhibiting the distinctive life style and culture which was still discernible well into the late twentieth century.)[33] As for the Celtic 'common people', they, like the Germanic-derived English 'common people' before them, were simply added to the rolls (though not the electoral rolls!), their descendants becoming the middle and working classes of later centuries.

In essence, England and the English colonised Britain and the Celts. Michael Hechter, in his major work on the subject, outlines the early stirrings of the English state from the Kings of Wessex outward under the title 'the expansion of the English state'. He also argues that the

Celts in the British Isles and in the British state did not, ultimately, meld into the larger ethnic group – the Anglo-Saxons – and thus create a homogeneous ethnic Britishness. There was no such 'diffusion'. Rather, the pattern of development between English and Celts in the new Britain (and the later United Kingdom) was essentially 'colonial' (or, as he calls it, 'internal colonial'). Conflict continued, separate consciousness did not dissolve, and Celtic nationalism remained a relatively serious force. As Hechter puts it:

> the union of the Celtic periphery with England, unlike the earlier unification of English counties during the Anglo-Saxon period, did not establish state-wide legitimacy for the government in London. The periphery's weapon of resistance to English authority was the nineteenth-century development which came to be known as 'Celtic culture', though in many ways this had little in common with its ancient counterpart. The renaissance of Celtic culture, the beginnings of Celtic nationalism, and the distinctive electoral behaviour of the Celtic territories were all responses to a situation which may usefully be described as colonial.[34]

Certainly many English people have always seen England in the driving seat of the new nation. This truth – embarrassing, insensitive – has often slipped out. There are a million examples. When George Orwell wrote his great paean of praise to the people in the islands who were winning the war his title was 'Socialism and the genius of the *English* people'. And in the Penguin Catalogue of Books (1994), under the heading 'History of *England*', there appears a number of books that are more properly 'History of Britain' books, for instance one entitled *Task Force: The Falklands War, 1982* and intriguingly, *Pax Britannica*. Even careful scholars like Correlli Barnett, in the inscription to his work on British history, *The Pride and the Fall*, writes: 'in the hope that *England* may yet prove stronger than the storms'.[35] Of course, Orwell and Barnett are probably right, calling it 'as it is' – but it still must be disconcerting for the Scots and Welsh to become un-persons and invisible.

Yet the English elite's take-over of Scotland, like its earlier take-over of Wales, did not mean that there was to be no popular, indigenous support for the new Britain or Britishness. Following the Reformation, Scotland, like England and Wales, became a Protestant nation. Thus, although Scotland would continue to flirt politically with the Stuarts, it shared with its English co-religionists an opposition to Catholic France.

And anti-Catholic sentiment (whether of the mainstream Anglican kind or of the Scottish Knoxian variety) could always be counted on, certainly during the nineteenth century, to unite majorities within the two nations.

However, it was the Empire, more than religion, which, over time, helped to somewhat reconcile Scots to England and Britain. After all, many Scots were to play a seminal role in both the creation and the administration of the British Empire.[36] And every time an English politician – whether Pitt the Elder during the Seven Years War, or Walpole as he tried to consolidate Whig popularity, or, later, Joe Chamberlain – stirred up imperial sentiment amongst the English, he was, at least by implication, including the Scots as part of the national imperial family.

So, as the eighteenth century came to its close – almost a century after the Union between England and Wales and Scotland, and well into the technology-driven widening of frontiers within the islands, and the literary 'amen chorus' for Englishness – Britishness, UK-ness, was developing behind it at least a measure of national sentiment.

National sentiment and national identity are asserted much more than they are ever measured. Yet, one way to measure them is to attempt to assess sacrifice, indeed the ultimate one. The willingness of young men to die (or to put themselves 'in harms way') for their country must represent some kind of test of national consciousness. Thus, patterns of responses (as between urban and rural, village and town, north and south) to voluntary military service may be a key to some kind of measurement of the reach of the long arm of British nationalism. Linda Colley has broken new ground in attempting such a measurement. By analysing the response of Britain's manpower (what she calls 'the map of war patriotism') to the survey of volunteers called for by the Defence of the Realm Act of 1798 – at the height of the country's reaction to post-revolutionary France – she concludes that 'the nation's call for large numbers of men to defend it after 1798 was answered, not indeed unanimously but certainly abundantly'.[37]

But she also concludes that nation-building – certainly a unified national consciousness – still had some way to go. Her results told her that 'the more industrialised and urbanised a region was, the more likely it was to produce a high level of volunteers'.[38] (If indeed the urban areas were more responsive than the rural and peripheral to a call to arms then it provides two intriguing insights. First, it critically re-visits the old saw that rural life and values are more patriotic than the cosmopolitan values of cityfolk. And secondly, it reinforces the notion that nationalism was, then at least, a function of modernity – influencing those, primarily in urban centres, who were in the catchment areas of the new communications.)

Yet, all in all, the makers of Britain had pulled it off. The UK-state was a going concern with a stable political order and even some popular support. This new, successful UK (the term *United Kingdom* was in normal usage by the late 1790s) became a perfect instrument for the English ruling classes. It was a useful front for England and Englishness. It enhanced their power base as well as broadening and re-invigorating them. And, perhaps most crucially of all, it resolved potential conflicts on the periphery of a nation which was increasingly wanting to concentrate upon its world role. It was almost as if the UK-state had been built specifically for imperial expansion.

THE LIBERAL IDEA DEFEATED

There was an alternative idea of England at work during the eighteenth century. It was the idea of England as the homeland of liberty. John Wilkes built his career on this idea. His political struggles (which included trial for sedition and expulsion from the Commons) built him into the English nationalist hero as 'became the personification of liberty, and liberty was the hallmark of Englishness'.[39]

Wilkes's Englishness – like the nationalism of other radicals before him – harked back to the idea of an ancient constitution of the English in which the 'historic rights of Englishmen' were enshrined. This 'lost democracy', so the legend had it, was, though, overthrown by the Normans as, after 1066, they established 'a Norman Yoke' over the honest, freedom-loving English.[40]

The seventeenth-century Levellers mixed their early democratic and radical ideas with more than a whiff of nationalism, as in this harrowing account:

And the last enslaving conquest which the enemy got over Israel, was the Norman over England. And from that time Kings, lords, judges, bailiffs, and the violent bitter people that are freeholders, are and have been successively: the Norman bastard William himself, his colonels, captains, inferior officers, and common soldiers, who still are from that day to this day in pursuit of that victory, imprisoning, robbing, and killing the poor enslaved English Israelites.[41]

This mixture of nationalism and liberty, although a favourite of radicals, was also adapted by those conservatives who developed the so-called 'Whig interpretation of history' – in which a past golden age of liberties becomes part of the 'entailed inheritance' of the 'long continuity of British institutions'. Edmund Burke became a proponent of this idea when he argued that there was an essential continuity – 'from Magna Carta to the Declaration of Right ... derived to us from our forefathers ... transmitted to our posterity' – a notion not without its contemporary adherents, such as the historian David Lindsay Keir.[42]

The idea (or myth) of continuity is not without its powerful, withering, critics. Jeremy Bentham savaged the idea of an ancient constitution of liberty as 'the wisdom of barbarian ancestors'; Tom Paine evoked the 'rights of *man*' not the rights of '*Englishmen*'; and, more recently, Ferdinand Mount has also questioned the validity of the idea of England's liberal exceptionalism.[43]

Even though the notion of a special English relationship to liberty may have been somewhat over-done by nationalist radicals, the English, of all the European national identities, can certainly lay some kind of serious claim to a uniquely powerful liberal heritage. The English certainly led the way in clipping the wings of monarchy while the rest of continental Europe was still living under various forms of absolutism. They did, in fact, experiment with a republican form of government at a very early stage in the story of the evolution of European democracy. And the 1688 settlement, although a fatal compromise between Parliament and Crown (which over the long term served to legitimise one of the most powerful executives in the Western world), was, for its time, a great democratic advance. Also, the off-shore islanders can surely count amongst their number the principal theoretical architects of the modern conception of individual freedom – Thomas Hobbes and John Locke.

This English radical tradition can also be credited with many of the radical ideas which expressed themselves in dramatic, and concrete, form during the American Revolution – arguably a classic example of the struggle (carried on thousands of miles from its home) between liberal ideas and the Tory culture and ideology represented by the aristocracy and court in George III's London.

Edward Countryman places the intellectual roots of the American Revolution within the 'British' liberal tradition. He argues, reviving the idea of a special history of liberalism, that what the colonists – primarily English, but Welsh and Scots too – shared in common was a 'Britishness'. They:

> ... may have acquired it by birth as did the puritans of New England and the Anglican gentry of the Tidewater, or by being conquered, as did the Dutch of New York, or by migration, as did the Huguenot French ... [but that] all of them were heirs to a political and cultural tradition that set them off sharply from the Creoles of Spain's American dominions or from the newly-conquered Catholic French of the St Lawrence Valley. ... To a Chinese or a Persian, of course, all Western Europeans must have seemed much the same. But in an age when absolutism ruled in much of mainland Europe, residents of Britain and its colonies could take pride in the fact that they lived in freedom ... Were they asked to define it, some colonials, like some Britons, would have answered that it lay in the security of person and property that the common law guaranteed. Others might have said that it lay in specific privileges and liberties given to them by their colonial charters. Still others would have pointed to the Whig settlement of 1688. ... They would have noted that the King could neither legislate nor tax without the consent of the people, who were represented in Parliament. They would have maintained that their own assemblies stood to them as the House of Commons stood to the people of England, Scotland, and Wales. ... British freedom ... blended the right to be left alone under the law's protection and the right to take part in political affairs.[44]

Thus the American colonists saw this 'Britishness' as ultimately guaranteeing them some kind of historic rights – the 'rights of Englishmen' – against the Crown and its church, against arbitrary executive power. This was the heart of the political message they had taken with them during the seventeenth and eighteenth centuries as they crossed the ocean from East Anglia and the West Country, from their dissenting churches and puritan sects. It was the kernel of the cluster of revolutionary liberal ideas which built the American Revolution, the formulation of the Declaration of Independence, the Articles of Confederacy and, ultimately, the Constitution of the United States. These

English-Americans and British-Americans were truly 'the posthumous children of the English revolution' and 'the Good Old Cause' of some 130 years before.

And there were indeed echoes of earlier English political liberalism, if not radicalism, in the domestic British response to the American Revolution – which was widespread, even within the aristocratic British polity (Edmund Burke supported the revolutionaries). Indeed, the revolution might easily have proved infectious.

Yet, it did not. For the growing domestic sense of individuality and 'rights' (the 'historic liberties of Englishmen') was always in a political contest with other home-grown, more organic (and reactionary) notions of society and state. Even as ideas of *individual* freedom were gaining a toe-hold in British life, the eighteenth century also saw the growth of the profoundly conservative *collective* identity of nationalism and national subjecthood.

The strange English mix of political liberalism and nationalism – starting with 'the Norman Yoke', running through the republicans in the seventeenth century, through to Wilkes in the eighteenth, 'Radical Joe' Chamberlain in the nineteenth, and on to aspects of Orwell, Benn and Foot in the twentieth – ultimately failed. Liberal ideas of universal rights could simply not be limited by state and nation.

Tom Paine understood this more than most. 'Britishness' or 'Englishness' could not, ultimately, be reformed, or swivelled into a progressive direction. Not himself limited by nation, Paine understood that liberal ideas were either universal or they meant nothing. As Countryman observed 'Paine attacked not one policy or another but the whole structure of Britishness, subordination, and monarchy within which colonial America had lived. The problem was not to explain what had gone wrong in a good system; it was to explain why the system itself was a problem.'[45]

So, this intriguing *alternative Englishness* – the vision of England as a land of liberty – was simply not as compelling as the Tory Englishness of land, class and race, an idea of England which perfectly suited the new era of empire upon which the country was about to embark. If pre-nineteenth-century British and English nationalism had exhibited decidedly progressive and liberal tendencies, then the Victorian experience of Empire would transform nationalism into a profoundly conservative proposition.

THE IMPERIAL SOUL OF ENGLISHNESS

The Empire was a decidedly *British* affair – as Scottish involvement in commercial, entrepreneurial, trading and financial origins of the empire, as well as in its building and running, was immense.[46] Yet it was the English, not the Scots, who were to become nature's imperialists. On questions of imperial rulership and administration it was the English, rather than the Scots, who took to empire as to the manner born. And it was the ideology of Englishness – a culture which only marginally touched the merchants, engineers and sailors who *created* the Empire – which guided the civil servants, top military and clergy who later *ran* the global enterprise.

Indeed, the ideology of eighteenth-century Englishness – with its imperatives of 'land, class and race' – was perfectly suited to the task of administering, if not forging, an Empire. After all, the power of the Empire, like power at home, derived from land – the Empire being simply a territorial expansion of the land mass over which the English aristocratic-cum-political class had control.

Also, the paternalism of the landed system at home was almost tailor-made for the colonial experience: a beneficent government by those who knew better would be administered to lesser breeds (whose loyalty, in return, would be demanded). Also, the fundamentals of the political class system, which England's rulers had established at home – where the majority of people were essentially incidental to politics (without the vote and without entrenched rights) – was simply extended to the new imperial territories.

And in the colonies political life was even easier. There was no middle class competing for power and attention, no 'working class' was becoming organised, and, because the newly-acquired peoples were racially different, no pretence had to be made about universal moral worth. Black and brown people were simply inferior.

Thus, although the imperial mentality flowed quite naturally from the ideology of Englishness, the whole experience of Empire provided a crucial new twist in the development of English identity: it added, to an already pretty elevated self-image of Englishness, the crucial ingredient of superiority.

This sense of superiority – an innate superiority accruing to the English, but particularly to the English upper classes – would tend to develop amongst all imperial ruling groups, not only the English. Yet the rulers of England were presiding over the most extensive, and most powerful, of Europe's empires – essentially leading the greatest country in the world and directly politically controlling a third of the globe.

It was heady stuff, and could be expected to leave its mark. A sense of national superiority was bound to breed in that environment. And this sense of superiority was enhanced, not diminished, by the nature of the English contact with their subordinate 'foreigners'. The English did not mix, they conquered, and then ruled. (So the colonial experience – though technically an internationalising phenomenon – hardly encouraged cosmopolitan instincts amongst the British.)

Lord Hugh Cecil, English landowner, imperialist, and High Tory, is a perfect representative of this English sense of superiority – class, national, and racial. In 1912 he proferred a view of the English mission which perfectly represented the sentiment of his fellow rulers during the height of Empire. In what was the very stuff of the ideology of Englishness he argued that 'our vocation in the world . . . [is] to undertake the government of vast, uncivilised populations and to raise them gradually to a higher level of life'.[47]

And another imperialist, Rudyard Kipling, revealed a similar mental framework in his famous poem:

> Take up the White Man's burden –
> Send forth the best ye breed –
> Go bind your sons to exile
> To serve your captives' need;
> To wait in heavy harness
> On fluttered folk and wild –
> Your new-court sullen peoples,
> Half-devil and half-child.

Thus English superiority was not simply cultural; it was racial as well. And the era of Empire saw the emergence in England not only of a general prejudice in favour of English and white racial superiority (Lord Hugh Cecil's views would have received near-universal support) but also of strains of literary racism (in, amongst others, the works of H. G. Wells), philosophic racism (exemplified by the works of G. K. Chesterton), even systematic, scientific racism (of which Stuart Houston Chamberlain was a leading exponent).

General theories of race – like general theories of politics – did not catch on amongst the English, and scientific racism became unacceptable amongst the political class, following the experience of the 1939–45 war and Nazism. However, a profound basic racial prejudice remained, invigorated by the experience of Empire. As one contemporary theorist has put it,

> with or without a theory of biological racism, whether derived from the work of Count Gobineau (1915) or some other source, a deep-seated unrefined belief in racial difference in performance, and in standards, probably owes its origin to the colonial relationship between white master and black subordinate. . . . The white man's civilising presence, the need to develop backward nations, the missionaries' vocation to convert the heathen acted as powerful justification for continued imperial domination. Such ideas deeply penetrated the culture of the British population and survive to the present day.[48]

Robert Colls has made the intriguing point that the imperial experience may have changed 'Whig' and Liberal perceptions of Englishness – away from ideas about Englishness being to do with liberty and constitutional development, and towards Englishness as 'race, language and custom'. Thus, according to this new view of Englishness, 'everyone who could possibly claim to have the right skins, show the right tongues, and be identified with the right feelings, was now invited across to the Whig celebrations'.[49]

Winston Churchill, the country's last unashamedly imperial leader, possessed a decidedly racist side – one shared by most of his contemporaries in the higher reaches of English imperial public life. The historian Andrew Roberts writes of the great man:

> Churchill's views on race did not spring up fully formed when he regained office in 1951, but were held consistently during his long political career. By the standards of today – and possibly even of his own time – Winston Churchill was a convinced racist . . . For Churchill Negroes were 'niggers' or 'blackamoors', Arabs were 'worthless', Chinese were 'chinks' or 'pigtails', and other black races were 'baboons' or 'Hottentots', Italians were 'mere organ-grinders'. . . . As the great tribal leader of 1940 his [Churchill's] speeches were peppered with references to the British race. . . Sir David Hunt, one of his Private Secretaries during his 1951–55 period of office, recalls 'Churchill was on the whole rather anti-black. I remember him sending a telegram to [South African President] Dr Malan and asking me whether he should say "My dear Mr President, Alles sal rect hom [all is well]. Keep on skelping the kaffirs!"' 'Blackamoor' was

also a term in normal upper class usage – indeed was used by another prominent figure of the fag end of empire, Elizabeth Bowes-
Lyon (now 'the Queen Mother').[50]

This kind of 'unrefined' racial superiority existed in Britain well into
the late twentieth century, and was revived by the arrival of mass third-
world immigration into the country, a process begun in the late 1950s.

The idea of racial and national superiority at the heart of imperial
Englishness was complemented by a mild and understated anti-semitism.
Victorian English society developed a certain tolerance for very rich
Jews such as the Sassoons, the Rothschilds and the Oppenheimers (as
its 'practical-man' persona tolerated big money from any quarter). Yet,
a disdain for Jewish people still surfaced regularly amongst English
leadership groups. Even as late as 1959 the then British Prime Minister, Harold Macmillan, could claim that 'the Jews, the planners and
the old cosmopolitan element' were playing 'no small part in the [Eu-
ropean] Commission'[51] A standard view, even as late as the 1970s,
would be that ' everyone knew very well that there was a gaping chasm
between them and us' and that although Jewish people are 'not really
Jewish here in England . . . of course they're not really English either'.[52]

Nevertheless, superiority had its obligations. The imperial version
of Englishness, conscious that it was the English role to administer
large tracts of the globe, and 'the vast uncivilised populations', developed a cult of rulership. Englishmen would be trained in the arts of
leadership. They would be trusted. And, like the feudal nobility, in
return for the loyalty of their subjects they would rule paternalistically
– over both the brown and black races and the domestic whites. They
would be 'firm but fair' (incredibly, as late as 1974, this was a paternalistic election slogan of the Conservative Party in the February 1974
general election).

And they would lead by example, setting standards of behaviour for
lower ranks and lesser orders to follow. This idea that rulers needed to
lead by personal example had been present earlier in English history,
but came into its own during imperial rule in India – when the needs
of administration coincided with the rapid growth, at home, of evangelical religion. Katherine Tidrick has argued that

this governing class [of India] owed much of its character to evangelical religion. . . . It . . . supplied a conception of authority which,
because it happened to take root in India under conditions which
were highly mythogenic, was of immense importance in defining

the ideal to which men of empire thereafter aspired. This conception of authority was rooted in the evangelical cult of personal example.[53]

An historian of English national character, Ernest Barker, writing in the 1920s, has gone as far as to say 'No one will ever understand Victorian England who does not appreciate that among highly civilised countries ... it was one of the most religious that the world had ever known.'[54] Evangelical religion was also the key ingredient in the education of the English upper-class young – the future rulers of empire – in the public schools of the nineteenth-century. The military historian Correlli Barnett has described how these young men were systematically imbued with a culture and an ideology which was purposely constructed for imperial leadership – and how Christian morality was at its heart. Dr Thomas Arnold, Headmaster of Rugby School from 1827 until 1841, exercised, according to Barnett, 'a decisive influence. He is quoted as saying

> ... rather than have it [science] the principal thing in my son's mind, I would gladly have him think that the sun went round the earth, and that the stars were so many spangles set in the bright blue firmament. Surely the one thing needed for a Christian *and an Englishman* to study is a Christian and moral and political philosophy.[55]

And, because these public schools were the point of entry not only to the older universities, but also to virtually every leading London establishment occupation, they became the breeding ground for a governing class. Those few young men who had not gone to public school but who, during the later nineteenth and early twentieth centuries, would get to university, would also, in all its essentials, be incorporated and absorbed into the culture of Englishness by their university environment and education. Philip Dodd makes the point that by 1900 'almost all' the history text books which were made compulsory in the secondary schools 'were written by academics', a factor contributing to what he describes as their [the ancient universities'] 'establishment as custodians of the national culture'.[56]

There was an elaborate structure of mimicry – lesser public schools mimicked 'better' public schools, and most of the newer provincial 'civic' universities which came on the scene during the nineteenth century mimicked Oxford and Cambridge. (London University would be something of an exception here. Although the London colleges were created some centuries after Oxbridge, many of them, having the advantage over Oxbridge of being located in the capital, felt able to construct a relatively independent identity. University College was an avowedly non-Christian foundation, the London School of Economics was quasi-socialist.)

So systematic was this Victorian public-school education that it produced a 'public-school type' who was instantly identifiable – primarily by accent, but by dress and attitudes as well. His education had purposely set him apart from the rest of his compatriots, a chasm which many found it difficult to bridge later on in life.

Diversity was not a Victorian public-school virtue. The boys were 'subjected to a powerful and uniform moulding process' and the schools were able to instil such a uniform education because they were able to virtually incarcerate the young men for months on end, thus depriving them of contact with families and wider community.[57] (It is a fascinating separate speculation as to why upper class Victorian English parents allowed this to happen.)

The educational philosophy of these schools also encouraged conformity, and positively discouraged individuality and spontaneity. 'Team spirit' was the watchword for these potential rulers of empire, 'dooming the variety, spontaneity and open-mindedness that had hitherto been the saving-graces of the British upper classes'.[58] It was something of an irony, but the liberty, freedom and, above all, individuality (and eccentricity) which were proclaimed as the hallmarks of England and Englishness, were, during the high-point of empire, being systematically drained from the minds and personalities of the country's future leaders.

The 'team spirit', conformity and orthodoxy taught in the public schools may have repressed the young men, but it served (and was meant to serve) the Empire well. A limited and predictable range of set responses to difficult situations – as opposed to random and spontaneous activity – was a necessary attribute for imperial rulers. Governing an Empire needed rules, not personality! Luigi Barzini, the Italian writer, in an essay on the English, has attempted an explanation of how this 'English' trait of imperturbability was important:

My friend Bernardo ... believed that it wasn't important for Englishmen to be intelligent (intelligence could be a hindrance) because, as I discovered, they could all behave intelligently when the need arose. This is how it worked. They all had a few ideas firmly embodied in their heads. He said 'seven ideas' ... whatever the number, the ideas were exactly identical and universal [that is, to all Englishmen]. That is why in older days, in distant lands with no possibility of communicating with their superiors, weeks or months by sailing ship away from London, admirals, generals, governors, ambassadors ... subalterns in command of a handful of native troops in an isolated outpost ... facing a dangerous crisis had always known exactly what to do ... and would have behaved in the same way in the same circumstances.[59]

It was from this cradle of repression that during the last three decades of the nineteenth century a new, revised and refined, culture and ideology of Englishness was brought into the world. And the Englishness so constructed amounted to a cultural form and totality as profound and peculiar as anything that happened in Germany in the thirties or Russia after the Bolshevik Revolution. Indeed, whereas the Nazification of the upper reaches of German society was to last for only a few years – eradicated by war – and Communist culture in Russia was to last for only a few decades before it collapsed, this culture and ideology of public-school, upper-class, imperial Englishness was to last for over a hundred years, and, undefeated in war or by domestic revolution, was still hanging around by the century's end.

This ruling-class, public-school cult of leadership, though it provided the leadership for the Empire, did not, though, lead to an authoritarian political and social system at home. Why it didn't remains an intriguing question. It possessed all the *accoutrements* of authoritarianism: an elite conscious of its leadership role, its propaganda and educational cells, an official ideology (Englishness), and control over the centres of economic and political power. Some historians argue that Britain in the late nineteenth and early twentieth centuries was too socially plural and politically liberal for any social group or ideology (even of the upper classes) to dominate. Katherine Tidrick, in a stark commentary, is not so flattering:

> We may ask ourselves in conclusion why it was that in a country where the cult of leadership enjoyed such favour as in England, fascism itself never acquired a hold. The answer must surely be twofold. First there was the empire to act as an outlet for the very emotions which it inspired: there were always brown races waiting to be led. Second, the mechanisms which developed to ensure that the imperial demand for leadership met with an unfailing supply also operated to rivet upon the British political system a governing class through which the leadership ethos was thoroughly diffused. In a land where the public school system worked to produce Fuhrers on the wholesale

principle, there was no prospect of any one of them arriving with the consent of his countrymen at supreme power.[60]

As well as attempting to foster a refined ideology of Englishness – and English identity – these same public schools then helped to impose it upon the still very hierarchical and deferential late Victorian, Edwardian and inter-war British society. One way in which this imposition took hold was through the creation of a standardised upper-class accent – which would serve as the authoritative voice of Englishness, and which would mark out rulers from ruled and serve as the standard for social aspirants. Philip Dodd, in an essay on Englishness, has argued that the term 'imposed' was too strong for the method by which English national culture came to establish a hegemony over the country.[61] He suggests that there were too many groups involved and thus no common intent to impose; and also that 'imposition' is too simple a term – as the 'establishment of hegemony' involves negotiation and active consent on the part of the subordinated. However, although there were indeed many groups involved in the process, none the less they did share a common position, culture and ideology, and tended to think, act and seem as one. Also, the Englishness they represented was, in its inherent character, incipiently imposing: possessing a sense of superiority and rulership.

Public schools such as Winchester are reported to have attempted to eradicate regional speech; in the late nineteenth century, at Bedford Modern School, local boys with a North Bedfordshire accent 'were so mercilessly imitated and laughed at that, if they had any intelligence, they were soon able to speak standard English'; and at Oxford University it had 'become virtually a condition of social acceptance amongst the undergraduates that one speak the Queen's English with a specific accent and intonation'.[62] And in the process of creating standard upper-class English the regional accents and dialects were devalued (by the most effective method in England – making them seem 'lower-class'). Future Gladstones (William Gladstone spoke with a Lancashire 'burr') and Peels (Robert Peel had a Brummie dialect) would, therefore, speak standard English.

This standard way of speaking (which later came to be called 'RP', Received Pronunciation) emerged in the public schools of the late nineteenth century as a new 'suitable' accent for imperial rulers. In the main it was precise, ungenerous, unengaging, high-pitched, controlled, non-confrontational, un-get-at-able, precious and slightly fey. In 1913 the Society for Pure English was founded, and worried about the growth of 'mongrel' versions (like the American) of the now standardised English. And a Henry Cecil Wyld, Professor of English language at Oxford University, 'was clear that the dominant English language was to be identified with certain English institutions – the Court, the Church, the Bar, the older universities and the great public schools'.[63]

In the 1920s, the BBC, through its Advisory Committee on Spoken English and its media monopoly power, not only sanctioned standardisation but, by and large, made the public-school kind of 'RP' standardised speech 'proper'.

Thus, the British people were asked to 'receive' the word, and a single accent of authority was born which was to last for well over fifty years. Any social, political or even economic aspirant – and there were thousands, if not millions amongst Britain's working, lower middle and middle classes – would need to make some genuflection towards this accent should they want to advance themselves. Some, like the late twentieth-century prime ministers Edward Heath and Margaret Thatcher, felt it necessary to take elocution lessons. This deadening cultural process amounted to an almost Orwellian attempt at social control, the nation's – and Englishness's – single most 'totalitarian' piece of cultural engineering during the twentieth century.

This newly refined imperial image of Englishness was constructed during the dawning of the 'age of democracy' – when the vote, if not the power, was being extended to more and more British males. And in this 'age of democracy' the images and values of imperial Englishness were transmitted to this broader public through the medium of this new 'official' standardised English pronunciation. We only have to hear the voice-overs of 1930s, 1940s and even 1950s Pathé News to understand the authority of these voices born to be obeyed.

It was also transmitted via the growing mass public-education system which was developing below the public-school level. The elementary education, under the Act of 1870 was, thus, a crucial aid to the spread of Englishness amongst the broader British population, as was the appearance of literature and history as core subjects in the vastly expanded schools of the period.

However, the most important factor in securing the acceptance of the new culture of imperial Englishness amongst the domestic masses was the hold and allure of nationalism – what some commentators, wishing to soften the term, call patriotism. It must remain an open question as to whether Victorian society (increasingly plural, quite mobile, and, although highly class-ridden, nonetheless highly economically productive), had it been able to develop free of the reality of nationalism, would have junked the culture and ideology of Englishness and developed along the American model: less class-conscious, more individualistic, more open.

Yet, Englishness was not junked: indeed it became nothing less than the country's 'official' idea of itself – to be aspired to and copied by the middle and working classes.

The selling of Englishness in Victorian Britain to the wider public was helped by the rapid growth of the nineteenth-century mass media. The sheer spread of this Victorian media is often not fully understood. Raymond Williams, the socialist cultural analyst and philosopher, has pointed out that as early as the mid-1900s a popular, and populist, mass media already existed. The 1840s saw 'the effective establishment of a popular Sunday press . . . the growth of new kinds of periodical, combining sensational romantic fiction with recipes . . . the coming of cheap fiction . . . the development of minor theatres . . . the rise of the music halls . . .'.[64]

Also, by the mid 1800s the circulation of popular Sunday newspapers (such as *Dispatch*, *News of the World* and *Chronicle*) had reached the startling heights of nearly 300,000 copies, whilst for a somewhat more selective audience the novels of Dickens, Thackeray, Reade, Marryat, Jane Austen and Mrs Trollope, Elizabeth Gaskell and Benjamin Disraeli were also widely read.[65]

Another key to the popularisation of Englishness lay in nationalism's, and patriotism's, unifying force. Because the working and middle classes were identifying with the state, Englishness was not seen as a separate distinctive culture for better-off people – the problem cosmopolitanism faced during the eighteenth century. Also, Englishness rode up and down on the tide of nationalism. Nothing succeeds like success: and the British nation-state (and its world-wide Empire) – and by extension its ruling class *and their culture and ideology* – was, by any contemporary test, a world-class success story.

National sentiment succeeded in dampening down the serious class divisions of the time. Indeed these class differences at the turn of the century were particularly sharp. In the period immediately before the First World War there was talk, not all of it utterly fanciful, about social breakdown, even revolution. Stark differences not only in wealth and income, but also in culture, manners and dress distinguished the classes. For instance, early photographs taken on the streets of London during turn-of-the-century summers reveal a rigidly classified society – boater hats (and some bowlers) for the middle classes and cloth caps for the working classes; and a segregated one too – for the classes did not mix, couples or clusters of people on buses or walking and standing in the streets were uniformly restricted to their own class only. Photographs of turn-of-the-century London are quite fascinating.[66] The same sharp differences applied to women. At the turn of the century, women were beginning to emerge from their traditional domestic roles in families into the wider world, but the class patterns seemingly remained:

> You could immediately recognise the social girl, the middle-class girl, the City girl and the factory girl. . . . The factory girl wore a black straw hat, ear-rings, a 'Mizpah' brooch, and hair dressed in rolls over her ears. The City girl was neat and severe. The middle-class girl was also neat, but added a touch of the style and chic which in those days could only be had by money. The society girl was consciously and demonstrably the society girl.[67]

Not only did nationalism act as a trans-class unifier, but, just as significantly, it enlisted the active support of all the classes of Victorian and Edwardian England. One such was the new industrial working classe in the cities, organising themselves into a trade union movement which was to become the most powerful in the world. The Victorian working class was patriotic, 'lousy but loyal', and their patriotism included support for the Empire. As Ellis Bartlett, a leading late Victorian jingo, remarked after the gathering of 40,000 signatures in favour of the retention of the imperial possession of Kandahar: 'It is a great mistake, as the Radical party will soon find out, to suppose that the working men of England are destitute of patriotism . . . the true working man is proud of his country . . . *is proud of its splendid and beneficent empire.*'[68]

Yet questions remain about the depth of popular support for the Empire. H. G. Wells wrote that 'Nineteen people out of twenty, the middle class and most of the lower class, knew no more of the empire than they did of the Argentine republic or the Italian Renaissance. It did not concern them.'[69]

It may not have 'concerned' them, but no section of British life ever turned decisively against the Empire – not the Scots, the Welsh the English, the industrial proletariat, the middle class, the nineteenth-century Conservatives or Liberals, and incredibly, not even the Radicals. There were votes in social-unity imperialism and in imperial preference. And there was no serious anti-colonial protest movement in the country until well into the second half of the twentieth century, not until after the Second World War made the Empire economically redundant. Indeed, the Empire possessed a popular constituency right

up to and beyond the Second World War. The Conservatives remained
the party of Empire right up until Winston Churchill died, and neither
the Liberals nor Labour (nor even the socialist intellectuals before the
Second World War) attempted any systematic rejection of the principle of Empire.

The imperial experience may not have reached deep into working-
class life, certainly not for those who never saw the colonies. Yet, the
Empire was a constant source of images and tales in the mass popular
media. And messages about the innate superiority of white Englishmen were produced and recycled in the educational texts and popular
newspapers, and by the propaganda surrounding Queen Victoria, the
'Empress of India'. And in the working-class areas of the cities – even
as late as the large council-house building programmes of the 1930s –
the Pretoria Avenues, Kyber Crescents and Mafeking Roads acted as a
constant reminder of British (and therefore their own) superiority. Through
association with Empire the working classes could feel superior to others
– the black and brown races. And it was their *nationality* (the only
thing they shared with the rulers of the Empire) that gave them this
sense of esteem and worth.

A source and sense of worth was also at the heart of the middle-
class reaction to Empire. Imperialism allowed the industrialists, the
merchants, the professionals, as well as to a lesser extent the clerical
grades, again because of their common *nationality*, to identify with
the aristocracy who ran the Empire – after all, they were all part of
the same enterprise! And through this act of identifying, the culture,
manners, and dress of 'official Englishness' became part of the life of
the middle class.

There can be little doubt that the Empire, as well as binding the
people to the leadership, also helped the nationalist (and Englishness's)
cause. It gave an added dimension of magic to the great nationalist
ceremonials which the late nineteenth-century political class were constructing to popularise the constitution – primarily the monarchy and
Parliament. The role of the monarchy was crucial here. For it was 'the
sovereign' who made the link between nation and Empire – being head
of both. And Disraeli – and Gladstone – helped turn Victoria into the
mythical figure: 'the Doyenne of Sovereigns, the Great White Queen,
the Shah-in-Shah Padshah, the Grandmama of Europe, *Victoria Regina
Imperatrix*'.[70]

But there were other forces at work which also helped send nationalism alive and well into the twentieth century – and they were the
very forces which limited and smothered the growth of a truly mod-

ernised liberal state and society. And they came from both left and right. Amongst the working class, and many of the middle-class intel-lectuals who gravitated to the nascent labour movement, the ideas of liberalism, and the Liberal Party, were increasingly losing out to vari-ous strands of socialist thinking. And socialism fitted quite easily into the nationalist framework. Socialist solutions were all nationalist solu-tions – as every reforming idea was aimed at change prosecuted through national structures. It could hardly have been otherwise, for the idea of international change, or international revolution, was indeed a ro-mantic fantasy. Yet, beyond these highly practical considerations, Labourists, and even left-wing socialists, were more than accepting of nationalist ideology. H. M. Hyndman, the leader of the Marxist Social Democratic Federation, could say 'patriotism is part of our heritage', and the Fabian Society could argue that it 'accepts the conditions im-posed on it by human nature and by the *national character . . .* of the English people'.[71]

As liberal ideas began to wane, the new and powerful ideology of socialism made an undeclared common cause with High-Tory tradi-tionalists to limit the emergence of what might have become a real threat to the ascendancy of nationalism (and indeed also to 'the landed interest' and its associated ideology of Englishness): a strong, self-confident, individualistic, bourgeoisie.

The historian Larry Sidentop has argued that one of the most interest-ing sociological insights about Britain is that it didn't, even during the age of Victorian capitalism, produce a robust and self-confident mid-dle class. Real middle classes are radical and liberal. They also tend to be internationalist, or at least less nationalist than social groups – such as aristocrats and peasants – who are linked to the land, and workers who are restricted to their locale. This historic weakness of the English middle class has lasted well into the late twentieth century. Neil Ascherson puts it in a constitutional setting: 'the middle class identifies with *the ancien regime* and is unable to see the advantages of overthrowing it and advancing to a condition of politically guaran-teed individualism'.[72]

THE MAKING OF THE ENGLISH 'GENTLEMAN'

In Victorian Britain Englishness needed its archetype and its champion, and the contemporary idea of 'the gentleman' was born. And the fellow was an 'English gentleman': for there was to be no such thing as a 'Scottish gentleman' or an 'Irish gentleman' or a 'Welsh gentleman' – except as used in a somewhat ironic and belittling way.

The idea of 'the gentleman' sprang from medieval times, based upon the feudal notions of chivalry and nobility. And his social position – linked to the land, not overly grand but certainly not associated with the lower orders – derived from 'the gentry' (or 'the mere gentry' as Hugh Trevor Roper once called them).[73] The term 'gentleman' was in general use during the Civil War – 'I would rather have a plain russet-coated captain who knows what he fights for, and loves what he knows', said Oliver Cromwell, 'than that which you call a gentleman and is nothing else.' And during the eighteenth century it was becoming established as a term describing all landed middle- and upper-middle-class adult males.

Yet, the emergence of 'the gentleman' in Victorian times had a much more moral aspect to it. As the representative of Englishness, the new 'English gentleman' gave moral worth to what essentially was Britain's power position in the world and the aristocrat's power position in domestic society. During the Empire, 'power had corrupted the British', argues Katherine Tidrick, 'by making them think it inhered in them personally rather than in the terror of their arms'.[74] And this cult of moral leadership (based upon evangelical moralism) involved no serious rupture with previous more genuinely aristocratic self-images of Englishness. In fact evangelicalism 'collided productively with aristocratic conceptions of honour to emerge as the Victorian ideal of the gentleman, acknowledged by his equals and adored by his inferiors'.[75]

Alongside this moral content, 'the gentlemen' possessed a degree of power, enough to be in control of his life, but not over-weaning power. And as well as moral worth, and a measure of power, the added ingredients of charm and social presence were thrown in. Charles Hampden-Turner has, from his own experience, captured the idea superbly:

If there was one abiding theme in my upbringing – one idea that held all others in thrall – it was the necessity for a commanding social presence. To be a gentleman, or to become one of the many modernistic transformations of a gentleman, was to command the attention of others with grace, style, wit, eloquence, self-possession and infinite subtlety. . . . The purpose of life was that stage itself, a scenario where ultimate ideas and great passions would play themselves out around me. And I was curiously dismissive of all those subjects which did not lend themselves to social fluency, i.e. science, technology, industry ... known to make people conversationally dull.[76]

The gentleman being moulded for production during late Victorian times (and given an outing in the works of Anthony Trollope) was always somewhat reticent and discreet, and certainly didn't show off. Yet, he was able to take command and was quite intelligent, but never, never, too clever and certainly not intellectual or meritocratic. Above all, and drawing upon the eighteenth-century idea of sincerity at the heart of Englishness, he was always honest and trustworthy.

In the twentieth century, P. G. Wodehouse produced an incontrovertibly dim kind of gentleman (the 'Bertie Wooster type' managed by 'Jeeves'), but he was never selfish or malign, remaining essentially a force for moral good, a 'good egg'. As was Agatha Christie's 'Hastings', the companion to Hercule Poirot.

During the twentieth-century this 'English gentleman' had a triumphant time. He was 'the officer' who led his men in two wars, and won them. He was – like Lord Peter Wimsey – the 'gentleman'-detective, the gifted amateur, who solved the murders whilst the plodding clerk of a policeman looked on. He was the romantic hero of novels. And, through the movies, this English gentleman also reached the postwar mass-market. The British 'Ealing Comedies' saw Ian Carmichael most perfectly representing the genre. And Hollywood, too, produced its own version of the English 'gentleman' – David Niven and Rex Harrison playing the part to a tee. James Bond, although initially played by the Scotsman Sean Connery, was the epitome of the cool, commanding and charming type demanded by Englishness's central casting.

And the English gentleman also made his appearance in the real world of postwar politics, portraying Englishness to a less English-dominated world, but still going strong, performing well. Prime ministers Anthony Eden, Harold Macmillan (an avid Trollope reader) and Alec Douglas Home (Lord Home of the Hirsel) acted the perfect parts, providing an image of Englishness which mixed old-world charm (Home was widely acknowledged to be genuinely charming) and world-weary imperial diplomacy – a combination which the English elite had then come to represent to the wider world.

TWENTIETH-CENTURY NATIONALISM

The English ruling classes continued to be beguiled by Empire long after the sun had set upon it. And, in consequence, the national culture of Englishness was to exhibit a decidedly imperial character well into the late twentieth century. Although H. G. Wells could assert in *Mr. Britling Sees it Through* (in 1916) that 'the middle class and most of the lower class knew no more of the empire than they did of the Argentine republic or the Italian Renaissance', this would also have been true of their knowledge of much of their own government.[77] A direct experience of Empire was not necessary in order to feel part of a great nation which had conquered a third of the globe, to feel, no matter how inchoately, superior culturally and racially to lesser breeds (and to have fixed in the mind a fairly clear racial hierarchy), and to believe that England and Britain was the centre of the world.[78]

For most of the first half of the twentieth century the national culture was pumping out its imperial messages – particularly to the young. In the 1930s schoolchildren were being told 'We're all subjects and partakers in the great design, the British empire. . . . The British empire has always worked for the peace of the world. This was the job assigned to it by God.'[79] And in the mid-1950s secondary schoolchildren throughout the country were still assembling for 'Empire Day' to be told that they were the inheritors of a world power.

Also, for most of the first part of the century the statecraft of the UK's political elite was governed by little else than the need to defend and protect the Empire – and its economic preference system. At the very beginning of the century Lord Salisbury had been deeply worried about the future of Britain once he had seen the writing on the wall for the Empire; during the 1930s Neville Chamberlain had constructed his whole foreign policy upon a last-ditch defence of empire; and, at the end of the Second World War, Winston Churchill set the victory in grand imperial terms – 'Once again the British Commonwealth and Empire emerges safe, undiminished and united from a mortal struggle.'[80]

And long after the formal demise of Empire, the imperial sensibility still lingered. Aphorisms of Empire – 'If Britain had to choose between Europe and the open sea, it will always choose the open sea', 'Britain is a trading nation or it is nothing', 'Trade Follows the Flag' – continued to dominate political debate. Winston Churchill, an avowed supporter of Empire, even during his postwar premiership, put a stop to Labour's process of de-colonisation, and further colonial independence had to wait until Harold Macmillan became prime minister. Although Churchill was the last imperialist prime minister, Anthony Eden acted like one, and his invasion of Egypt in 1956 possessed all the hallmarks of the imperial mentality. And as late as 1962 the Labour opposition leader Hugh Gaitskell was evoking not only 'a thousand years of history' but memories of 'Vimy Ridge' and 'Gallipoli' as part of his anti-Common Market campaign.

Yet, the sun was slowly setting on this extraordinary imperial venture; and as, during the 1950s, it finally dipped below the horizon, the whole culture and ideology of British imperialism (particularly the central feature of national 'greatness' and superiority) could be expected to fall with it.

But a fortuitous rescue was at hand. For the idea of Britain – and its dominant culture, Englishness – was to be given a huge boost by the two devastating world wars which were to disfigure twentieth-century Europe. The fires of patriotism, and nationalism, were re-stoked as war reinforced the sensibility of not only a separate but also a virtuous English and British identity.

The sheer nationalistic fervour of 1914–18, the last time in British (and Western) history when millions volunteered to fight (and die), is, to much contemporary thinking, still inexplicable. Yet it was real, and so was the full participation of the country's ruling-class youth. Quite simply 'the great war' against Germany saw the English public-school 'Christian gentleman' go to war *en masse* – thus precluding a re-run of the eighteenth-century radical taunt that the upper classes were unpatriotic. And the 'classlessness' of this sacrifice may help explain why the ineptness and bungling of many within the senior officer corps during the carnage of the trenches provoked no revolutionary reaction once the war was over.

Yet the seeming triumph both for the British state and for Englishness didn't last too long. The sheer human toll taken in the trenches – as well as the lack of a clear ideological enmity between the Allies and Germany, propaganda about 'the hun' notwithstanding – all conspired to somewhat dim the glow of patriotic triumph and pride. Indeed, in the two decades which followed the carnage, internationalism and pacifism came to dominate political thinking, and were also rife amongst the general public.

Although nationalism received something of a set-back politically, it was nevertheless sustained culturally. The 1930s British cultural scene was dominated by a dense literary network which epitomised prewar Englishness. Elizabeth Young suggests that:

The briefest glance will suffice. Louis MacNeice, John Betjeman and Anthony Blunt, art critic and spy, attended Marlborough. Eton's cultural litany included Harold Acton, Cyril Connolly, George Orwell, Henry Green and Anthony Powell. A variety of public school friend-ships were consolidated at Oxford. Cecil Day-Lewis, MacNeice, Stephen Spender, Auden, Waugh, Graham Greene and Cyril Connolly clustered beneath the gleaming spires. . . . Valentine Cunningham makes it clear to what extent 'a small enclave of the English bourgeoisie' dominated cultural life during the first part of this century. Two out of the three main First World War poets – Rupert Brooke, Siegfried Sassoon, Wilfred Owen – were drawn from the officer class. Eng-lish nationalism, the tendency to close ranks around favoured sons could ultimately militate against Celtic outsiders like MacNeice.[81]

World War Two revived national, and nationalist, sentiment. And Englishness, too, had a very good war. The country faced, alone for some time, a clear, unambiguously evil, enemy. Unlike the French, it successfully repelled an invasion. And, 'it won the war', thus provid-ing the country and, through the glamorous lens of the burgeoning film media, the wider-world, with a number of heroes, most of them upper-class southern English types. In addition to the bulldog 'Churchill' stereotype, there was also the handle-bar moustached RAF fighter-pilot type (even though the RAF fighter pilots who, in Churchill's phrase, 'knocked the hun out of the mid-day sky' were, by and large, gram-mar-school boys from working-class and lower middle-class backgrounds, a point recognised by Churchill himself during the war).

The month of May, 1945, provided the image of Englishness with its last serious psychological boost. Field Marshal Bernard Law Montgomery was an Ulsterman, but could easily pass – by accent and bearing – as an archetypal public-school Englishman. On 5 May, com-manding the 21st Army group, he presided over the surrender of all German forces in North-West Germany, Holland and Denmark. Three days later, Winston Churchill – the ultimate symbol of warrior Eng-lishness – appeared alongside the royal family on the balcony of Buck-ingham Palace to salute 'Victory in Europe'. The British people could be forgiven for believing that the English governing class had pulled it off yet again; that Britain – of which admittedly they were only a marginal part, but a part none the less – was still the most powerful nation under the sun; and that the ideology of Britain's rulers, and the culture of Englishness, personified in the 'English bulldog' personality of Winston Churchill and the decent 'English reticence' of King George VI, would resonate around the globe as an emblem of eternal steadfastness, courage and ingenuity.

Following the war a major myth-making industry appeared which fed the illusion of British (normally meaning English) centrality in the defeat of the Germans. To some extent national identities serve the function of hiding awkward truths. Britain played an important though subsidiary part in the landings in Normandy in 1944, but the 'turning point of the war' was more likely to be located in the 1942 Battle of Stalingrad, or even in the first invasion of the European mainland in 1943 in Italy – under the leadership of the Americans. But the postwar British cultural industry and media vastly exaggerated the British contribution, as they did the role of Winston Churchill – who, as his own records more than abundantly testify, was very much the junior partner to Roosevelt throughout the last three and a half years of the war.

Churchill's postwar standing, particularly in America where he became a statesman and hero (and rivalled the posthumous popularity of Roosevelt) did wonders for the traditional image of upper-class England and Englishness – even though he himself was half-American. It gave it a new lease on life. For the Americans and their increasingly influential mass media, Churchill, the Englishman, was not only a war hero, he was also a political poet (in President John Kennedy's words, written by Theodore Sorenson, he 'marshalled the English language and sent it into battle').

Following hard on the heels of Churchill came Elizabeth Windsor and the 'new Elizabethan age'. Once the postwar Labour government was out of the way, the official national identity, Englishness, was most perfectly represented by the official duo of Queen and Prime Minister. Churchill was its political, and Elizabeth Windsor its cultural, face. And the 1950s – the first time the mass of working-class Britons had a taste of a consumer society – seemed to promise a country which could deliver mass 'peace and prosperity'.

Politically Britain still counted in the world as one of a 'magic circle' of Western nations – she had a seat at the United Nations, a privilege denied to Germany, and, for a while, was one of 'the big three'. Even as late as the late 1950s Harold Macmillan could, just about, get away with being considered a world leader, and, through the Commonwealth of Nations, the UK political elite (and particularly the Queen) could still present themselves as leaders of a multi-national alliance of states.

Even the emergence of the USA as a world power had a rub-off effect upon the English, particularly their upper classes. The English elite could claim pride of authorship of this newly powerful nation. In the immediate postwar period, during American world supremacy, the levers of power and culture in the USA were still largely controlled by Anglophile white Anglo-Saxon Protestants. English was the language of this new super-power and for some time, well into the 1970s, there remained a 'special relationship' between the USA and Britain.

Yet, this new dawn for Englishness was really its Indian summer. It all began to fall apart in the early 1960s when it became abundantly clear that Britain had suffered a major economic defeat. It was becoming apparent that the unreconstructed British economy was not going to perform, in the long term, on anything approaching a level of parity with the country's major competitors. Britain was slipping down the various economic 'league tables' (a term, from soccer, introduced in the early 1960s by Labour leader Harold Wilson to highlight Conservative economic failure). Thus a loss of confidence in the country's economic performance compounded the political humiliation of the country's ungainly retreat from its Suez operation in 1956.

THEME-PARK ENGLISHNESS OR 'ENGLISHNESS FOR EXPORT'

For many English people, even as the twentieth century drew to its close, the traditional idea of Englishness, although weakening, was still alive and well. Indeed, national self-consciousness had arguably somewhat intensified with post-1940s political and economic decline. With every passing postwar decade, almost as a feature of decline, the English appeared increasingly interested in themselves, in what Englishness meant in the modern world, in the search for the essence and deeper meaning of their nationality.

There was also a relatively clear view of what Englishness amounted to. In a recent, typical, depiction, one writer suggested that 'a group of dinner guests in their thirties' would describe Englishness as:

A bowl of scented roses on a sunlit table and the muted thwack of leather against willow. Umbrellas clashing on city streets and felt trilbies brim to brim at the races. A cup of tea, or a pre-prandial glass of sherry. The first cuckoo of spring and the first Pimms of summer. Kipling and *Just William*. Royal Doulton figurines and talking about the weather.[82]

In a somewhat similar vision of the meaning of Englishness, the 1990s saw the country's prime minister – John Major – evoking a nostalgic theme of nationality by quoting approvingly George Orwell at his most sentimental: '... the clatter of clogs in the Lancashire mill towns ... the old maids biking to Holy Communion through the mists of the autumn morning ...', and a leading advertising agency – with 'voice over' quoting from Shakespeare's 'sceptred isle' soliloquy – establishing for millions the images of cottage and countryside (set against 'less fortunate lands' with the channel 'defensive as a moat') for a television advertisement for tea.

This Englishness exists for export. It is the 'English product' which is sold around the world, particularly so in North America, but which is also aggressively marketed – mainly to upper income groups and to the international super rich – in continental Europe and amongst the third world elite, particularly in the Arab countries and East Asia. Increasingly it is becoming a key ingredient in the broader English heritage industry, which as part of the leisure and tourist industry can be expected to grow in a country increasingly relying upon the service sector. The Conservative Party under John Major recognised its importance when soon after Margaret Thatcher left Downing Street it established a 'Heritage Minister' with cabinet rank.

This 'English' product is primarily about lifestyle. Englishness is sold as a way of life. One of its flagship publications is *Country Life* (which publishes every week of the year, and can be acquired as an annual subscription in the United States for around $200). *Country Life* tells its audience how to acquire Englishness (at a price, of course). And it suggests that the heart of the matter of Englishness is the grand house or country cottage, and the related furnishings (advertisements for which take up almost half of the magazine), the English garden and the English dog, all of which appear in a rural setting. *Country Life* presents 'A week in the country' by the Duchess of Devonshire, and has even developed a series entitled 'Hero of the Countryside'.[83]

Country Life also presents a highly self-conscious 'how to do it' kind of Englishness. In an article entitled 'How a Gentleman should dress', the Duke of Devonshire advises: 'At Cambridge I wore flannels and tweed. Cavalry twill was just coming in and it was rather laughed at as the jodhpur in June brigade.'[84] And an 'English look' is presented for parading at the races, Ascot, the Badminton Horse trials, the Royal Windsor Horse Show, Henley, and of course, polo – at 'the events which make up our summer season'.[85] In promoting this 'English look' diversity is not encouraged – for instance, the men all tend to look like Charles Windsor in corduroys and tweeds, 'dressed in the best British country style' as *Country Life* put it.[86] Similar advice is offered over a range of pursuits from sports cars (normally referred to as 'motors' or 'motoring') to the proper way to picnic – Roy Strong offers, in 'A Question of Taste', advice on the traditional English picnic 'before the corporate clients promoted conspicuous wealth'.[87]

This 'stage Englishness' has been so successful that it has caused imitation: the inventing of an 'English' personality. An extreme, and somewhat sad, contemporary example is the amazing career of Stanley Olson. During the late 1960s, Stanley Olson, a Jewish-American from Akron, Ohio, left his country in his early twenties and set about re-inventing himself. He acquired what he considered to be an 'English' persona. In 1969, Olson, at the age of twenty-two, left America and set about 'rectifying nature's error: he would create himself anew – live as if born without parents, siblings, family history and religion, midwest education and cultural trappings. He moved to London and transformed himself – thoroughly, wholeheartedly, impeccably – into an Englishman.'[88]

He adopted the accent, the clothes, the mannerisms, indeed the *persona* of an English gentleman until, according to his biographer, 'Englishness [fitted] him like a glove.'[89] In his nearly twenty years in London – he died of a stroke at the early age of thirty-nine – he lived the manufactured life of an 'English Gentleman', an aesthete, a man of letters, a social lion with a circle (including, appropriately, the Duke of Devonshire) which he entertained, often lavishly, on the Akron-based Olson family fortune.

Olson's story is not so odd. It is the story of large numbers of Britons too. It is the journey taken by umpteen intelligent and aspiring working-class, lower middle-class and bourgeois young men from Britain's provincial towns and cities. Faced with so stark a chasm between mainstream British life and the life of an 'English gentleman', some have engaged in just as brutal a switch of identity as did Stanley Olson. Others have adopted the manners, lifestyle and ideology of Englishness more naturally and less abruptly. Even so, the journey from Akron to Englishness is hardly any further than the journey from Bristol or Birmingham or Manchester.

In any promotion of Englishness, of the 'English product', the upstairs–downstairs image needs to be catered to. Upstairs is covered by lashings of royalty – royal tittle-tattle primarily. And downstairs also makes regular appearances, though normally bathed in ladles of condescension and bordering on the kitsch. Identikit servants and 'loyal working folk' appear in the pages of *Country Life* – under the title of 'Living National Treasure', a hayrake maker, a basket maker, a gypsy caravan restorer and, inevitably, a housekeeper have been profiled.[90]

Of all the icons of theme-park heritage Englishness the most exalted must still be the game of cricket, particularly village cricket. No aspect of Englishness induces such sentimentality as the 'leather on willow' images:

> When the late squire of Crowcombe, Major Thomas Trollope Bellew, was buried last year, he was escorted to his grave not only by uniformed hunt servants, but also by his cricket team in their whites. The image of village cricket is enduring and endearing: it has its stock characters, its folklore, its champions, its literature and its idyllic settings – the green, with the church behind, and the pub somewhere handy. . . .[91]

This kind of rhapsodising is, of course, not really about the game of cricket. Those who play the game, and take it somewhat seriously, are often oblivious to its mystical cult status – for many of them it remains a game like any other, though more intelligent and competitive. Rather, the game – and its 'Englishness' – has in reality become a metaphor for the celebration of the English village and rural nostalgia. It has other attributes which make it attractive as an icon of nostagic Englishness. Of course, it was invented in England, and is largely played by Englishmen and those considered 'honorary Englishmen', from the ex-colonial lands, thus restricting it to the old imperial family. (Continental Europeans and Americans do not play the game.)

It also, particularly in the three-, four- or five-day game, and to a lesser extent at league or club level on Saturday and Sunday afternoons, exhibits and encourages a range of supposedly 'sturdy' 'English' qualities: perseverance, patience, 'team spirit' (although in truth, cricket, unlike soccer, is not much of a team game, involving at its heart a contest between bowler and batsman only) and, of course, 'fair play'. It is a measure of the extraordinary success of cricket as an English ritual and totem of national character that, more so than the real national game (in terms of popular support soccer would qualify for this prize), so much of the terminology of the game has entered into the mainstream of everyday usage in the language of contemporary British-English. 'Sticky wicket', 'end of play', 'stumped me', 'hit for six', 'straight bat', 'had a good innings' and the like are 'very English' phrases.

This contemporary theme-park Englishness also embraces a notion of English national character. According to the standard self-image promoted during the twentieth century the essence, the 'quintessentialness', of the Englishman and woman involved very prosaic qualities. The stereotype had it that English people were essentially practical and not overly-bright (certainly not, in the national phrase which mocks intellectualism, 'too clever by half'). Yet, at the same time, they were loyal and trustworthy ('sturdy' again suffices to describe the attribute). By contrast, foreigners (and 'foreignness'), particularly continental Europeans, were altogether more exotic: they were theoretical and – particularly southern Europeans – emotional, given to grand gestures and ideas, qualities which can easily make for instability.

Paul Addison has argued that it was Britain's role during the Second World War that induced this particular self-image of national character: 'On all sides publicists proclaimed that the key to victory lay in the native genius of a people who were sturdy, industrious and unimaginative – not very clever in fact – but moved by an inner spirit that expressed itself in such things as patriotism, a love of the countryside and a love of liberty.' He suggests that so powerful is this stereotype in the films and literature of the postwar period – the product not simply of Dunkirk, the Blitz and the subsequent mass-media legends, but also deriving from the English elite's reaction to the French Revolution and Napoleon – that 'it remains there to this day, a massive chunk of patriotic legend that still defies the best efforts of historians to break it up'.[92]

This notion – that the essence of Englishness combines ordinariness with a 'sturdy' love of liberty (and a concomitant need for privacy) – was extolled by two wartime English writers, J. B. Priestley and George Orwell, whose influence on the contemporary image of Englishness was profound. Priestley, both a novelist and a playwright, helped make his name by evoking Dunkirk as an obvious example of this English characteristic of sturdy independence. And the essayist and novelist George Orwell virtually exalted the concern for privacy and freedom (particularly from 'bossy' bureaucrats) as a unique attribute of Englishness.

Intriguingly, both Priestley and Orwell, who cornered the market in describing and evoking the life of England in the war-time and early postwar years, are themselves often both depicted as being 'very English'. One writer suggested that J. B. Priestley was so English that he still nestles 'in the nursery wing of the Anglo-Saxon mind'. And George Orwell was described by one of his leading biographers as being 'a specifically English writer and a specifically English character, both in his seeming amateurism ... and in his eccentricities' (a depiction which begs the question as to whether 'a specifically English' writer can possibly be both professional and normal!).[93]

To some extent this may be because Orwell and Priestly added to this contemporary idea of Englishness a certain glorification of English insularity and provincialism – an aspect, too, it is argued, of the works of the less political, though 'most English of writers', Alan Bennett.[94] They were the founders of 'Little England'. For them, England's reduced circumstances were no bad thing. No lovers of Empire and the aggrandising imperial mission, they domesticated the idea of Englishness. The true English spirit, they argued, was to be found at home, was provincial and practical – not outward looking, cosmopolitan and full of grand visions.

The domesticity of Priestley's and Orwell's Little Englandism was in part a reaction against the terrors of the grand designs of Fascism and Communism (and, to some extent, those of American Capitalism too, for both Priestley and Orwell were moderate socialists). Thus, the sheer cosiness of English life, instead of provoking a reaction against its limiting, unimaginative and unproductive qualities, was built into a virtue. And in the process one of the most revered values of Englishness became familiarity. Although current theme-park English images such as 'the muted thwack of leather on willow' or 'the first cuckoo of spring' may have been a little over-ripe for Orwell and Priestley – and, also too middle-class: for they were both determined to depict Englishness as a phenomenon existing beyond the home counties – they none the less both prized familiarism. In his famous essay 'The Lion and the Unicorn', George Orwell was at his sentimentalising best when describing familiar English scenes:

English civilisation ... is somehow bound up with solid breakfasts and gloomy Sundays, smoky towns and winding roads, green fields and red pillar-boxes. ... However much you hate it or laugh at it, you will never be happy away from it for any length of time. The suet puddings and the red pillar-boxes have entered into your soul.[95]

Little Englanders saw the country not only as cosy, but also as stable, indeed uniquely so. This idea of England as a peaceable island in a troubled world, and of Englishness as a stable pillar of cultural security, has carried itself forward from Orwell and Priestley into the contemporary debate about England's role in Europe. Almost fifty years after the end of the Second World War one of England's, and Englishness's, leading polemicists, the prolific Eurosceptic Paul Johnson, still sees Britain as uniquely stable, and continental life as somehow threatening this stability – indeed as redolent with images from the Second World War, of 'conflagrations' and of Hitler's panzers hurtling with a 'speed and intensity' through France. In an extraordinary commentary, one which is not unrepresentative of much contemporary English opinion, he argues:

> There is a feeling throughout Europe that democracy is not working and that the gap between what people want and what they are al-lowed by their rulers is too wide. That means trouble, and exactly how and where it starts is less important than the speed and inten-sity with which it will spread. A European conflagration will bring the Channel (as opposed to the Chunnel) back into fashion . . . as the continent slithers into anarchy – or worse – and we watch the exciting drama from our grandstand seats on the White Cliffs . . .[96]

So powerful is this Little England image of Englishness (stable, cosy, even twee) that it has increasingly assumed the proportions of an 'of-ficial' idea of Englishness. In the latter part of the twentieth century this theme-park Englishness (with its stage Englishmen and women) has become so dominant that it has forced aside other, more realistic, images of Englishness. It remains a mental strait-jacket which imposes itself upon the diversity and plurality of the real life of the country and its peoples. And it is, of course, as illusory as any of the other stage nationalisms (Irish, French, German) the English still laugh at.

As with any 'official' culture or ideology, Englishness presents us with problems of conformity. Inevitably, there remains a tendency to dismiss as un-English those things which do not meet the standard, approved style or product – even though they may represent the life and culture of millions of people living in the real England. For in-stance, Priestley himself once observed that the society emerging in England in the mid-1930s – clean, bright . . . factories, palatial cin-emas . . . crowds as rootless as the car which symbolised the age . . . *wasn't really England at all*'.[97] (Such a starkly narrow assessment begs large numbers of questions – some of them not wholly facetious. What about those English people who don't play cricket? Are they considered not really English at all? Is a writer who does not write like Betjeman – that 'most English of writers' – in fact under the influence of 'foreign' canon? What about those who play cricket, but are obviously not Eng-lish? Are they honorary English?)

This theme-park Englishness (cosy, soft in temperament, steadfast, and stable) – although perhaps unrecognisable to earlier generations of English – is, none the less, the end-product of some three centuries of the making, and refining, of a national identity. Of course, the idea of what it means to be English has changed, often radically, over time.

For instance, Englishness during the high-point of Empire became an imperial identity: conquering and hegemonic. Beram Saklatvala captured a somewhat romantic side of this dynamic Englishness when, in the late 1960s, he could write that:

> From their tiny kingdom lying off the northern shores of Europe the Anglo-Saxon people went out over the world taking their laws, their method of government, and their language with them. They built the colonies in North America, setting out their farms in the white plains and green valleys of the New World. They peopled Australia and New Zealand. They went into Africa and into Asia – governing many different people to whom they taught their language and their laws. They planted Parliaments in many lands, believing that representational government and government by consultation and consent were unarguably and self-evidently the best. . . . The Anglo-Saxon people . . . have given much to the world, perhaps more than the world now cares to acknowledge.[98]

As well as retreating into a more provincial aspect, Englishness has also recently undergone a softening process – a far cry from some of its previous images. For instance, the fifteenth-century printer William Caxton was described as a 'thoroughly English character' possessing attributes such as 'business acumen' and 'gusto' – terms not normally appended to the English in the late twentieth century, either by themselves or by foreigners.[99] In the nineteenth century, to be English often meant to be tough, indeed ruthless, coarsely commercial, adventurous and restless – to be world travellers (like Walter Ralegh or the explorers Richard Hakluyt and Francis Drake) or conquerors of more peaceable peoples (like Clive of India).

Yet, it is hardly surprising that today's Englishness – the homely, cosy, provincial and somewhat insular Englishness of the English theme-park – is less grandiose and imperial than its strutting forebears. For Englishness, like the nation it purports to represent, is now living in considerably reduced circumstances.

2 An Audit of Englishness

Compared with the sense of progress of the eighteenth and the triumph of the nineteenth, for Britain and the British the twentieth century has been one of unremitting decline. In 1890 the country was the leading political and economic European power, and in 1914 its national income was just below that of Germany, and its per capita income was almost double that of France and significantly higher than that of Germany. By 1980 Britain had almost half of the GNP of West Germany and had fallen well below France – and, later, was to fall below Italy. In 1914 Britain had just under a third of the national income of the United States. By 1980 she had about one-sixth.[1]

As well as this economic competition, Britain during the twentieth century also had to face the age of democracy. Throughout the West the franchise was vastly extended, individual rights became a major feature of social, political and economic life, and the old feudal orders and social hierarchies, never a feature of American social life, were progressively put to rest throughout Europe. Throughout the West, the new managerial techniques of the company have been introduced to somewhat match the changes in the political world. And on top of democratisation, the British were faced with, perhaps, the most difficult of all the changes: the internationalisation of economies and cultures.

The dominant English national culture of the British Isles was incapable of adapting to this new world. The harsh truth seems to be that by the very beginning of the twentieth century Englishness had become frozen in place, a settled culture, unable to change (except into the triviality of media-determined theme-park Englishness). The guardians of Englishness suddenly stopped looking forward, and 'the conviction that English culture was to be found in the past was stabilised'.[2] In sum, the Englishness of the late nineteenth century was the final product. As Philip Dodd argued, 'the people of these islands with their diverse cultural identities were invited to take their place, and become spectators of a culture already complete and represented for them by its trustees'.[3]

Yet, the national culture which had been constructed during the two preceding centuries hardly suited this new age. In the age of decline the traditional pretensions of Englishness fostered illusions of power and superiority; in the era of democracy Britain remained stubbornly hierarchical and traditional; and in the age of science and industry it remained captured by the allure of the rural.

Incapable of reflecting real changes in the real Britain and the real England, this frozen Englishness (representing little more than the modern remnants of the old imperial class) degenerated into a reactionary identity and ideology. It helps explain why, virtually alone amongst the peoples of the West, the British seemed unable to accept the erosion of 'sovereignty', and why they found it so difficult to adjust to European integration. It had become an identity wholly inadequate for the peoples of the British Isles during the twentieth century, hobbling their ability to compete and survive.

ILLUSIONS OF POWER

'We're in a very big world and we're now very lonely' argued the Archbishop of Canterbury in the spring of 1994. He suggested that 'we have lost nearly all our navy and air force and so on' and that 'We're a pretty ordinary little nation and yet we don't realise it.'[4]

This seemingly prosaic depiction was, none the less, unusual – particularly from so establishment a figure. It flew directly counter to the dominant postwar rhetoric of Britain's political class – a language of politics still couched in the self-importance, if not of Empire, then of a world role.

Even as late as the mid-1950s Winston Churchill could argue at a State Department dinner that 'only the English-speaking peoples count: that together they can rule the world'.[5] Incredibly, some forty years later, Prime Minister John Major could go even further, leaving the United States out of it. He argued, in a speech which one columnist said was difficult to believe unless 'you heard it with your own ears', that 'The United Kingdom – the greatest cradle of culture and academic and scientific and political achievement in modern times – that's not some trifle to be lightly set at risk . . . it is the highest cause this party knows – and we will defend it with every fibre of our being.'[6]

And this extraordinary sense of national self-importance was not restricted to Conservatives. In the aftermath of war the Labour-supporting *Daily Mirror* displayed an imperial tone (with a nice touch of condescension for all Britain's allies, particularly the brown peoples) which had echoes of pure Churchilliana as it remembered 'the grand Canadians who, when our peril was greatest, came to nourish and sustain our resistance . . . the Australians and New Zealanders who bore the brunt of the battle in Egypt and Greece . . . the loyal Indians and sons of Colonies who won new battle honours . . .'.[7] So did Ernest Bevin's belief in British exceptionalism – that Britain was 'not just another European country' – which became the guiding strategy of the foreign policy of the postwar Labour government.[8] This was the mental framework which, for the Labour right, was determined to create a 'British bomb', and, obversely, for the Labour left, sought 'to give moral leadership to the world'.

This sense of national self-importance found the loss of Empire extremely difficult to swallow. And in consequence it invented the idea of the Commonwealth, of the mythic notion of Britain as 'the centre of the Commonwealth of Nations':

> The conventional explanation of Britain's (or, better, England's) turning away from the world . . . is still summed up in Dean Acheson's aphorism: we have lost an empire but failed to find an alternative role. Not Europe, not a civilised and quietist insularity, not a rediscovery of nationhood in Britain's historical diversity. One escape route from this dilemma is to insist that we still have a kind of empire – the Commonwealth of Nations which continue to look up to us even if they are abominably rude much of the time.[9]

Britain's continuing, though diminishing, global links were to serve as a distorting lens through which a generation of political leaders saw Britain in relation to the world. Arguably it led to a series of foreign and defence policy blunders. The 1956 Suez adventure might not have been attempted had the realities of Britain's new relationship both with the emerging third world and, more importantly, with the United States been fully understood. Britain's refusal to involve herself in the negotiations leading up to the formation of the European Community was also based upon an over-blown view of Britain's global position.

Over three decades later Britain's political establishment was still not connecting with reality – as it entered the pound in the European Communities' Exchange-Rate Mechanism at an unsustainably high level, a level later proved, by the freely-floating regime, to be far too high for the country's economic performance. Later, during John Major's second administration, even the British Foreign Office, whilst accepting that Britain possessed a much reduced role, none the less revelled in a new kind of self-importance: a belief that the country, and its Foreign Secretary Douglas Hurd, 'punched above her/his weight'.

The sense of self-importance which the national culture of Englishness induced served to reinforce British insularity. In late twentieth-century commentary and journalism many purely British events were still regularly depicted as 'moments in history' (as though what happened in Britain was still of global consequence), and a wide range of British institutions were still being described as 'the best in the world'. The BBC was often a candidate for such exultation, so it was not unusual for a new director-general of the BBC to be described by a national newspaper as having 'the most important job in the world'.[10]

High-Tory ideology – a key intellectual component of Englishness – tended not only to evoke, but also to encourage, a disposition towards the familiar. Lord Hugh Cecil could suggest that 'distrust of the unknown and the love of the familiar' should amount to nothing less than the guiding principle of the Conservative Party in the twentieth century. More recently, Michael Oakshott has suggested that 'change is a threat to identity, and every change is an emblem of extinction'.[11]

The two prime ministers of appeasement typified this insular attitude. Stanley Baldwin rarely travelled abroad, and made something of a point about it. Neville Chamberlain was also uninspired by anything outside of the country, treating the European mainland in a cold and disdainful manner – not, as is often argued, as a supplicant. In many ways he most perfectly represented the British imperial mentality in the early twentieth century. 'His vanity was monstrous, his ambition ruthless.' 'After Munich, when he was asked by a fellow guest at a dinner party why Hitler's promise should be trusted, after so many promises made by him had been broken, he replied that, this time, it was different: "this time he promised *me*".'[12]

Insularity mixed with superiority to produce a powerful continuing belief in British – and English – exceptionalism. Geoffrey Elton has argued that ancient prejudices have given 'lasting currency to two English convictions: that every other realm groaned under despots and that everywhere else the peasantry had to live on mere vegetables, while in England Kings governed with the active consent of their subjects and people ate good red meat'.[13] There was also the notion that the rights of man were 'the rights not of Man but of English men and women'.[14] And: 'this Island was blest, Sir' says Charles Dickens's Mr Podsnap 'to the Direct Exclusion of such Other Countries as – as there may happen to be'.[15]

These sentiments echoed down the centuries to produce a British chauvinism which has exhibited itself in varying guises throughout twentieth-century British society. These attitudes can take a stark form

– as when English football supporters chant 'we won the war' in European cities or 'two world wars and one world cup' in front of German supporters. And they can also induce some visceral views about the inadequacy of other nations – particularly France. A Methodist grocer in Lincolnshire, the father of the country's most famous post-Churchill prime minister, could say that the French nation was 'corrupt from top to bottom', and a leading journalist could argue that the national experience of France amounts to 'a bureaucratic oligarchy punctuated by popular reigns of terror'.[16]

Anthony Smith has argued that a distinction needs to be drawn between

> two kinds of nationalism, ethnocentric and polycentric. The former or 'weaker' kind was a movement of resistance to foreign rule in order to preserve the group's culture and freedom. The outsider was the 'barbarian', the 'heathen'; and value pertained only to one's own group and its gods. The 'polycentric' kind of nationalism sees the world as divided into nations, or collective individualities, each with its own value, each requiring a state of its own to realise its communal potential and sovereign autonomy, and each seeking to join the 'family of nations' by contributing its peculiar experiences to the common fund of humanity.[17]

The legacy bequeathed by the unadapted national culture of Englishness to late twentieth-century British national sensibility was to help shape it into the former, not the latter, kind of nationalism.

These nationalist illusions of power and superiority were increasingly to clash with the realities of the world which Britain was inhabiting. The country's humiliation during the Suez affair and the jolting experience of joining the European Community both served to emphasise these new realities; though there was little in the way of a body of domestic opinion which sought to point the new awkward realities out. Increasingly, though, foreign opinion was filling this void. Britain's partners in the European union were beginning to become outspoken about Britain's traditionalist attitudes. As was much of third world opinion. A Malaysian journalist, writing in 1994, argued that

> Britain needs to adjust to the emerging post-modern world, which requires cultural awareness and sensitivity to the concerns and attitudes of others. Today, Britain is the beggar; it can no longer insult others with impunity or parade its ingrained prejudices. In the increasingly prosperous economies [of Asia], paternalism and cultural

ignorance will be penalised where it really hurts: in . . . [your] pockets.'[18]

A REACTIONARY IDENTITY

Nationalism was not the only discordant note sounded by the national culture of Englishness – for it was also decidedly uneasy about the age of democracy. In fact, Englishness, like most of the country's institutions, was born and formed in a pre-democratic age.

The politics of Englishness is certainly pre-democratic. Its great institutions – monarchy, Lords, Commons, the established church – were all forged in much earlier times, and have had to adapt to the age of democracy. The monarchy, the Lords and the established church have adapted by lessening their formal roles in the life of the evolving nation. The Commons has adapted by widening its franchise. Yet the basic structures of a state created in feudal times have remained – and this continuity is the primary reason why the British constitution, with its unwritten rules, seems so incongruous amongst the democratic nations.

Yet, democracy is more than a constitutional form, it is also a way of looking at the world. And Englishness looked at the world from rather a great height. Class hierarchies simply couldn't allow the national culture to be anything else than an expression and celebration of the culture of its ruling classes. Thus the culture never came to terms with mass society. As Jack and Adam Lively argue in their excellent survey of British democracy, 'there is not the same tradition in British literature of celebrating "democracy" as a broad, almost aesthetic idea that there is, for example, in America'. In fact, they go further, suggesting that 'British writers have been variously attracted and repelled by this idea.'[19]

In the political culture of modern Britain, 'we the people' is a phrase with little resonance or meaning. There was, and is, no 'British dream' to match 'the American dream' – the idea that in a democratic culture anyone can do well and share in its full fruits. The ultimate political authority of the British state has rested with the crown, and subsequently in 'the crown in Parliament', not, as in the American republic, with 'the people'. Historically, this role of 'the crown' – together with working-class social deference and a deep-seated belief in inequality amongst the rulers – has limited the notion of citizenship, and served to instill a widespread idea that the people of Britain do not own their own country. Thus can Edward Carpenter, in his late nineteenth-century essay on democracy, say that 'I see a great land waiting for its own people to come and take possession of it.'[20]

This sense that 'the people' – either collectively or individually – did not own their own country was a reflection of the undemocratic reality of a ruling class. Even that great advocate of English cultural unity, George Orwell, could argue in 1941, at the height of the Second World War, that 'at the moment of writing it is still possible to speak of a ruling class'.[21]

It was the essentially undemocratic ruling values of this ruling class which allowed the country's seismic industrial experience to be carried through with hardly any concern for the lives of the people. Both the socialist historian E. P. Thompson and the more conservative historian Correlli Barnett agree that the period of industrialisation was a top–down affair, guided by a small, ruthless, elite and, in Thompson's words 'unrelieved by any sense of national participation in a communal effort. . . . Its ideology was that of the masters alone.'[22] Barnett agrees. He paints a picture of life in nineteenth-century Britain, the life 'which moulded the character of the new working class: a home life in a mean brick hovel without piped water in an unpaved street with open drains'. According to Barnett the working classes were no better off than 'Bantu coolies'.[23]

Professor Robert Cowan has described the scene in Glasgow in 1844:

In all districts of the burgh, and in the suburbs, there is a want of sewerage and drainage . . . the streets, or rather the lanes and alleys, in which the poor live are filthy beyond measure . . . the houses, in the disease-haunted areas, are ruinous, ill-constructed, and, to an incredible extent, destitute of furniture. . . . In many there is not a single article of bedding, and the body clothes of the inmates are of the most revolting description.[24]

As well as being ill-clothed, ill-housed and insanitary, the working classes – and other social groups too – were ill-educated. A Royal Commission in 1868 linked this low standard of life to potential economic decline:

We are bound to add that our evidence appears to show that our industrial classes have not even the basis of a sound general education on which alone technical education can rest. . . . In fact our deficiency is not merely a deficiency in technical education, but . . .

in general intelligence, and unless we remedy this want we shall gradually but surely find that our undeniable superiority in wealth and perhaps in energy will not save us from decline.[25]

Richard Cobden made much the same point some thirty years earlier, in 1835, when he suggested that 'national prosperity lies in the timely re-modelling of our system, so as to put it as nearly as possible on an equality with the improved management of the Americans'.[26]

Industrialism was forged in a pre-democratic age – and a modern democratic sensitivity was hardly to be expected. However, the effect of the deeply undemocratic ideology of Englishness upon the human capital of the country was truly devastating. As was the inability of the governing ideology of Englishness to comprehend the link between a dismissive attitude to 'lower orders' and economic competitiveness. Coolies have consequences. There is an initial economic pay-off in treating people as hardly human; yet ultimately it is self-defeating, as skills, work-rates and commitment become just as important as costs. (It was probably not by chance that Cromwell's new model army – which was not only better trained and better run, but also better treated than the royalist military – won the day.)

And this historic lack of concern for the capability of the country's human capital finds an echo today in the skills-gap between Britain and its competitors, and in the more generalised corporate view of the dispensable workforce – the idea that short-term profitability not medium-term market strategy should govern employment levels and conditions.

The way in which Britain's industrialisation was forged took its toll on the self-confidence and self-esteem of the working people. But the culture and ideology of Englishness took its toll on the confidence of virtually everyone outside the ruling groups. Englishness evoked power, assuredness and effortless superiority, but only for those who could participate in it. And Englishness was not constructed for, or meant for, everybody. In fact, exactly the opposite. It was to be lived by a few only; the rest assigned to the status of onlookers and servants. This lack of a citizenship culture – of a general public belief that they have a stake in and own the state – is what led David Lloyd George to assert that living in Britain was like 'trespassing in your own land'.

This deeply exclusive and exclusionary culture (the idea that some people are 'worth more' than others) – when added to the social apartheid and economic deprivation of the early capitalism – can help explain why there were, and are, low levels of self-esteem and high levels of social deference in twentieth-century Britain.[27] The socially-deferential

Briton may have been the right kind of social product for an ordered society, but was of less use in the more assertive, market-oriented, competitive era.

THE GENTLEMAN CULTURE

If the continuing hold of the ideology of Englishness precluded the British from adapting to their reduced international status and to a more democratic age, it may also – although these things are very hard to measure – have taken a toll on the competitiveness of the nation.

The central social character of Englishness – the 'English gentleman' – may have been noble and good, but his wider influence was certainly less than positive. He became a powerful traditional social image in a society which was slowly modernising. Associated not only with elitist values in a democratising society, but with pre-industrial values in an increasingly industrial society, and with rural manners in the most urban country in the world, the power of the idea of 'the gentleman' – still alive in post-Second World War Britain – certainly acted to constrain social and cultural change. With him at the helm the country entered the highly competitive post-1945 global economy under a severe disadvantage and with a large handicap.

The gentleman culture was resistant to industry. As the American cultural historian Martin Weiner has suggested:

> In the world's first industrial nation, industrialism did not seem quite at home. In the country which had started mankind on 'the great ascent' economic growth was frequently viewed with suspicion and disdain. Having pioneered urbanisation, the English ignored or disparaged cities. The more I explored these incongruities, the more important they seemed to become. . . . Taken together they bore witness to a cultural cordon sanitaire encircling the forces of economic development – technology, industry and commerce.[28]

This anti-industrial aspect of Englishness reflected itself in the less than adequate support offered to science and technology in schools and universities. David Coates, although warning analysts not to 'swallow whole' the cultural explanation of UK underperformance in the twentieth century, nevertheless sees some force in what he calls the 'pre-industrial class pathology' of the country. He suggests that there was in the nineteenth-century educational system a 'generalised antipathy to science, and an inflated view of the importance of religious and literary education'.[29] And other academic analysts give some life to this thesis by reporting that Britain's 'failure to support science in schools and universities ... gave [the UK] an annual output at the beginning of the [twentieth] century of 300 chemistry graduates, fewer than the science staff at one German university, and about the same as the number of research chemists at one German dye firm'.[30]

The reason for this bias against industry, science and technology in the culture and ideology of Englishness was to be found in the landed character of the national culture. The English political and economic elites who helped forge Englishness in the eighteenth century were the inheritors of the system of primogeniture. The Celtic social system had allowed 'partible inheritance' (the breaking up of inherited land amongst numbers of inheritors), but the English system kept large land aggregations intact, helping the formation of an aristocracy.[31] And, naturally, this politically and culturally influential aristocracy, a class based in the economy and culture of rural England, saw to it that the values of rural life were protected and projected.

This powerful reactionary landed ideology was so dominant that it held sway way beyond culture – for it served to inform the structures of English, and later British, government itself. Indeed, 'the rural gentleman was the purest and most authentic embodiment of the ancient national character ... the surest guarantor of authentically representative government'.[32] The argument that it was 'representative' is intriguing, but is based upon the aristocratic view that 'society' did not include the vast majority of the British people. And, for the next century or so, the landed character of Englishness continued to determine the composition of the House of Lords and, to a considerable though lesser extent, the character of the Commons.

This culture of ruralism also helped to devalue the virtues of commerce – primarily prosperity – and evoke the virtue of 'poverty' (as long as it was restricted to the lower orders.) As Thomas Gray looked down the Vale of Grasmere in the latter half of the eighteenth century he declared 'Not a single red tile, no flaring gentleman's house, or garden walls, break in upon the repose of this little unsuspected paradise; but all is peace, rusticity, and happy poverty in its neatest most becoming attire.'[33]

This culture of ruralism was still dominant during the early days of state education. In the later decades of the nineteenth century it became one of the prominent images in the teaching of English:

The hymns that children sang every day were, of course, completely
rural in imagery and pre-industrial in sensibility: 'We plough the
fields and scatter / The good seed on the land'. 'There sheep may
safely graze.' 'All things bright and beautiful'. 'The rich man in his
castle / The poor man at his gate.' There are simply no hymns which
acknowledge the urban experience. Likewise the proverbs and say-
ings that were taught were largely pastoral in origin: 'Might as well
be hanged for a sheep as for a lamb', 'Casting pearls before swine' . . .
'what is sauce for the goose is sauce for the gander', 'It's no good
locking the stable door after the horse has bolted.'[34]

Nineteenth-century English rural enthusiasm was, at its core, reactionary and nostalgic. In J. B. Priestley's *The Beauty of Britain*, published in 1933, the English, not the British, countryside 'was projected
as an emblem of true Englishness, polite and reticent, a landscape without
the dramatic contrasts of foreign scenery'.[35] Alex Potts suggests that
'the "Hay Wain" became a visual cliché'[36] and that J. H. Massingham
[a 1930s writer] sought to define, through his picture of an 'old England' of beautiful countryside, a national tradition based upon the conservative idea of the virtue of organic life as opposed to 'abstract'
progress. He also argued that the rural instinct at the heart of Englishness was essentially anti-industrial and anti-capitalist and was seen by
many leftists as providing a bulwark against 'such horrid foreign mod-
ernities as Fascism and Stalinism'.[37]
Proponents of this arcadian vision were still well represented amongst
the country's late twentieth-century intelligentsia. Jonathan Raban describes Highgate Hill in the 1970s:

> On the clear windy top of Highgate Hill there is a community of
> ardent villagers. They wear country clothes – riding macs and head-
> scarves, tweeds and Wellington boots – and talk in gentry voices,
> braying bravely over the tops of taxis. They have their church, their
> tea-shop, their family grocer, their village green, three village pubs,
> and the Highgate Society with its coffee mornings, its knighted presi-
> dent and its evening lectures.[38]

This gentleman culture – forged in the land, anti-scientific and industrial – was the central reason for Britain's inability to develop a technical education which could compete with the continental competitors.

The Royal Commission reporting on technical education in the year 1900 suggested that technical higher elementary schools similar to those on the continent were 'singularly lacking in our own country', and that 'your commissioners cannot repeat too often that they have been impressed with the general intelligence and technical knowledge of the masters and managers of industrial establishments on the Continent'.[39]

Instead of a solid education in technology, the English 'Christian gentleman' was schooled in a high-minded classical and liberal arts education. Herbert Spencer, the country's leading proponent of business values, could argue in the middle nineteenth century that English education too often omitted that 'which most nearly concerns the business of life' and that 'our industries would cease were it not for the information which men begin to acquire, as best they may, after their education is said to be finished'.[40]

Cardinal Newman summed up the dominant Victorian view about the objectives of education: 'Liberal education makes not the Christian, nor the Catholic, but the gentleman. It is well to be a gentleman, it is well to have a cultivated intellect, a delicate taste, a candid, equitable, dispassionate mind, a noble and courteous bearing in the conduct of life . . .'[41]

John Stuart Mill and Thomas Huxley also squared off in this debate. Mill argued, in 1867, that: 'universities are not intended to teach the knowledge required to fit men for some special mode of gaining their livelihood. Their object is not to make skilful lawyers, or physicians, or engineers, but capable and cultivated human beings.'[42] Whereas Huxley, some ninety years ahead of C. P. Snow, offered science and technology as an alternative educational foundation for creating Mill's 'capable and cultivated human beings'.[43]

In the roster of Englishness Mill, not Huxley, would take pride of place, and the educated 'gentleman', the amateur, the cultivated 'all rounder', was to form the archetype and the ideal around which British education was to be constructed for the next century. And the continuing dominance of the public schools and the ancient universities – where this bias was most entrenched – was to ensure that the culture of education contributed little to the country's industrial performance. The life of industry – and the prosperity of the people – limped on regardless.

THE RADICAL FAILURE

Testimony to the continuing strength of the culture and ideology of Englishness was the weakness of the political opposition to it. Post-1945 Britain has seen three avowedly radical governments (the Attlee, Wilson and Thatcher administrations), yet none of them directed their radicalism towards the structures and ethos of Englishness, or even targetted the 'gentleman culture' as a serious obstacle to their reforming zeal.

The Attlee administration came to power whilst Britain still possessed a world-wide empire, and after the culture of Englishness had received a huge shot in the arm by 'victory' in the war. And neither primary faction on the British left – the Labourists around Ernest Bevin and Herbert Morrison and the socialists around Aneurin Bevan – saw the traditionalist and aristocratic culture of Englishness as meriting much attention. Many right-wing Labourists were socially deferential and not only identified with the Empire, the monarchy, and the whole paraphernalia of the Westminster–UK state, but embraced the nationalism and the racism of the national culture. The Labour left – and the developing Marxist alternative within it – also contained traditionalist elements, many of them imperial and national in their underlying assumptions. A strain of socialist thinking was heavily Anglo-centric, believing not only in English exceptionalism (in the English as an historically democratic peoples) but also in the contemporary moral authority of the English and British people – an authority which needed to be exhibited by renouncing Empire and nuclear weapons. And the harder left (the less romantic, more scientific, socialists) saw overhauling, and transforming, capitalism as the central strategic objective – *not* the democratisation of the institutions and the culture.

These two strands of British left-wing politics were still flourishing during Harold Wilson's Labour administrations in the middle to late 1960s. In the small number of years before the Labour government was 'blown off course' (and concentrated wholly upon economic crisis-management), radical political ideas – based upon propositions for modernising Britain – found some currency. An emerging group of revisionist social democrats – centred around Tony Crosland and Roy Jenkins – were beginning to challenge the traditionalism of both the Labour right and left. And Tony Crosland, by far the most intellectually gifted of the social democrats, had articulated some of these modernising sentiments in his book *The Future of Socialism*, published in 1956. The strong American connections of some of these social democrats gave them a glimpse into the more modern, egalitarian and open culture of the United States, and into Britain's less than central role in the wider world.

This modernising strand of British social democracy was the theme chosen by Harold Wilson – 'the white heat of the technological revolution' – to win the 1964 general election. Wilson also, during the campaign, unleashed some modernising – anti-aristocratic – rhetorical flourishes against the Conservative prime minister, 'the fourteenth Earl', and against 'the gentleman and players society'. This was the very first time that a British party leader had talked in these almost cultural terms (it echoed Lloyd George at the beginning of the century); and Wilson's political advisor and fellow cabinet minister Richard Crossman even initiated a serious attempt to reform the House of Lords (a proposal blocked by an alliance between Michael Foot and Enoch Powell). However, this flirtation with modernisation was put to rest once the economic problems overcame the Labour government.

The few twentieth-century opponents of the country's governing national culture and ideology had always tended to seek constitutional change as a mechanism for deeper change in social and political attitudes. This had been the strategy of the old radicals and of the radicals within the reforming Liberal Party of the pre-1914 era. And post-Second World War modernisers – such as John MacIntosh, the Labour MP and revisionist social democrat who pioneered the idea of devolution and parliamentary change – also saw the constitution as a reactionary agency. Yet constitutional change had hardly been on the agenda since the Liberals had 'taken on' the House of Lords in the pre-First World War period. The crisis in the monarchy during the abdication had been averted by secret political pressure and a media black-out, and economics and foreign policy had dominated the 1930s – as they did the 1940s. In the 1950s, when the world-wide post-war boom gave the country something of a respite, the Conservative governments – still heavily dominated by the 'knights of the shires' – pursued their traditional stance of uninterest in constitutional change.

The 1970–74 Conservative government of Edward Heath was, intriguingly, very different from the earlier Tory administrations. Heath was the first elected leader of the Conservative Party, he was a grammar-school product and an avowed moderniser. There was no rhetoric of opposition to the bastions of Englishness – like the monarchy and the Lords and the established church – and no overt flourishes of radicalism (Heath was a Conservative Prime Minister!). Yet, Heath became extremely impatient with what he considered to be old-fashioned management practices and a reactionary trade union movement. And, constitutionally, he engineered the country's entry into the European Community – thus forging a new constitutional instrument which ultimately would become poised like a dagger at the traditions of Englishness.

It was from the administration of Margaret Thatcher that an overt attempt at a 'cultural revolution' was to come. Thatcher was an almost perfect candidate to overhaul the traditionalist national culture. A woman, therefore an outsider, provincial from a small town in Lincolnshire, middle to lower middle-class in social attitudes, highly ambitious, restless, bright and determined.

Indeed, once she had become Prime Minister she was to pitch the rhetoric of Thatcherism against the idea of the squirearchy, 'the gentleman'. Increasingly annoyed by the upper-class male Tories who surrounded her in the cabinet, she seemingly developed a theory which sounded very much like that of the old radicals – and the new analysts of decline, Martin Weiner and Correlli Barnett. The Thatcherite thesis went that: the aristocratic 'toff' classes were part of the problem of decline. It was their semi-feudal concern for the masses – their tenants and estate workers – that made them support the Keynesian consensus and the welfare-state and made them hostile to the radicalising force of the free market. Britain needed to end this paternalism and to create a market-oriented 'enterprise culture' which would open society up to the talents at its disposal. (Thatcher even said she supported a 'classless society' – a theme which annoyed her more traditionalist Tory supporters.)

Thatcher (and Thatcherism) was, though, schizophrenic about English traditionalism. Part of her saw the need for a major assault upon this national culture, and yet another part of her was rather fond of it. Whereas Heath had abolished hereditary peers, Margaret Thatcher, peculiarly, brought them back. And she presided over a serious increase in the powers of the central government in Westminster, a process which, by denying diversity and plurality, actually enhanced the culture of Englishness.

Following the Falklands War she resolved the tension in her (and in all modern Conservatives) between economic liberalism and national sentiment by siding with nationalism – and, by associating herself with an implacably hostile attitude to the European Community and Union, a growing current of chauvinism. For the later Thatcher, Englishness was not to be overcome – in order to create a truly open and competitive society – rather, it was to be evoked, lauded, gloried in.

Yet, the question remains as to why the radicalism inherent in market consumerism – as it challenges traditional ways of doing things, breaks up old tribal and communal bonds, and makes nations and national cultures increasingly redundant – made such a small impact upon the traditional national culture of Britain. Indeed, by the time Margaret Thatcher left office it was arguable that there had been something of a recrudescence of national sentiment.

Of course, Margaret Thatcher's own effort to raise national consciousness probably played a part. So too did the recession and job losses of the early 1990s – which tend to reinforce solidarities. However, ultimately the explanation may lie in the somewhat sophisticated argument that dramatic shifts to a market economy may not, after all, alter underlying culture, but rather, simply reinforce it. Charles Hampden-Turner has argued that markets are not independent of culture. He suggests that 'market forces, like weather systems, have prevailing winds and known currents. To "leave it to market forces" in the hallowed tradition of classical economics is not . . . to submit to an impersonal mechanism of allocation, but rather to the *forces of British culture*. Laissez faire is equivalent to the injunction "let British culture be".'[44]

If Hampden-Turner is right then the market revolution of Thatcherism – the privatisation, the de-regulation, the diffusion of ownership in shares and housing – simply reinforced what he calls 'the forces of British culture'. Without parallel constitutional and institutional changes, these market-driven reforms – together with the taxation changes – may simply have served to provide the country's land-based 'old money' (and, thus, the culture of Englishness) with a new lease on life. The Conservatives, even during the radicalism of the Thatcher era, were unable to create the necessary impetus behind a modernising bourgeois revolution which would sweep away the old culture. (Perhaps only a modernising Labour government, unhindered by the lingering allure of the aristocratic legend, can do that?)

Thus, Thatcherism – coming when it did – became a force of continuity, bolstering, not shattering, the pre-existing culture of Englishness. And after all the exertions of the 1980s, all the restless activity, the 'permanent revolution', the claims of 'new era's' and 'irreversible changes', by the early 1990s Britain remained twenty-first of twenty-three nations in 'Anticipated Net Increase in New Business'.

Britain's domestic radicals have not caused the national culture and ideology any serious trouble. The real 'cultural revolution' was coming from outside the shores, from beyond the water's edge.

3 Identity Crisis

CLIENT-STATE

Although the national culture of Englishness was strong enough to withstand domestic challenges, it was the crisis of the British nation-state – of the UK – that was to prove its undoing. Britain had entered the Second World War as a 'sovereign' independent power. Only a few years later it had lost, along with its empire, this precious independence. The power which had 'won the war' had lost its independence because its economic base was inadequate to sustain such independence.

The economic decline was comparative. Throughout the twentieth century Britain's GNP was generally rising and the condition of her people was broadly improving, certainly so during the 1950s and 1960s – the very years when Britain was falling behind many of its continental competitors. Yet, comparative decline was of crucial importance. If Britain had been able to match the economic performance of the United States then not only would it have been able to retain its independence of action, but (as was the case in the nineteenth century) it would have been able to construct, lead and guide a world economic system. As it was, comparative decline was a cruel task-master: for, under its sway, Britain not only ceased to remain an independent nation, an independent player on the international scene, but became, in all but name, a client-state of the United States.

The comparative decline was precipitate. In 1870, at the height of Victorian power and prosperity, Britain's share of world manufactured exports was 45 per cent; by 1950 it had fallen to 26 per cent; and by 1989 to only 9 per cent. Britain's share of manufacturing output reached 22.9 per cent of the world level in 1880; by 1913, on the eve of the Great War, it was 13.6 per cent and by 1938, on the eve of World War II, it was 10.7 per cent. In 1890 Britain was second only to the United States in iron and steel production (producing 8 million tons of pig iron) but by 1913 the country was ranked third (producing only 7.7 million tons of steel, compared with Germany, 17.6 million, and the USA, 31.8 million, who were ranked second and first respectively).

One reason for Britain's rather swift fall from economic pre-eminence was that its Victorian economic performance, though impressive, was not much of a launching pad. Britain's economic growth in the nineteenth century was, by today's standards, relatively slow; investment rates were fairly paltry – particularly in education and training. As late as 1870 the average number of years of schooling for male workers was as low as 4.3, and share of GNP invested in machinery and equipment never exceeded 2 per cent. As the economic historian Nick Craft has pointed out, the basic enterprise in the growing Victorian economy was 'small-scale family capitalism rather than the joint-stock multi-divisional corporations which were to give the United States its great capitalist boost in the twentieth century.' Americans pioneered the development of the large corporation with the associated investments in highly trained management which this required 'whereas in Britain managers continued to be poorly trained and recruited from a narrow social elite'. In the new century, the conditions needed for economic success were changing, and in ways which were not good news for Britain: 'a much higher level of investment, more skilled workforce and more sophisticated management' were becoming the order of the day.[1]

On the eve of the First World War Britain still possessed a high per capita income (amongst the great powers, second only to the United States), yet the writing was on the wall. Indeed, in 1913 – when national economies still had meaning – Britain was slipping well behind its competitors in a whole range of industrial sectors. It was first in rail and shipping, but third in textiles, fourth in alcohol and tobacco, and, crucially, way behind in many of the lighter industries which were to dominate the new commercial age (eleventh in chemicals, twelfth in cars and aircraft, thirteenth in books and films, fourteenth in bricks and glass, fifteenth in wood and leather and eighteenth in electricals).[2]

From its pre-eminence at the height of Empire, Britain had fallen so far and so fast that by the late 1930s it became increasingly dependent – for its very survival – upon another country: the United States. There were two phases in this unfolding dependence. The first began when the country's inter-war re-armament programme became utterly reliant upon American industry and technology. American machinery was needed to equip British industry for the production of tanks, aero-engines and weapons and 'Britain had to turn to America even for steel, the very foundation of an advanced industrial economy in peace or in war.'[3] By 1940 Britain was bankrupt, 'incapable either of waging war or of sustaining her national life. In that summer of heroic attitudes, therefore, when the English scanned the skies for the Luftwaffe and the sea for the German army, and thrilled to Churchillian rhetoric on the wireless,

England's (sic) existence as an independent, self-sustaining power was reckoned by the Government to have just four months to run'.[4] (Although the national culture – the English way of life – was about to receive a new, though short, lease of life from the war, it must indeed have seemed in 1940 that, along with its country and its nation-state, it was about to expire then and there.)

After 1940 Britain's war effort – particularly the output of guns and aircraft – would have been out of the question without the American machine-tool industry: the country's domestic machine-tool industry was simply too inefficient and unskilled to produce the quality and output of guns and aircraft needed. The design and manufacture of British tanks (particularly the Covenanter, described by Barnett as 'junk') remained a problem, and by the summer of 1942 the famous British Eighth Army was equipped with almost twice as many American (Grants and Stuarts) as British (Crusader) tanks. Even in the sensitive and crucial radar industry Britain became reliant upon North America for sophisticated parts – such as magnetrons for the airborne interception radar for night fighters. It was estimated in 1943 that annual imports of radio components and equipment from the USA equalled four-fifths of British production. As with other war technologies, British inventive and theoretical science was first rate, but production and design were often below the standards of allies and potential competitors.[5]

Britain also became reliant upon American financial goodwill. British reserves had run out by the early spring of 1941 and the country was in no position to repay America for war supplies. However, the 'Defense of the United States Act' – otherwise known as 'lend-lease' – was passed by Congress in March 1941 and thenceforth, for the rest of the war, Britain no longer needed to wage war 'within her own means'. She became 'as dependent upon American strength as a patient on a life-support machine'.[6]

By 1944 so dependent upon the United States had Britain become that it played host to hundreds of thousands of American troops, the only foreign army to be stationed on British soil since the Norman invasion. Britain was unable to prosecute a second front without the United States, and her new subordinate relationship to her American protector was soon revealed when an American, General Eisenhower, became the supreme allied commander. And it was under his leadership that the British, from British soil, encouraged the first non-European army to set foot in continental Europe since the Mongol invasion. In such an environment the idea – central to the ideology of Englishness – of Britain as an independent, 'sovereign' nation was extremely difficult to sustain.

These American troops left Europe and Britain immediately upon the armistice. And for a time it seemed as though, the exigencies and desperations of war over, Britain was regaining her independence, returning to a 'sovereign' state. Yet, the second phase of Britain's dependence upon the United States was about to begin. When, after the Marshall Plan and the setting up of NATO, the Americans returned to Britain and Europe – both economically and militarily – Britain became a key player (for a time, the key European player) in the American-led Western system.

It was a role – soon dubbed 'the special relationship' – which was able to appease national sensibilities and pride, at least for a while. Yet, the reality was that Britain, yet again, became utterly dependent upon the United States: *and more so than during the war*. Whereas the wartime dependence could at least be sold as a temporary emergency, the cold-war dependence, it seemed at the time, was open-ended, even permanent. There could be no more poignant sign of the dependence of a once independent and proud (not to say arrogant) imperial English ruling class than having to shelter under the American nuclear umbrella, and seek protection – in the form of an ultimate nuclear guarantee – from a foreign government against an even more 'foreign' nation-state.

Britain's own nuclear bomb was built, originally by the postwar Labour cabinet, as an attempt to retain some independent influence and to keep a seat at the geo-political 'top table'. Yet, the British bomb's delivery system increasingly became dependent – certainly so after the 1962 Nassau agreement on Polaris between Prime Minister Macmillan and President Kennedy – upon American goodwill. If nuclear independence was a test of national independence, then France (which under De Gaulle insisted upon a genuinely independent and self-sufficient nuclear system) remained an independent nation much longer than Britain.

The history of the early postwar years is littered with examples of reluctant British acquiescence in American policy. In January 1951 John Strachey, the British Minister of War, and other ministers including Aneurin Bevan, argued for a show of British independence during the Korean War, but was over-ruled by the cabinet, particularly the very pro-American Hugh Gaitskell, who argued that if Britain supported an anti-American resolution at the United Nations it could lead to the break-up of the alliance and the Americans leaving Europe.[7] And during the international crisis sparked by the Iranian nationalisation of oilfields in 1951 the British only backed away from a confrontation because the United States had determined that no force should be used.[8]

British dependence upon the United States, and subordination to her world view, became more than apparent during the 1956 Suez crisis when the British Tory Prime Minister Anthony Eden organised the Anglo-French invasion of Egypt following the Egyptian leader Colonel Nasser's nationalisation of the Suez Canal. Eden was forced to abandon the military operation in humiliating circumstances primarily because of the American government's displeasure. Even more revealing of Britain's lack of independence was the subsequent discovery that the American President had virtually conspired in forcing not only a policy change upon Britain, but possibly also the resignation of the Prime Minister.

The historian David Carlton has reported that during the crisis President Eisenhower not only refused to have dealings with the British Prime Minister but, even more brutally, bypassed him altogether and dealt separately with a selected group of pro-American cabinet ministers (Harold Macmillan, Rab Butler and Lord Salisbury). At one point the President instructed his ambassador in London to 'get the boys moving' – in other words to activate his pro-American sympathisers in the British cabinet (in much the same way as the Soviet Politburo might have activated their own supporters in their East European client-states).[9]

The Suez affair was a major blow for English national sensibility. Here was an archetypal Englishman – representing almost perfectly the culture and ideology of Englishness – being brought low not only by the American leadership but, much more piquantly, by an upstart Egyptian colonel. It was an early sign that England and Britain was no longer the centre of the world, and that 'the voice born to be obeyed' no longer carried as much authority as many thought it did. It was also a measure of American influence in the new postwar order and of the emptiness of the notion of British national 'sovereignty'.

Following the Suez adventure there were to be no further serious independent British geo-political initiatives. The British decision to enter the EEC in 1973, although in part prompted by a residual conservative reaction against American influence over British foreign policy (an instinct shared by Prime Minister Edward Heath), had none the less been a long-term American goal. And the 1982 Falklands War, conducted by an ostensibly independent government pursuing independent foreign-policy objectives, was, in reality, virtually a joint exercise with the Americans.[10]

As it became increasingly apparent that postwar Britain was little more than a junior partner to the United States, perhaps even a client-state, those English elites who took an interest in foreign policy (some of the most fervent supporters of the culture and ideology of Englishness) formulated a face-saving formula which, it was hoped, would allow them to live with the new realities. Quite simply Britain suddenly became 'Athens' to America's 'Rome'. Drawing on a somewhat presumptuous throw-away remark by Lord Halifax, Britain, or rather its foreign-policy elites, were deemed to have 'all the brains' whilst America had 'all the power'. In a biography of Foreign Secretary Edward Halifax, Andrew Roberts reports a British diplomat as saying that during the loan negotiations in December 1945: 'Lord Halifax once whispered to John Maynard Keynes . . . it's true they [the Americans] have all the money-bags but we have all the brains.'[11]

Yet, these Americans, although diplomatically very courteous, hardly began to act as though this formulation was an apt one. As the cold war progressed, and the United States began to guide and direct the West's global policy towards the Soviet Union, Britain, although remaining a major lobbyist in Washington, was increasingly supplanted as the major European ally by the emerging Federal Republic of Germany.

This more lowly role for Britain was not, though, essentially the product of a failed statecraft – for the breach with Washington in 1956 was only a temporary one, restored quite quickly by the very pro-American, Harold Macmillan. Rather, it simply reflected Britain's economic performance. The British economy had, in the very early postwar years, achieved a very temporary boost over Germany and France, her devastated European national competitors. Yet the postwar period was to see what one leading economic historian described as the 'the acceleration of the industrial decline of Great Britain'. The country's share of world manufacturing production fell from 8.6 per cent in 1953 to a mere 4 per cent in 1980, and its share of world trade from 19.8 per cent in 1955 to 8.7 per cent – and still falling – in 1976.[12] And during the last quarter of the twentieth-century Britain's Gross National Product was to slip below that of Italy and hover around that of a resurgent Spain. Paul Kennedy, in his mammoth work *The Rise and Fall of the Great Powers*, argues that by the early 1980s Britain had become 'an ordinary, moderately large power, not a Great Power' – a development which, as it increasingly came to be understood, shook to the core the more self-important aspects of English self-image and identity.

The scene was set for the greatest challenge traditional Englishness ever faced – the invasion of Britain not by American military bases but by American culture.

CULTURAL INVASION: THE AMERICANISATION OF
ENGLISHNESS

If the 1940s introduced large numbers of American troops and large
amounts of American money (through the Marshall Plan) to Britain,
then the 1950s saw an American cultural invasion. It was not resisted.
The appeal of democratic American culture to a people slowly emerging
from the embrace of Empire and hierarchy was considerable – and is
still so.

This Americanisation of Britain would probably have happened
anyway – even if the United States had remained a great, rather than
a super, power. Indeed, some time before the outbreak of the Second
World War (and America's new world role) the high priests of Englishness were already lamenting American influence.

In the mid-1930s J. B. Priestley's *English Journey* identified three
Englands – the old England (where 'Englishness' had reigned supreme),
the industrial north of England (intriguingly not counting as part of
old England), and a 'new England'. This 'new England' of 'clean,
bright, art-deco factories, palatial cinemas and eating houses and the
young, anonymous people who frequented them' and of crowds 'as
rootless as the car which symbolised the age' drew its 'models from
sportsmen and film stars, not the old upper class'. The historian David
Starkey suggests that Priestley was right in believing that this 'new
England' 'wasn't really England at all' and that he was prescient in
believing it to be another country altogether: 'America'.[13]

This American challenge to the culture of Englishness, well under
way in the 1930s, was enhanced by the wartime role of the United
States and its immediate post-war economic hegemony. And in the
heyday of postwar affluence and optimism (the 1950s and 1960s) the
American challenge turned into a great cultural contest – a battle in
which the ideal of Englishness (essentially built around the image of
the gentleman) had to compete with American culture and 'the American dream' (of prosperous property-owning families inhabiting a mass
consumer society) in its own backyard – for the minds and loyalty of
the British. American movies, television, mass catering, clothes, even
many aspects of American music, literature and art, engaged Englishness in fierce competition, and the American dream won. Hands down.

It was hardly surprising. The American dream had some powerful
advantages over Englishness. First, it was democratic. It said to anyone who would listen and aspire that they could participate in it, that
'you too' can be like this. By contrast the English ideal – essentially

that of the English country gentleman – remained purposely elusive and exclusionary, a life which certainly allowed itself to be admired, but was available only to a few. It reduced the population to onlookers. In Britain, the increasingly odd – by world standards –idea of royalty set the ultimate social standard, but could not, ever, and by definition, be emulated. Whereas the American dream was providing an attractive suburban life for American women, and the possibility of upward social mobility – 'rags to riches', 'log cabin to White House' – for 'blue-collar' working-class Americans, the ideal of the English gentleman or of English royalty had little to give to either of their British counterparts.

Also, the themes of American culture transcended national boundaries. Whereas Englishness was about one particular national cultural elite's lifestyle and approach to manners and behaviour, the American way of life dealt with the universal and accessible themes of love, ambition, money, sex and violence. And the American dream had the financial and technical power of the US economy and the propaganda arm of Americana, Hollywood, behind it.

The American dream spoke to the postwar British population in their own native language, but with the appeal of a democratic accent. Thus, the English language, for so long the preserve of the ruling culture of Englishness, conveyed to the British people an alternative, and *more democratic*, culture. As the twentieth century progressed, and more and more foreigners spoke English, then not only American culture, but other cultures too, would be able to transmit their values and life styles to the domestic British population. And as new information technologies took advantage of the new post war mass market, mass-circulation newspapers, paperbacks, magazines, movies and, finally, television, brought this alternative culture to millions, arguably making Americanness even more widely diffused than had been Englishness.

The American influence on British 1960s popular culture was immense. Stephen Amidon has suggested that in the 1950s and 1960s 'Great Britain' became so Americanised that it 'became a 51st state of mind, without ceding her national identity'.[14] The sociologist Arthur Marwick, in his influential work on contemporary British Culture, *Culture in Britain since 1945*, does not share Amidon's view of American culture being so dominant, but the over-all impression received from his survey is of American influences being extremely powerful.

In the 1950s and 1960s the arrival of popular music amounted to a social revolution. On one level it was a revolution in public taste; but on another it was a revolution in sociology, as the previously dormant social category of 'the teenager' was discovered, and a mass market for this new social group was created. Both the United States and Britain (primarily New York and London) became world centres for this new, highly commercial popular art form. Yet, at the same time, much British popular music was essentially a derivative of a slightly earlier American experience. Arthur Marwick argues that British popular music's origins 'lay solidly in America, with black rhythm and blues, transmitted to Britain by the white imitators and adaptors, principally Bill Haley and Elvis Presley'.[15]

The list of British popular musicians who owe much of their inspiration to American artists is impressive. Marwick suggests that the American artists Little Richard and Chuck Berry gave birth to the British artists the Rolling Stones, while 'the great Chicago bluesmen' – and other blues singers – were the inspiration for Eric Burden in Newcastle and for the very popular British singer Eric Clapton. He sees the British bandleader Ted Heath as but a (poor) response to the American Swing bands, and Vera Lynn – the 'wartime forces sweetheart' – and the crooner Donald Pears as essentially imitative of the American crooners and ballad singers Bing Crosby, Guy Mitchell and Doris Day. Also, Keith Richard in London, it is argued, modelled himself on the guitar-playing of such rock 'n' roll stars as Chuck Berry.[16]

Charlie Gillett has suggested that Britain's most successful popular music group, The Beatles, were 'derivative of two American styles which had not previously been put together, the hard rock 'n' roll style like the singers Little Richard and Larry Williams, and the soft gospel co-and-response style of the Shirelles, the Drifters, and the rest of the singers produced by Leiber and Stoller, Luther Dixon, and Barry Gordy'.[17] Stephen Amidon argues that one of the main reasons that 'there was a beat on the river Mersey' in the first place was that the port of Liverpool was the arrival point for the crates of popular music record and records albums being imported from America. Apart from any direct American influence on British popular music taste in the postwar years, the propensity of generations of British pop singers to adopt American accents in their performances is another tribute to the power of American popular music.

Postwar American literature was also extremely influential, both as an inspiration for many British writers and directly with the public. American novelists, most notably Saul Bellow and John Updike, have inspired a generation of British writers. In popular literature, and the seemingly English preserve of detective stories, the American Hank Jansen catered to a huge British audience, and even Peter Cheyney 'who was English to the core . . . had his characters speak the weirdest kind of pidgin American'.[18] And in the theatre the great postwar British genre of the 'angry young man' lent heavily on some of the works of Arthur Miller and Tennessee Williams.

In painting, a host of American Abstract Expressionists and 'Pop artists' have inspired a whole generation of British painters, most notably David Hockney, who left Britain to live in the United States. And American influence upon the built environment was also pronounced. Many of Britain's most prominent architects spent considerable time in the United States, where they were influenced by modernism and 'high tec' architecture.

Yet it was in the world of film – the movies – where American culture scored its greatest success with the British public. Cowboy films (heroes like John Wayne, Randolph Scott, Gary Cooper and later Clint Eastwood) provided a new frontier for the imagination of Britons. American detective stories, like Philip Marlow (by Raymond Chandler) or Perry Mason, and even some of the early gangster movies, possessed, for the postwar British a certain romantic charm. American musicals (such as *Annie Get your Gun*, *Oklahoma* or *West Side Story*) were huge box office hits.

The Hollywood star system provided role models for British youth, and for many British women the female roles in American movies – many of them strong and assertive – proved attractive and, to some extent, subversive of the lowly role assigned to women by the 'gentlemanly' ideology of Englishness. It also provided role models for some of the best British actors. In the land where the profession of Shakespearian actor still held sway, 'Albert Finney's hard man monologues in 1960s *Saturday Night and Sunday Morning* have a lot more to do with Brando and the Method than they do Olivier and the Royal Shakespeare Company.'[19]

By contrast to the democratic content of American movies, the British movies of the period were invariably about class. The Ealing Comedies (and the films starring Ian Carmichael and Norman Wisdom) purveyed class themes, as did the 'anti-class' movies like *Look Back in Anger* and *Room at the Top* and other movies starring Richard Burton and Lawrence Harvey.

Intriguingly, British movies produced no real heroes or role models from amongst the 'blue-collar' working-class majority. In the postwar British movie industry Britain's largest social group were assigned the roles of 'chirpy cockneys' or the role of joker, loyal deferential (who blurted out 'gor bless ya guvnor' as he went over the top in the First War trenches), or bitter young talents who turned into 'angry young men' as they railed at the establishment and the system. Nor were British women assigned particularly strong roles in the new mass medium of film – a reflection of the dominance of male life in the national culture. It was not surprising that 'the world of Ealing and Norman Wisdom was swept away when a new generation of film makers such as Tony Richardson and Karel Reisz, weaned on American directors such as Sidney Lumet and Elia Kazan, came to the fore.'[20]

With this huge cultural invasion it is little wonder that an Americanisation of the English language used in Britain took place. American-English increasingly interpenetrated English-English and British-English. Greetings such as 'Hi', words such as 'hike', 'wise', 'sure', 'guy' entered British-English. An Englishman, Captain Marryat, travelling in the US in 1838, singled out a number of American-English words with meanings strange to the British-English ear. Few of them are unfamiliar any longer. Amongst them were: 'reckon', 'calculate', 'guess' (colloquial synonyms for 'think' or 'believe'); 'clever' (for 'good natured'); 'smart' (for 'clever'); 'fix' (for 'repair'); 'mean' (for 'ashamed'); 'great' (for 'fine' or 'splendid'); 'stipulated' and so forth.

Other American words or phrases now in common use in British-English are: from the wild west – poker, saloon; from the Gold Rush 'bonanza' – 'pan out', 'strike', 'hustler'; from the railroad era – 'in the clear', 'make the grade', 'right of way', 'off the rails'; from Mark Twain – 'take it easy', 'get over', 'a close call', 'gilt-edged'; from German-Americans – 'check', 'delicatessen', 'ecology', 'fresh' (meaning impertinent), 'hoodlum', 'kindergarten', 'yes man', 'no way', 'will do', 'let it be'; and from American-Jewish – 'enjoy' and 'I should worry'. The twentieth-century wars created some common words between the Americans and the English: such as barrage, camouflage, 'going over the top', 'digging in' and the like.[21]

With the arrival of mass television (a process largely complete in Britain by the mid-1960s), American influences upon the culture of the postwar British became ever more potent. Also, North American ownership of the mass culture industry – the American citizen Rupert Murdoch in both television and newspapers, Canadian Conrad Black in newspapers and magazines, and the large American corporate penetration of Britain's top ten publishing houses – helped propagate American cultural forms and attitudes.

This process of Americanisation was not, though, some kind of alien implant in the British cultural body politic. Apart from mutterings amongst some English cultural elites (many of whom were also able to accept American resources when they were offered), the American cultural invasion was hardly contentious, and certainly not resisted. There were no serious political moves (as in France) to limit its reach.

In a sense, Americanisation might more properly be defined as modernisation – a metaphor for the growth of cultural democracy and the spread of consumerism, a feature first perfected in the USA but a product of all Western societies in the post-Second World War period. Even in France, the Western society most self-conscious about its national identity and most resistant to Americanisation, it is now increasingly realised that 'Gallic accusations of materialism, social conformity, and status seeking were a caricature of America . . . these faults were as inherently French as they were native to America.'[22]

And in inter-war Britain this process of modernisation – producing those 'clean, bright art-deco factories, palatial cinemas and eating houses and . . . young, anonymous people who frequented them . . . as rootless as the car which symbolised the age' – owed as much, if not more, to indigenous industrialism and the first stirrings of mass democracy as it did to early twentieth-century American influences.

America was also a metaphor for globalisation. America itself was (and is) a collage of international ethnicities and cultures, a kind of forerunner – captured within the confines of a single continent-wide nation-state – of later globalisation. And it should not be forgotten that the British input into contemporary American culture is formidable. After all, it was British people who founded the nation-state and took the primary role in setting the language, the industrial system, the financial system (including modern accountancy), the original industrial management techniques, the framework of American law and politics – indeed all the 'Anglo' structures and values of the contemporary life of the United States. American culture bears the imprint of English and British rebels, of British people who left their native country before the national culture of Englishness took hold in the eighteenth century. As Alex de Tocqueville once observed, 'the American is the Englishman left to himself.'

Thus, 'Americanisation' or 'modernisation' or 'consumerism' could, relatively accurately, be viewed as a refined and developed successor of an earlier British commercial puritanism – which, denied its full development at home, found its most perfect outlet, and internal market, in the United States. During the decades following the Second World War it had simply, like the prodigal son, returned home. J. B. Priestley was missing the point when he suggested that the 'new England' – of mass consumerism – 'wasn't really England at all'. It was as English, certainly as British, as it was American. The commercial

and democratic instinct of British popular culture was simply express-
ing itself at last, and in modern terms – having been occluded and
repressed for so long by the hold of official Englishness.

The problem for Britain and the British, though, was that in the late
twentieth century the American cultural industry – primarily the mass
media and mass tourist sectors – increasingly needed a separated and
'distinct' English and British culture which it could sell to its customers.
Thus it promoted its ersatz version of theme-park Englishness. And as
the culture of Englishness came under threat it reacted militantly, yet
in a manner needed by the growing world-wide leisure and tourist industry – by becoming more and more rural, more and more nostalgic,
more and more contrived and artificial. The British broadcasters pro-
grammed even more reruns of *Brideshead Revisited* and *The Jewel in
the Crown*.

For the British, the post-1945 era had witnessed the loss of the prized
independence of the country's elites and they had found their official
national culture under serious challenge from across the Atlantic. Yet
these postwar decades were a time when the world capitalist economy
(no longer located primarily in America) was forging seismic changes
throughout the world – undermining the role of the nation-state and
the stability of national identities. It was providing nationalists, not
only in Britain, with a bumpy ride.

THE END OF THE 300-YEAR REALM

The Americanisation of Britain – both geo-politically and culturally –
was an early sign that the old nostrums of British national independence and 'sovereignty' were wearing thin. The three-hundred-year realm
– the nation formed by the Act of Union in 1707 (an extension into
Scotland of the 1688–9 settlement), which had grown during the age
of nationalism into one of the world's most impressive nation-states –
was obviously nearing the end of its effective life.

Yet, the hold of the idea of national sovereignty, of British sovereignty, was very difficult to prize open. It had had a long run and was
firmly established. The more general notion of 'sovereignty' was first
revived in modern form – that is, after the long period in the Middle
Ages during which the classical notion of sovereignty had collapsed –
by Jean Bodin in *De la Republique* (1576 in French, 1606 in English).
Bodin 'worked to find some basis of ideas on which the harmony of

the political community could be restored'. Thomas Hobbes also played a crucial part in the development of the idea of sovereignty 'by substituting for the Prince the abstract notion of the state'.[23]

Over time, in Britain, the idea of sovereignty became a veritable holy shrine. It was meat and drink to monarchists and to those who supported hierarchy and centralisation; and it came to represent Sir William Blackstone's 'quintessentially Anglican version of the traditional English unitary and absolutist doctrine' of governmental authority.[24]

Later, Hegel also got in on the act. During the latter part of the nineteenth century the influence of Hegel's ideas, particularly his conception of the state 'as the realisation of the moral ideal and as an absolute end, had made headway, even in supposedly liberal societies such as Britain; and this renewed interest in the sovereignty of the state went hand in hand with the rise of nationalism, and thus the "sovereign state" quite easily became interchangeable with the "sovereign nation": they were, in fact, one and the same thing.'[25]

In Britain, 'national sovereignty' became intertwined in the political mind with other ideas – the Empire, monarchy (the *sovereign*), Englishness, parliamentary *sovereignty* – which reinforced its appeal. Of these, 'Parliamentary *sovereignty*' was by far the most important. Invented by Albert Venn Dicey in the late nineteenth century, the idea of 'Parliamentary *sovereignty*', a nostrum which precluded the idea of separated powers, became the perfect legal, constitutional and 'democratic' cover for the huge centralisation of British power in the executive branch. Thus, the sovereignty of the state became the sovereignty of the nation, and, in Britain's case, also became the sovereignty of Parliament – a veritable holy concept, still being appealed to by anti-Marketeers in the 1970s and Eurosceptics in the 1990s.

Of course, ideas of nation-state sovereignty rarely went uncontested, for they ran up against some other, contradictory English liberal beliefs. During the nineteenth century the powerful free-trade ideology and instinct rejected – mainly implicitly but sometimes openly – national sovereignty. So, too, did that aspect of liberalism which elevated individual conscience, and pacifism, over the demands of the nation-state. Indeed, Lord (Harold) Acton was very influential, though ultimately forlorn, in trying to persuade his contemporaries of the unfashionable idea that nationalism was not a liberal idea at all. And, of course, the business class was always wanting to limit the role of the state, and thus, at one remove, the nation. Scepticism came from the democratic left too. The potential for absolutism at the heart of the idea of sovereignty led the political theorist Harold Laski to argue that 'it would be of lasting benefit to political science if the whole concept of sovereignty were surrendered ... it is at least probable that it has dangerous moral consequences'.[26]

Yet (as has been argued earlier) both the collectivism and the wars of the twentieth century boosted the nation-state and the idea of national sovereignty. And, strangely, so too did the rules of international law and practice drawn up by both the League of Nations and its successor the United Nations. The UN based the fundamentals of post-Second World War diplomacy on the 'sovereignty' of nation-states, only admitting to its ranks places that were deemed to be nation-states and only recognising them as the principal actors. And as far as the 'British sovereign state', the grandiosely-called United Kingdom, was concerned it was not only so recognised as an independent 'sovereign' actor, but as one with a seat on the Security Council, a favoured place which was only to be questioned in the 1990s.

In recent years, though, the idea of British national sovereignty has held less glitter. Revived somewhat during the Falklands War in the early 1980s – by some very archaic rhetoric from Margaret Thatcher and a nationalist 'amen chorus' in the tabloid press – it has nevertheless become associated, certainly amongst opinion-formers, with Empire and war, indeed being seen as one of the causes of violence.

Even more deadly for the concept of 'national sovereignty' is its increasing redundancy. Quite simply, the processes of globalisation are making the territorially-bound nation-state increasingly irrelevant. And at the very heart of the pressures forcing globalisation is the revolution in technology. Intriguingly, it may have been in the military field – traditionally the bastion of nationalism- where changing technology made a decisive breakthrough against the nation. During the 1930s in Britain the policy of appeasement was suddenly given a serious boost when it became clear that one of nationalism's great imperatives – the defence of the territory of the nation-state – was no longer possible. The frightening slogan of the time – 'the bomber can always get through' – displayed in vivid terms the limits of the nation. And the nuclear age, with its technology of intercontinental missiles and space weapons, opened traditionally secure national territories to instant destruction – and from thousands of miles away. There was little sovereignty – either inherent in Britain or in its 'mother of parliaments' when the Soviet politburo sitting at the other end of a continent could destroy the country in a matter of minutes.

Changing technology is also one of the primary forces behind the emergence of a global economy and the erosion of the viability of borders. For instance, the transportation, communications and computer revolution has allowed transnational corporations – the single most dynamic force weakening national sovereignty – to develop and expand on a truly global basis: 'Its [the transnational corporation's] access to knowledge is central to its success: to its production techniques, to its distribution and marketing, to its financial operations. . . . In sectors ranging from financial services to management consultancy to commodity trading, there is no longer *production* as it is traditionally understood. There is only *information*, communicated efficiently within, between and among companies.'[27]

'Sovereign' British economic decision-making can hardly exist in a global economy in which transnational companies, many of them with financial resources the size of small nation-states, can move those resources around the world at will. Anthony Sampson suggests that 'the huge flow of foreign funds, whether from Arabs, mafias, or multinational corporations, tests the integrity of every institution to the limit' and rightly concludes that 'in the global context, national politicians or administrators begin to look more like local councillors confronting big-time developers.'[28] When meetings about investment or mergers and acquisitions in Bonn, Paris, Brussels, Washington, Riyadh or Tokyo may possess a greater purchase upon Britain's future than any decision taken in Westminster or Whitehall, then Britain's national decision-makers have indeed become 'local councillors'.

'Sovereignty' is also eroded by the very institutions set up to attempt to manage this global economy, to attempt to give some order to this increasingly anarchic world marketplace. The International Monetary Fund, the World Trade Organisation, and more particularly the international meetings, both formal and informal, of national politicians, all serve to limit sovereignty even further. Indeed, it could be argued that the single most important institution affecting the economic lives of ordinary Britons in the late twentieth century was the G5 or G7 meetings of finance and other ministers, for it was often within this framework (or other ones very much like it) that Britain's so-called 'sovereign' economic destiny was co-ordinated with those of its major Western allies, that its interest-rate policy, exchange-rate policy and, ultimately, its taxation and unemployment levels were all effectively determined. Increasingly, as the European Union began to take hold, then British interest rates, exchange rates, taxation and unemployment levels were being decided in European forums (in the Economic and Financial grouping of the Council of Ministers and in the European Monetary Institute), and in the interplay between European

politico-financial actors – an environment giving the British government even less room to manoeuvre than they possessed in the old,
looser, Western Economic Councils. In this environment the model of
a British Chancellor of the Exchequer, representing the *sovereign* British Crown, reporting to a cabinet which in turn reports to a *sovereign*
Parliament, is no longer even a legal fiction.

This globalisation of the economy has enormous implications for
culture. In the age of national sovereignty culture too was largely national. Public information was controlled by domestic media outlets
(principally the BBC); and public taste was dictated by what amounted
to a group of rather provincial upper-caste guardians. Now, though,
'sovereign' control of culture is a thing of the past. Changing technology – satellites, telecoms, computer networks – will enable a massive penetration of the domestic market by 'foreign' culture (principally,
initially, American).

Also, the global economic market will allow increasing foreign control of media outlets. Traditionally, British culture (which ultimately
meant 'English' culture) was supported by a nationally-owned media
(including, powerfully, the mid twentieth-century Reithian BBC and
the press barons of the old Fleet Street, many of them articulating
patriotic, jingoistic and imperial sensibilities). Now, though, the increasing cosmopolitan character of media ownership, the increase of
foreign-based satellite television, together with the increasing plethora
of television and newspaper outlets, will, inevitably, take its toll upon
indigenous cultural production.

In the process the culture of the British will inevitably become both
more cosmopolitan and more egalitarian. There will be no turning back;
the world of 'sovereign' British culture – the world bounded by 'kings
and queens', by 'garden gnomes' and 'castles and cottages' – is already dissolving amidst a cloud-cover of receiving dishes from John
O'Groats to Lands End.

And in the place of the old clear-cut idea – and reality – of 'sovereignty', of 'national sovereignty', of 'Parliamentary sovereignty', there
is already arising a more fluid, tangential and plural theory to fit the
new reality. The writer Neal Ascherson has already been reaching towards
a new conceptual framework. He argues that 'sovereignty [in Europe]
will cease to be a one way flow, going either downwards (as in Britain) or upwards (as in Germany). Instead it will become a sort of all-
permeating medium, like water in a swamp, in which clumps and floating
islands of self government will relate to one another in many different
ways. The 21st century will be a period not only of fuzzy logic but of

fuzzy democracy.'[29] Put in another way: 'the theory of sovereignty will seem strangely out of place in a world characterised by shifting allegiances, new forms of identity and overlapping tiers of jurisdiction.'[30]

The dissolution of the sovereign British state of the United Kingdom of Great Britain and Northern Ireland – and the emergence of new, more indeterminate and malleable relationships between polities – will inevitably take its toll upon national sensibilities, upon the resilience and resonance of the idea of nation in the British psyche.[31] After all, the state itself was a major transmission agent for the idea of nation. Yet, with the state seriously weakened, rather like a croaking and sputtering radio with its message becoming fainter and obscured by other stations, national identity itself may also be on its last legs.

THE WANING OF NATIONAL IDENTITY

People need to identify with something bigger than themselves, and the British are no different from anyone else. For the British, as for others, sense of self can be secured, honed and developed by a relationship with others. Indeed it has been suggested that the sense of identity

> is inseparable from an awareness of ourselves as members of a particular family or class or community or people or nation, as bearers of a specific history, as citizens of a particular republic; and we look to the political realm as a way in which we can develop and refine our sense of ourselves by developing and refining forms of community with which we can be proud to identify.[32]

Yet, how important is the nation in all this? How central as a 'community' with which to identify is an old-fashioned European nation-state like Britain? How does 'belonging to Britain' compare with, say, belonging to, or identifying with, the family, the immediate locale, with the city or village, with the local sports team, with the office, with the network of friends? And, crucially, how intense is an identification with the British nation-state as compared with an identification with sub-national entities – Scotland, Wales, the English 'South', Yorkshire or Cornwall or London – or with multi- or supra-national entities like the European Union, the United Nations or even the OECD? Certainly the nation-state used to compare extremely favourably with

any of the above. Alan Milward suggests that the ultimate basis for
the survival of the nation-state, including the British, 'is the same as it
always was, allegiance'.[33] And the nation-states certainly appeared to
generate quite remarkable levels of loyalty in their peoples. During
this very century millions of British people have apparently displayed
their allegiance by making serious sacrifices for their country, including a willingness to make the ultimate one.

Yet, the genuine level or intensity of allegiance, or loyalty, is very
difficult to measure. The nation-state has also been the ultimate political and legal authority over the lives of its people. It could, still can,
fine, tax, imprison, even take life. There was no higher appeal, and
most people were powerless to leave its boundaries. In such circumstances a degree of 'loyalty' or 'allegiance' was hardly surprising, perhaps
more a measure of *force majeur* than genuine feeling. Linda Colley
has attempted to measure loyalty – by the yardstick of willingness to
serve in the armed forces. She reports that by early eighteenth-century
standards, 'They [the statistics organised by the government in 1798
and 1803 to find out who would serve in the armed forces] confront
both those who argue on the one hand for widespread loyalty and deference throughout Great Britain . . . and those who claim on the other
hand that the mass of Britons were alienated from their rulers.'[34]

What it is possible to measure is a real shift amongst the post-Second World War generations away from military service – perhaps the
ultimate test of allegiance to nation. Fighting and dying for one's country
is no longer a test of young manhood in most Western nations – and
joining the military has become a job like any other. In the United
States the middle-class young's resistance to conscription during the
Vietnam War was in marked contrast to the kind of self-sacrifice prevalent
during that earlier ill-defined bloody conflict of the First World War.
And in Britain, too, the willingness of young men to risk being killed
for their country, or any other abstraction, also declined. The abolition
of conscription was a popular act. And the supposed war fever and
xenophobia unleashed by the Falklands War was, for most of those
who engaged in it, more a case of vicarious valour – the real fighting
was safely distant, in colour, on television.

The late twentieth century's tests of national loyalty and allegiance
are much less rigorous. A leading nationalist Conservative politician,
Norman Tebbit, declared that one test of national loyalty might be to
ask whether a person supported England at cricket. National sentiment
and national loyalty has indeed become an aspect of the leisure and
consumer society – primarily expressed (often vociferously) through

support for national sporting personalities and teams. In Britain identification with nation – in football, as it happens, with England, Scotland and Wales – becomes little more than taking sides in an
entertainment. It is not ultimately serious; nor are the plethora of empty
rituals – for example, the recent 'inventions of tradition' such as the
Trooping of the Colour and the State Opening of Parliament –
which the entertainment and tourist industries offer up as authentic
'national' experiences.

The decline in national allegiance – indeed in national identity –
which has overcome the British, as it has overcome other nation-states
in the West during the latter quarter of the twentieth century, still sur-
prises many observers. The 'resilience' of the nation-state is still the
currency of much comment and analysis – particularly so the 'resilience' of the British nation, which, alongside that of the French nation,
is often thought of as one of the classic, centralised nation-states of
the modern world.

Yet there is nothing particularly inevitable or immutable about the
nation-state or nationalism. A national sensibility has only held sway
over the imagination for a small portion of the time of the existence
of recognisably civilised life on the territory of the British Isles. The
nation-state, and a sense of nationalism, were absent during both classical
times and the Middle Ages. Indeed, during medieval times 'nation'
connoted 'race' (in the *Cursor Mundi* of the fourteenth century 'English'
meant the English race).[35] Then, traditional organisations such as blood-
based tribes, kingdoms and empires were the primary political units.
And most of the serious analysts of nationalism agree that there was
little or no nationalism in the world until the end of the eighteenth
century, and that only since the French Revolution has it dominated
'the political thought and action of most peoples'.[36]

Kenneth Minogue has sought to find 'a general condition of things
from which nationalism seems primordially to spring' and suggests a
general answer: 'Our clue may be that nationalism in both France and
Germany became the spearhead of an attack on feudalism.'[37] Ernest
Gellner has also portrayed it as the inseparable ideological counterpart
of modernisation, of the transition from agricultural to industrial society.
He argues that the ideology of nationalism provides 'an integrative
structure both assisting and easing the shocks of modernisation in all
its facets – the breaking down of tribal, social and intellectual barriers,
the reorientation of politics, the spread of education and literacy, the
expansion of equal opportunity, the introduction of agricultural and
industrial techniques'.[38] Other analysts of nationalism do not dispute

its modernising character, its crucial role in the transition from a feudal order, but argue that the nation, and the nation-state, was not the sole transporter of modernity. Gerald Newman suggests that the modern era was formed during 'the nationless universalism of the early enlightenment, the age of Locke and Pope and Voltaire.'[39] And English, and British, nationalism was no exception. The 'integrative structure' of the new British state certainly helped absorb the exceptional dislocations ushered in by the rapid commercial, industrial and technological changes which swept over the British Isles during the late eighteenth, nineteenth and early twentieth centuries.

As well as being essentially modern phenomena, the nation-state, and nationalism, are also less than natural, or popular, in their derivation. Some experts believe that far from being a popularly rooted aspect of political life, the nationalism of modern times was all got up by the intellectuals. 'Nationalism is, at the outset, a creation of writers', argues Gerald Newman.[40] And Minogue has described the initial phase of nationalism in eighteenth-century England as being created by native intellectual 'stirrings' against French domination of literary life. There is little doubt that in the forging of English, and later British, national sensibility the role of writers, thinkers, polemicists – and others with a reflective temperament and time on their hands, what the eighteenth-century writer Richard Hurd called 'dextrous people' – was utterly crucial.[41] As was the wider dissemination of the ideas of the intellectuals that was secured by the burgeoning internal market and the advances in printing and publishing.

The idea of a new community – a 'national' or 'English' community – developed by writers as part of a literary reaction against the French – fitted in well with the new political reality of the 1707 British Union state. Political and intellectual life were for a time pulling in the same direction. Together, the landed families who controlled the politics and the 'stirrings' of nationalism amongst the literati cemented the new nation-state – the realm of Great Britain, and later of the United Kingdom of Great Britain and Northern Ireland. Thus, like most of the other contemporary Western nation-states, the British variant, constructed well before the age of mass democracy, was forged by elites.

The British nation-state was born in the pre-democratic age. Therefore, not only its structures – those deriving from the compact of 1688–9 – but also its ethos was decidedly aristocratic. 'We the people' had to break into the structures, they hardly informed them – as they were to inform the late eighteenth-century Constitution of the United States. Nor was the new nation-state particularly liberal. Nationalism may have been a modern phenomenon, but it was not a liberal one. Harold Acton was one of the few ninteenth-century political thinkers who understood the inherently illiberal germ at the centre of the ideology of the nation. Thus, not surprisingly, there was no place in the body or structures of the new British state for entrenched individual rights.

THE INDIVIDUAL AND THE NATION

Indeed, it was the powerful new liberal idea – involving the primacy, indeed the 'sovereignty', of the individual, and his or her autonomy and consciousness- which, over time, was to shake the very fundamentals of the collectivist nation-state – more so even than the later arrival on the scene of globalisation.

The 'sovereign individual' has always been at the centre of British liberal thought, yet Britain during the height of its nationhood has seen its liberalism constrained not only by class (of both the High-Tory and trade union varieties) but also by the collective sensibility of nationalism itself – a collectivism fuelled by two world wars. Yet, a decisive breakthrough for the idea of the individual took place in the post-Second World War era with the arrival of a mass consumer society. The industrial and commercial age, as well as fostering a technology (mass communications) which *enhanced* 'national' sensibility, also set in train, and more decisively so, the rise of the individual – the phenomenon most likely to *destroy* the idea and hold of 'nation'.

The growing political culture of individual rights met up with the economic development of mass markets catering to individual needs and desires to produce a powerful boost to assertive individualism. 'In the modern variant of capitalism, the individual's relationship to the economic system is a highly atomized one. Individualism, not collectivism, typifies consumerist society, even for those who do not possess the wealth required to fulfil their desires: I consume therefore I am.'[42] Increasingly, individuals began to count. And selflessness came to be seen as self-sacrifice or self-abnegation – whether of the mild kind like 'public service' or of the egregious kind like the sacrifices made by millions for 'country' in the First World War. In this environment the collectivities – including nation, one of the most important of collectivities – were bound to weaken.

British reactionaries – many of them fervent nationalists – saw this threat very clearly indeed. George Eliot in 1879 summed up the fear of nationalists when presented with an early glimpse of the modern individual consumer:

> Not only the nobleness of a nation depends upon this presence of a national consciousness, but also the nobleness of each individual citizen. Our dignity and rectitude are proportioned to our sense of relationship with something great, admirable, pregnant with high possibilities, worthy of sacrifice, a continual inspiration to self-repression and discipline by the presentation of aims larger and more attractive to our generous part than the securing of personal ease or prosperity.[43]

Although such appeals to 'repression' and 'self-discipline' were not, likely to advance the cause, in the latter part of the twentieth century the echoes of this anti-individualism could still be heard from British Tories. Lord Hinchingbrooke was horrified by the damage done by '*individualistic* businessmen, financiers and speculators' who were 'creeping unnoticed' to 'injure the character of our people'.[44]

In this individualist environment identity itself – 'the condition of being a specified person' – begins to weaken its hold.[45] The assertive and self-conscious individual seeks to become his own man or her own woman, less constrained by reference to groups – particularly large and relatively anonymous groups like nations. Schiller's advice to his fellow Germans: 'Do not seek to form a nation, content yourself with being men' nicely captures this dichotomy between nation and individual.[46] As the Marxist historian Eric Hobsbawn has put it 'the cultural revolution of the late twentieth century can thus best be understood as the triumph of the individual over society, or rather, as the breaking of the threads which in the past had woven human beings into social textures'.[47]

And in this environment whatever group consciousness – and identity – continues to linger may no longer be national or even local, but rather, more personal, based upon 'individual' characteristics such as being male, female, young, old, middle-aged, 'thirty-something', tall, short, disabled, homosexual, heterosexual and so on. Thus, being English, let alone British, becomes much less important than being young, or being a student, or being a woman. And, geographically, being a Londoner certainly becomes more important than being English or British.

One of the features of individualism was a slowly growing scepticism of authority, an inclination which, by the last decade of the twentieth century, may have turned into something near contempt. Institutions, including the nation-state itself, were increasingly becoming subject to market consumerism – judged on their performance, not their historical import. This 'individualistic', market approach to nation-state was intriguingly exhibited some two centuries ago when a London coachman, way ahead of his time, provided a superb description of the instrumental citizen of today. Asked whether he would fight for his country during the heightened anxiety over a French revolutionary invasion in 1803, he replied:

> No law or power under the canopy of heaven shall force me to take up arms. . . . I pray to God, that I may never live to see my country become a province of France, but if this war is suffered to go on I know it will be conquered, for I am positively sure that the King, Lords and Commons . . . have long since lost the hearts, goodwill and affection of a very great majority of the people of this nation.[48]

National feeling, severely weakened by the rise of individualism, is also threatened by the growth of more local and regional loyalties and identities, principally the emergence of ethnic nationalisms. Since the collapse of the Soviet Union the intensity of ethnic identification that existed within the former Soviet empire has been revealed – and in the case of Yugoslavia a 'new' identity so powerful that thousands are willing to fight and die to defend it. And sub-national ethnicity may also be unleashed by the European Union as it weakens the hold of those other mini-empires – the larger European nation-states. As Neal Ascherson has argued, 'we can formulate a law of politics here. When European Union advances, so does regional autonomy.'[49] Although the Scots, unlike the Serbs or the Bosnians or the Croats, may not be prepared to die for the cause of their 'ethnic' nation, they are likely to identify with Scotland and Scottishness more intensely than any Briton will identify with Britain and Britishness.

A RATIONAL CALCULUS

In western Europe, including Britain, the dramatic weakening not only of the sovereignty of the nation-state, but also of people's emotional and psychological ties to nation, will inevitably mean that a more rational view of political organisation may become possible. Publics will no longer invest sentiment in the political organisations which govern their lives. Rather, they may increasingly make what amounts to a rational calculus of functions and needs.

And, in any such rational calculus, the British nation-state, like many others in Europe, must increasingly appear as ill-equipped to perform the functions of twenty-first century government. Britain is a perfect case of this incapability: for, like France, Germany, Italy and Spain, it is both too small and too big. It is too small to perform the functions of geo-politics and geo-economics – the foreign, defence and strategic, international trade, international economic, environmental and transport network policies. It is also too small to properly enforce a regime of individual rights against incursions by large-scale transnational enterprises. Yet, at the same time, it is too big to provide the democratic participatory functions increasingly demanded by citizens – and more effectively provided by local and regional government.

THE LAST HURRAH

Thus, the loss of national sovereignty (and national identity) caused by globalisation, the rise of individualism and sub-national ethnicity, means that the eighteenth-century nation-state – the major positive force during the transition to modernity – is not only incapable and irrelevant but also ultimately doomed.

Even so, such intimations of mortality do not necessarily mean that eruptions of national sentiment are no longer possible. Indeed, quite the opposite. Some of the starkest nationalist sentiment has found expression in the 1970s, 80s and 90s. Conservative politicians such as Enoch Powell made stirring and evocative nationalist speeches during the period when Britain first entered the European Community. And, later, Conservative ministers Nicholas Ridley and Patrick Nicholls gave vent to remarkably hostile anti-German and anti-French sentiments associated more with the Second World War than with life in the European Union. Yet expressions of national sentiment often become raucus when national identity is weak, and when it is under threat either from other nationalisms or from universal forces of change. And during the latter quarter of the twentieth century British national identity, along with the British nation-state, was certainly both enfeebled and under threat.

4 True Brits, Real England

REAL IDENTITIES

This late twentieth-century crisis of nationalism naturally led directly to a crisis of national identity, and thus of 'Englishness'. It became increasingly difficult to identify with a political unit – the nation-state – that contained less and less meaning. 'Englishness' was also weakened, fatally so, by Britain's comparative economic decline. Constructed upon an identity involving superiority and confidence, 'Englishness' needed England – through Britain – to be a world, imperial power. And, as Britain not only lost its Empire but sank down the European league tables, to below Italy in GDP per head, it became extremely difficult to assume the role of a 'gentleman' whilst existing on an increasingly threadbare inheritance, and embarrassing to be John Bull whilst a junior partner – both to the United States and to the Franco-German alliance in the European Union.

Yet there was one priceless advantage deriving from economic decline and the consequent tattered national ideology of Englishness. For the first time, arguably since the late eighteenth century, the realities (and thus the real identities) of Britain, and of England, and of their peoples, could begin to reveal themselves; and, as they did so, they displayed a very different world from that conjured up by the manufactured national ideology.

'Englishness' was thus a false identity. And the unreality it propagated was as complete as it was audacious. Virtually every field in which the country and its people had excelled was denied by this official ideology. The home of the industrial revolution was devalued by an idea of Englishness which was dominated by older, landed virtues; the country's massive contribution to scientific enquiry went largely uncelebrated, certainly compared with its literary output. It was no wonder that, in Martin Weiner's words, 'in the world's first industrial nation, industrialism did not seem quite at home. In the country that had started mankind on "the great ascent" economic growth was frequently viewed with suspicion and disdain.'[1]

The powerful mix of science, commerce and industry – the defining quality of the modern English (and British) experience – was denied by a self-image which, promoted by a powerful combination of aristocracy and literati, defined Englishness in terms of its own narrow reality. And, as this literary elite controlled the images and helped form the identities, it was not surprising that England's primary contribution to the Western world came to be seen exclusively for its artistic output, its land, its country houses – and not at all for its steam engines, its industrial organisation, accountancy practices or jet engines. No wonder, too, that the world's most urban country was exalted for its country-side; and, later, one of the most suburban of nations still projected itself as a land of broad acres.

And nowhere was this inversion of image and identity more total than in the attempt to re-write the country's philosophic traditions. Britain has been one of the most practical of nations, with the most empirical of philosophic traditions – one of the most secular and, above all, the most rational. Indeed, British thinkers helped pioneer the Enlightenment, the age of reason and science. Yet we now tend to tell ourselves that the Enlightenment was essentially foreign (principally French, therefore certainly foreign!). Quite simply this idea of Britain as a foremost intellectual champion of reason has been 'written out of history' by conservative writers such as Edmund Burke as part of the making of the myth that Britain possessed no serious radical tradition which, based upon reason, appealed to universal principles. And, in the process, this myth even succeeded in marginalising the centrality and importance of Isaac Newton, Charles Darwin and T. E. Huxley. 'Abstract theories' (or 'abstractions' or indeed 'crazed abstractions'), conservatives told us, had no roots in Britain, certainly not in Eng-land; we British stood for history, tradition and 'accumulated wisdom'.

Only lately have revisionists sought to correct this record. Richard Crossman has argued that 'only a moment's serious consideration is necessary in order to see that theory and speculative thought are by no means foreign to the British mind'.[2] And in the world of contempor-ary commentary it has taken a foreigner, the American Irving Kristol, to attempt to set the record straight by commending the British on their contribution to the age of reason. He argued that the Protestant Reformation, 'a British mood if there ever was one', played a seminal role in advancing secular ideas by severely weakening the irrational authority of the church; that Francis Bacon 'exemplifies perfectly' the primacy of reason; and that Britons have taken the lead in 'modern scientific modes of thinking about natural phenomena'.[3]

Also, there is now an increasing understanding that an English En-lightenment predated the French. It was English radicals such as John Toland, Charles Blount and Matthew Tindal and other freethinkers –

many of them setting themselves in opposition to the priestly character of the Church of England in the late seventeenth century – who
developed many of the ideas later taken up by French thinkers such as
Voltaire and Diderot.[4] Many of these ideas sprang from the notion
that reason as much as religion should be the basis for constructing a
just society.

More importantly still, official Englishness distorted the very identity of the people themselves. The official ideology insisted that the
image of the Englishman – the epitomy of the country's success – was
an aristocrat, or at the very least an aristocratic gentleman – tied to
the land. Later, during the age of Empire, this typical successful Englishman would become an imperial administrator, a person still, of course,
possessed of the aristocratic, paternalist values. Yet, again, the reality
was very different. Britain's success as a nation was based upon its
unique economic performance in the eighteenth and nineteenth centuries, an economic lift-off engineered by the commercial prowess of a
new and vibrant business class – drawn from a much wider social
base than the aristocracy. As one writer put it, 'the wellspring of its
unique expansion came not from the aristocracy but from more practical, less well-born men of the middle or even the working classes'.[5]

And the social attitudes of these business Englishmen were inherently commercial. Many of them came from dissenting Protestant faiths
– Quakers, Presbyterians, Congregationalists, Methodists – imbued with
Calvinist instincts. Joel Kotkin sees this Calvinism as utterly crucial
to an understanding of the British, and their economic success. Calvinism united capitalism and religion by arguing that work had a spiritual dimension. Work was good, not just necessary. And it was this
precept that helped the new British business classes develop their famed
'work ethic'. Calvinism was also crucial in helping the business classes
reject the feudal, anti-commercial ethic of Catholicism – and much of
Anglicanism – which still sought to subordinate individual economic
achievement to the moral authority of the church. It was also scornful
of aristocrats: 'To Calvin the profits of the artisan, merchant or specu-
lator were no less worthy than the rents harvested by the land-owning
aristocracy.' Calvin himself asked 'what reason is there why the income from business should not be larger than that from landowning?'[6]

Of course, these commercial instincts of Britons and Englishmen
were very much to the fore during the building of Empire (though not
necessarily during its later administration). Kotkin has argued that
what he calls 'the British diaspora' (the Empire) had little to do with
la mission civilitrice (the French idea of civilising and politically

incorporating the colonial peoples) and much to do with 'money, not glory', with 'the search for markets, resources and, where possible, prospective lands for new economically viable colonies'.[7]

Yet these business British – with their Protestant, work-ethic values – were to become of little account in the forging of the national identity which was proceeding during the nineteenth century and emerged as a finished product in the popular press and media world of the twentieth century. In 1863, Richard Cobden, during the height of the great British capitalist boom, could reveal his great despair that feudalism's instincts and habits were returning:

> We have the spirit of feudalism rife and rampant in the midst of the antagonistic development of the age of Watt, Arkwright and Stephenson! Nay, feudalism is more and more in the ascendant in political and social life. So great is its power and prestige that it draws clear to it the support and homage of even those who are the natural leaders of the newer and better civilisation. Manufacturers and merchants as a rule seem only to desire riches that they prostrate themselves at the feet of feudalism. How is this to end?[8]

It was not to end. For by the mid-twentieth century Britain, the home of the bourgeoisie, the first society to create a serious middle class, none the less evoked as its national image the life of the aristocracy. And, just as perversely, the land of the Protestant business ethic – and the broader 'work ethic' – portrayed its national virtues as upper-class leisure, effortlessness, even idleness. Working for a living became somewhat socially suspect; money should be inherited not earned, hidden not flaunted.

In the political realm the idea of Englishness also served to deny reality. By any test Britain (and earlier England) possessed a rich history of political liberalism. Magna Carta, the English Civil War and Commonwealth, the settlement of 1688 – all confirmed the country as a leader in limiting the power of kings and centralised executive authority. Indeed the politics of England, before the French Revolution, was not only considered liberal by the conservative, traditionalist European standards, but positively anarchic, even revolutionary. Britain 'had a European reputation, whether admired or abhorred, as a politically volatile people given to regicide and rebellion', indeed possessing 'a revolutionary past'.[9]

Also, any society which over the years could produce Thomas Hobbes, John Locke, Adam Smith, Jeremy Bentham, Herbert Spencer, and James and John Stuart Mill must take pride of place in the history of individual and civil rights (even though Britain has not, even yet, codified or entrenched these rights).

Yet this most liberal of national histories – that same history which was to produce the great Victorian liberalism (of the Liberal Party, free trade, and, for its time, open government) – never quite translated into a modern liberal identity for the twentieth century. As the growing United States took over the mantle of liberalism, then Britain began to pride itself not on its history of liberties and rights – far too abstract! – but rather upon the *traditions* of its polity and the merits of its slowly evolving constitution. Twentieth-century constitutionalists like Sir Ivor Jennings, Professor Hood Phillips and Sir Kenneth Weare have all followed in the footsteps of the nineteenth-century conservatives Walter Bagehot and Albert Venn Dicey, who perfected the notion of Britain's traditionalism and organic development as being virtuous.[10]

By the mid-twentieth century, the reality of national decline tended, for a time, to reinforce this denial of Britain's history as a dynamic, liberal, industrial culture. As the country lost its industrial, scientific and technological lead then the initial reaction was to turn even more fervently to the alternative identity of England and Englishness as essentially artistic, literary, spiritual and contemplative – the presumptuous image of 'England as Athens' to 'America's Rome'. 'England as Athens' must have seemed all that was left. Yet, by the time, in 1959, when C. P. Snow fluttered the intellectual dovecots with his 'two cultures' thesis – the great *crie de coeur* on behalf of the country's lost virtues of science and reason – the long-awaited reaction was setting in. The country, for so long force-fed with the drug of 'Englishness', was beginning to dry out.

TRUE BRITS

As the contours of the real Britain began to emerge, and the British slowly began to emerge from under the conformity of Englishness, and discover their true selves, the essential *diversity* of Britain and the British became increasingly apparent. Instead of *one* identity – the single, total (totalitarian), official, conception built around the idea of 'the English gentleman' and the United Kingdom (*Ukania* as Tom Nairn has incisively described it) – the real Britain possessed several identities. Instead of 'one nation' the real Britain played host to several of them.

The theory of British nationhood rests upon the proposition that Britain's unitary constitution is rooted in the foundation of a broadly uniform culture where Britons share a common identity. Those who promote this 'one nation' thesis – amongst political scientists, analysts such as Jean Blondel and Samuel Finer – argue that modernisation has created in Britain one of the most homogeneous of all the industrial nations – and that social differences based upon nationality, language and religion have virtually been eradicated.[11] 'One nation' theorists have also tended to argue that regional economic inequalities are much less pronounced in Britain than in many other industrial countries – that levels of income and social provision are broadly similar throughout Britain.[12]

Furthermore, 'one nation' proponents argue that in modern times this essential homogeneity has been reinforced by the the heavily centralised London-based mass media who provide the same messages and shared experiences to a British-wide audience.

Yet, one of the intriguing aspects of this 'homogeneity' is the way in which Northern Ireland is often left out of the analysis. Because of its deep religious (and ethnic) divisions, not only between the two antagonistic Northern Ireland communities but also between the Irish of Northern Ireland (and their religiosity) and the rest of the British (with their primarily secular culture), Northern Ireland and the Northern Irish fit uneasily into the United Kingdom; their support for the Union (of Northern Ireland and Great Britain) being more to do with necessity than with a homogeneous 'one nation' common identity. So weak is the common identity between the Northern Irish and the rest of Britain that the Liberals almost succeeded in releasing the whole of Ireland from Britain in the 1920s, only to be thwarted by a last-minute military insurrection caused by Protestant fears rather than common loyalties and identities.

In the rest of Celtic Britain, in Scotland and Wales, a 'common identity' – between Scots and Welsh and the various regional peoples of England – is also fairly weakly felt. One of the most intriguing aspects of Celtic consciousness, of Scottish and Welsh separateness, is that, after centuries of British structures and Union propaganda the last half of the twentieth century has seen Scottish and Welsh political nationalism – parties which specifically reject not only the Union but the idea of a common identity within Great Britain or the United Kingdom – on a rising curve. The two separatist parties (the Scottish National Party and Plaid Cymru, the Welsh Nationalist Party) achieved a paltry 27,288 votes between them (0.1 per cent of the total UK electorate) in the general election of 1950. By 1964 this figure had risen to 133,551 (0.5 per cent), but by October 1974 it had risen to over 1 million (1,005,938, or 3.5 per cent of the total UK population, and in Scotland providing 14 seats to the SNP). Ever since this breakthrough year of 1974 certainly the Scottish separatist political movement has always been a serious electoral player, constantly threatening to become Scotland's largest single party. As the writ of the European Union runs ever deeper, then the Celtic nationalist parties may be expected to achieve even more significant results in the next century. One of the SNP's major electoral problems was that it lost votes because many Scots felt it would be isolated should it become independent. 'An independent Scotland Within Europe' (the slogan of the SNP in recent general elections) would seem to overcome that particular disadvantage. (Should Scotland secede from the British Union, the UK-state, there are still some unresolved questions about whether such a 'successor' nation-state could automatically become a member of the European Union with all the rights that entails. There is also a question about whether, in these circumstances, England would also be a 'successor' state and thus have to reapply for membership. It was, after all, the United Kingdom – and not England, Scotland, Wales and Northern Ireland separately – that joined the European Community in 1973.)

The obvious conclusion is that the spread of industrialism, the British single market, and the later 'homogenising' consequences of the media and information revolutions, and, of course, the common nationhood which the ideology of Englishness attempted to create, were simply not able to fully forge a common identity throughout the British Isles. This failure may have several causes. One, of course, may simply be the debilitating morale-sapping effects of national decline. The Scots and the Welsh, like everyone else, prefer to back winners, and Britain and the UK can no longer deliver (as they certainly could during the Empire) success, or even much of a sense of progress. Another explanation may lie in the economic realm. Although present levels of social provision, even income, may not vary (between the regions and nations of Britain) as much as 'North–South' divide protagonists tend to suggest, the phenomenon of Celtic nationalism may, in part, be the product of regional economic and social inequalities built up during the early, and defining, era of industrialism.

But, just as importantly, the lack of a strong common identity, of an unbreakable British national sentiment, may simply be because of the *colonial* character of the construction of Britain and the United Kingdom. The Union between England and Scotland (and earlier between

England and Wales) was not forged by mutual agreement, common affection and identity, or by votes (as was Britain's accession to the Treaty of Rome in the referendum of 1975); rather it was settled on the battlefield, a product of bloodshed and *force majeure*. According to Michael Hechter, Scotland and Wales were essentially colonised (by southern English elites and their collaborators). He suggests that two models of development can be set out to explain the historic relationship between Britain's two largest ethnic groups – the Anglo-Saxons and the Celts. First, the 'diffusion' model in which the smaller group (Celts) slowly melds into the larger, leading to ethnic homogeneity and a lasting common identity; and secondly, the 'internal colonial' model in which contact between the two groups is never completely resolved, leading to conflict and continuing separate consciousness.[13] The continuing robustness of Scottish and Welsh nationalism suggests that the latter model was the more relevant.

This cultural diversity – or lack of a common identity – also reflects itself in the racial and ethnic make-up of Britain. The 1991 census revealed that over 2,600,000 people whose head of household had been born in the new Commonwealth now lived in Britain (433,641 from the Caribbean, 312,155 from East Africa, 149,835 from the rest of Africa, 161,179 from Bangladesh, 692,692 from India, 441,869 from Pakistan and 175, 477 from South–East Asia). It also revealed that over 780,000 Britons were Irish by derivation and just under 1,500,000 were from the 'rest of the world'.[14] Thus, the British Isles is unquestionably a multi-racial and multi-ethnic society. And in the absence of a national – or, in the event of a transfer of Home Office functions to the European Union, a European – policy of repatriation, it will remain so.

Racial and ethnic diversity in the British Isles has been further entrenched by the pluralistic approach to new racial and ethnic communities adopted by successive British governments. No serious attempt to integrate (compared, say, to the French model which seeks assimilation into 'French culture') has been undertaken. As in the multi-racial United States, so in multi-racial Britain: separate racially-based societies exist in urban ghettos and produce separate political leaderships bargaining and manoeuvring for group benefits. Thus a 'common identity', a sense of common Britishness, remains somewhat chimeric.

There is little that is new in this racial/ethnic diversity and separateness. Rodney Hilton suggests that

> it could be argued that since prehistoric times the country has been
> invaded and settled by successive ethnic groups – Celts, Romans,

Angles, Jutes, Saxons, Danes, Norwegians, Normans, Bretons, French
– who sufficiently kept their separate identity to deprive England,
during this period, of any Englishness ... [and the idea that there
was no such thing as Englishness] could be re-inforced by pointing
to an indigenous population speaking one language and a ruling class
[Normans] speaking another, its cultural identity still outside this
newly conquered land.[15]

Later, Huguenots and Jews, like more recent immigrants seeing their
port of entry as the large cities, further added to the ethnic diversity
of Britain. Of course, by the time the West Indians, the Pakistanis
and the Indians came to Britain – during the late 1950s, 1960s, and
1970s – the earlier ethnic immigrations had already become assimilated to the point of invisibility. These new immigrants will not be
invisible in the same way – a distinctiveness, together with new religious identities, which will serve to intensify cultural diversity.

The story of British cultural diversity, though, does not end with
the multi-racial scene. Late twentieth-century Britain may no longer
be divided by religion in the sense that sixteenth-century England was;
however, a survey of religious belief (and non-belief) shows a pattern
rich in diversity. In 1992 Roman Catholics represented the largest single
Christian religious grouping (over 2.04 million church members), slightly
ahead of Anglicans (1.81 million) and Presbyterians (1.24 million).
More interestingly there were more Muslims (over half a million) than
Methodists, more Sikhs (over a quarter of a million) than Baptists,
and more Hindus than Jews.[16] And the new Islamic presence in some
of the inner cities, and the growth of Christian fundamentalism – *in
the midst of Britain's essentially secular society* – will hardly foster
'one nation' common identities.[17]

And this racial and religious diversity often leads to violence, as
did class divisions. The idea – perpetrated by the ideology of Englishness – that the English were a peaceable people, living a tranquil and
civilised, largely rural, existence was, of course, mythical. The country's history was as violent as that of any other of its kind, and even
in the twentieth century its racial, religious and class divisions have
often spilled over into social unrest. In August 1958 serious race disturbances broke out in London's Notting Hill district. During the 1980s
– in Bristol, Manchester, Brixton and other inner city areas – the country
witnessed race riots on the American model. Earlier examples of street
violence, though, were hidden from view by censorship of information. In the summer of 1919 in Cardiff, Newport and Liverpool there

were race riots which never reached the headlines. Mining villages saw disturbances during the 1920s and 30s. Religious differences – between Protestants and Catholics – sparked numerous instances of sectarian violence in Glasgow and Liverpool during the first half of the twentieth century. Violence erupted at football matches and at marches of unemployed people – although films of these events were regularly banned (in 1932 the violence on a hunger march was filmed by Paramount Pictures but not shown publicly). And, again in the 1930s, the regular clashes between Blackshirts and Communists often turned violent.[18]

In such a society of diversity – of national, ethnic, racial, religious (let alone class and regional) differences – what is it that unites the peoples of the British isles? What, in the late twentieth century, does it mean to be British? What is it that provides the 'common identity' so often claimed by 'one nation' theorists? The answer is: increasingly little.

Certainly, for the moment (in the late twentieth century), all the peoples of Britain share a common political and legal life. All Britons, irrespective of national ethnic, religious, class and regional divisions, live under common laws in a common political unit. Yet, this legal (and legalist) form – the British nation-state – is a waning reality, as both the European Union and the pressures of globalisation bear down upon it.

As well as a common legal status the peoples of Britain share a common language. Whether you are a Scot from the Highlands, a Pakistani in Bradford or a Welsh hill farmer your primary means of communication will be English. Yet, this commonality provided by the English language – which some Britons believed helped define them and 'separate them off' from others – is eroding fast: for this 'common language' of English is now shared with millions and millions of others outside of the home base. Today, English ranks second only to Chinese in the numbers of speakers, and its world-wide reach is increasingly hegemonic. It is the world's leading 'second tongue', it is the language of science and international business, and – because of the influence of American popular culture and media technology – the language too of the global 'infotainment' industry. Most importantly it is becoming, unofficially, the primary language of the European Union.

Even an emerging trans-European economy will likely do little to reduce English's leadership. Already both German and French firms employ English as their lingua franca for international business. Similarly, German, the language of Europe's premier economic power, has not even expanded beyond the less than 100 million speakers it possessed in 1925.[19]

As with German, French seems unlikely too to be able to challenge English in the European Union – particularly amongst the peoples! The English language appears simply unstoppable; and although it no longer defines the English it begins to appear as the greatest of all gifts from the English to the world.

DOES ENGLAND EXIST?

If the modern British do not possess the characteristics necessary to forge a common national identity, what of the English? What of England, the heartland, the home of 'Englishness' itself?

Like Britain, England is essentially a geographic unit – comprising the counties bounded in the north by Hadrian's Wall, in the south by the English Channel, in the west by the Welsh border, the Atlantic Ocean and the Irish Sea, and in the East by the North Sea. It is not a nation-state, and it is not represented at the United Nations, yet it does appear on formal governmental political documents, usually referring to laws and policies for 'England and Wales', and in a peculiar hang-over, it – together with Scotland, Wales and Northern Ireland – possesses its own 'national' football team.

Yet, although 'England' has for almost three centuries been subsumed by 'Britain', many British people still think of themselves as 'English', and some, echoing John Wilkes down the centuries, viscerally so. The use of the self-description 'English' is a feature of many amongst the majority white, non-Celtic population of the British Isles. Yet, does a sense of commonality, a sense of common 'English' identity, really exist even amongst these non-Celtic English? In England, and amongst the majority population, are there serious binding commonalities to be discovered beyond the simple assertion of 'Englishness'?

One problem for the 'one nation' theorists is that the majority non-Celtic English population are about as seriously diverse and fragmented a people as are the wider British. When, inevitably, the idea of England as a common singular idea has been conjured up – as in 'England Expects' – the question was always, still is: which England?

The fact is that the hold of the attempted unifying culture – of

'Englishness' – was always patchy. In large parts of the north of England it hardly existed. In the land far from London, Oxford and Stratford-upon-Avon – of chapels and industry, pit villages and working-class communities – 'Englishness' imbued little. And even in the south of England (South of a line drawn from the Wash to the Severn) its writ did not run universally. The heartland of heavy Englishness was to be found in the home counties and most of the small towns, but there was less of a presence in the big cities and their suburbs. Indeed the light industrial suburban 'ribbon development' which spread out to the west of London during the inter-war period was the raw material for J. B. Priestley's 'New England' – so new, he argued, that it was 'not really England at all'.

Disraeli helped to unmask the myth of a common English identity when in *Sybil* he coined the term 'two nations'. Yet, of course, England was, and is, a land not just of two but of 'many nations'. And a sign of the sheer profundity of England's 'many nations' is the fact of the persistence, right up until modern times, of the cultural distinctiveness of the English regions. In the very means of communication, in the markedly varied accents and dialects (with all that implies for attitudes and lifestyles) the tale is told. And are the real distinctions between Cockneys, Brummies, Scousers, Yorkshiremen and women, Geordies, East Anglians and West Country people any less marked than between any of them and, say, the populations of the more recognised 'nations' of Scotland and Wales? And, aren't some of these serious cultural distinctions amongst the English much more pronounced than those that exist amongst people in more homogeneous cultures such as the United States, Germany or Scandinavia?

These cultural regions have persisted through, and beyond, the onslaught of 'Englishness'; indeed they survived the massive attempt to standardise dialects following the introduction of Received Pronunciation (RP) in the early twentieth century. Developed during the late nineteenth century in the public schools – as a 'suitable' accent for an imperial governing class, RP was adopted after 1920 by the BBC, who used its monopolistic power over information and manners in an emerging mass society in an attempt to standardise the way people spoke English. In the process regional accents and dialects were derided socially – as being 'lower class', even though in previous eras regional accents had possessed no class connotations:

Sir Robert Peel (Harrow and Oxford) one of England's most famous Conservative Prime Ministers, never disguised his Midlands speech.

Lord Stanley, later Eighteenth Earl of Derby (Rugby and Cambridge), spoke a 'sort of Lancashire patois'. His Liberal Opponent William Gladstone, spent his childhood in Liverpool and his Lancashire 'burr' survived both Eton and Oxford, which suggests that there was virtually no social pressure to lose it. Even at Eton, the shrine of English private education, the Revd J. L. Joynes, one of the poet Swinburne's tutors, is known to have pronounced 'died' as 'doyed', and to have attacked the 'oidle' in his sermons.[20]

Yet, the attempt to impose a standard dialect ultimately failed. This failure can be seen in the skin-deep character of RP (or 'posh') English. Those elites in Britain who speak RP often picked it up quite consciously (or even, like Margaret Thatcher, by elocution lessons), and, like Margaret Thatcher, will in moments of crisis or intense feeling often revert to their original regional accent – in her case Lincolnshire. This failure can also be seen not just in the persistence of regional accents, but in their triumph. For instance, in the south–east and the 'home counties', the supposed homeland of RP and standardised English, it is the regional accent of Cockney (or Cockney mixed with 'standardised speech') which increasingly holds sway. Cockney is the genuine dialect of London, the original sixteenth-century accent of all Londoners who were not part of the court. Its centre of gravity was the old East End – the area which runs from Bethnal Green through Limehouse to Aldgate in the City of London – but it also possesses rural, French and Yiddish roots.[21] As Cockney – under the influence of Londoners moving into the surrounding countryside – tends to crowd out both the standardised UK-wide Received Pronunciation of the upper income groups of the 'home counties' and the original accents of North Essex, South Suffolk, Kent, even Hampshire, a real south-eastern consciousness – akin to that, say, of Yorkshire or the north-east, has begun to emerge.

This still powerful English cultural regionalism – with its attendant identities and loyalties – can, should a federal or devolved political system become a reality, give real meaning to new political regions in England. The North (comprising Cleveland, Cumbria, Durham, Northumberland, Tyne and Wear), Yorkshire and Humberside, The East Midlands (Derbyshire, Leicestershire, Lincolnshire, Northamptonshire, Nottinghamshire), East Anglia (Cambridgeshire, Norfolk, Suffolk), the South-West (Avon, Cornwall, Devon, Dorset, Gloucestershire, Somerset, Wiltshire), the South-East (Bedfordshire, Berkshire, Buckinghamshire, East Sussex, Essex, Greater London, Hampshire, Hertfordshire, the Isle of Wight, Kent, Oxfordshire, Surrey and West Sussex), the

West Midlands (the county of West Midlands, Hereford and Worcestershire, Shropshire, Staffordshire, Warwickshire) and the North-West (Merseyside, Cheshire, Lancashire and Greater Manchester) – are all real regional-cum-cultural territories with media-centres ('capital cities') and local economies. And the loyalties and identities of their respective populations (certainly outside of the South-East and East Midlands) are arguably more regionally-grounded than they are national and 'English'. And in London, identity as a Londoner may be just as strong as, in some cases stronger than, that of an English man or woman.

Yet as well as being divided 'horizontally' – by region and nation – the English are also seriously divided vertically – by the old-time religion of class. In modern England there remains a fairly strong relationship between 'regionality' and class – in the sense that, broadly-speaking, those people rooted in regional localities and possessed of regional identities and accents tend to be lower on the social and income scale than the trans-regional national elite (many of whom still tend to identify with 'Englishness' and with a national London-based culture). Britain's fundamental 'class problem' (the one which distinguishes it from the 'class problem' of most other Western societies) remains, at root, a cultural one. It involves divisions between people based as much upon corrosive social and psychological inequalities as on economic ones; and deep inequalities of dignity and worth, of aspirations and self-confidence, of education and life chances. England's private education sector (the public schools) still creates a somewhat separated and self-conscious elite (with dense social networks that provide a lifetime's advantage for their members); and the country, even very late into the twentieth century, has been incapable of producing a self-confident middle class (a bourgeoisie on the American or French model) which would in its turn create a modern commercial society in which old-style class divisions would subside.

Alongside these cultural class distinctions the English are also riven by striking inequalities in income and wealth, inequalities that are normally, though not always, co-terminous with the cultural and psychological inequalities. Old regional distinctions created by industrialism, and sustained by more recent disparities between 'North' and 'South', have left their mark on living standards. Whereas Greater London is 23 per cent better off than the average, the south-east generally is 16 per cent better off than the average, and East Anglia is 2 per cent better off than the average; on the other hand, Yorkshire and Humberside is 7 per cent less well-off than the average, the south-west is 6 per cent less well-off, and England's poorest region, the north-west is 10 per cent worse-off.[22] The debate about how to rectify these disparities will no doubt continue; but the *fact* of them punches a serious hole in the 'one nation' illusion. When people in the south-east are over 30 per cent better off than those in the north then even should a 'common identity' exist it will be placed under considerable strain.

As well as these quite sharp regional distinctions, late twentieth-century England also exhibits severe national ones. 'A common identity' is difficult to sustain when the most wealthy 5 per cent of the population own 50 per cent of the wealth of the country. Nor are the late twentieth-century *trends* particularly encouraging for 'national unity' – the share of income of the bottom fifth of households fell between 1981 and 1990–1, and only the top fifth of households had a larger share of total income in 1990–1 than they had in 1981.[23]

Traditionally, sharp differences in income and wealth – indeed large-scale poverty – may have threatened the social fabric and the political stability of the British state, but they posed no threat to national identity and sensibility. Now, though, the time when the disadvantaged could be reconciled to a common identity by appeals to patriotic or imperial glory are long gone.

THE MEANING OF 'BEING ENGLISH'

So, in such a diverse society what does it mean to be English? What is unique, and exceptional, about it? What are the commonalities that separate Englishness off from Scottishness or Welshness or Frenchness – or, indeed, Chineseness? And in the late twentieth century is there anything more to being English than the simple fact of living within the borders of the geographical unit called England, the group of counties bounded in the north by Hadrian's Wall, in the south by the Atlantic Ocean and the English Channel, in the west by the Welsh border and the Irish Sea, and in the East by the North Sea?

It is easiest to determine what Englishness is not. It is not, and never has been, a racial category. Thomas Sowell has argued that 'race is one of the ways of collectivising people in our minds'; yet the English cannot properly be so 'collectivised'.[24] If the non-whites living in England were excluded from calculations, then, racially, the English would certainly share the commonality of the Caucasian racial category – but, crucially, they would also share being Caucasian with all the other Caucasians in Europe and North America. Thus, in this racial sense, *Englishness* is hardly a definition of Caucasian.

Yet, of course, the non-Caucasian populations of England cannot be excluded from the analysis. And the reality within the land called England of a multi-racial (multi-ethnic) society robs Englishness not only of a racial definition, but also of a potential sense of separateness: the English are no different, in this respect, from the rest of the Western multi-racial and multi-ethnic world. If race (or ethnicity) is no longer a uni-fying and defining 'commonality' for the English, what of the English language? Certainly the English language is a form of communication which the diversity of peoples in England share in common. Yet, as a source of unity, it should not be over-stated. The still sharply diver-gent dialects – Cockney can probably still be understood England-wide, though not a broad version of Scouse or Brummie – remain a major source of cultural distinctiveness and continue to limit a common identity.

Indeed language has little automatic connection with nation-states. There are certainly examples of national identity being forged out of a common language. One such is Romania – which separates itself from the Hungarian and Slavic languages surrounding it. Also, 'the use of German helped Bavarians and Saxons and Wurttembergers to see them-selves as German and to identify with one another at a higher level of identity'. And Japan represents the 'clearest and most outstanding example of the type in the whole world'.[25]

But there are also numerous examples of nation-states which do not possess a common language. Switzerland is an example of the 'one nation–several languages' model. So too is Belgium (Dutch and French) and Britain (English, the various Celtic languages, and a host of Indian and Asian languages). In the USA several languages now essentially compete with English, and the US authorities still refuse to designate English as an official language.

Indeed, 'nationality may predict the language but the language will not predict nationality'. English-speakers can be British, American, Australian, New Zealanders or Irish. Arabic-speakers can be Iraqi and Egyptian. Portuguese-speakers can be Portuguese but also Brazilian. An analyst argues: 'It is because of its potential to establish identities that have nothing to do with local self, the family self, the national self, that I regard the "one language–many nations" model of language use as the most promising for the future.'[26]

Indeed the English language, although often promoted as a crucial attribute of Englishness (as a distinctive cultural form – separating us from the rest of Europe), is no longer – if it ever was – the property of the people of England only, and thus a source of *separate* identity.

The English people now share their English language with the world. Under the influence of Empire – and, more recently, because of the popular success of American international business, information and media, and, of course, the appeal of Hollywood, English has now emerged as the world's most influential language. A language spoken by only 1.5 million people on an off-shore island in the eleventh century 'today ranks second only to Chinese in the number of speakers, with as many as 700 million users. . . . Most important, it is spoken commonly in more countries, and on more continents, than any other language. . . . By 1980, nearly 100 million non-English speakers – three out of five of them Asian – were studying some variant of the Queen's English.'[27]

English is the unofficial second language of the European Union; when Germans and French people wish to speak to each other they do so, usually, in English. English is increasingly the lingua franca of international business, and is already the language of science and technology and, crucially, information. It has been estimated that 80 per cent of the information stored in electronic retrieval systems is written in English.

This world-wide appeal of English begs the large question (around which a lively debate still swirls) of the importance of language in informing national identity.

The view that 'nationality' classifications are essentially 'cultural' ones, and that these are (or rather must be) linguistic classifications' – in other words, that 'the criterion of nationhood is language' – is broadly supported by the philosopher Ernest Gellner. Yet this view is challenged by Professor Anthony Smith in his major work on nationalism, where he casts a critical eye over the importance of language to both culture and nationality. He argues that 'culture' is a far broader concept than 'language' – 'culture includes customs, the ancestry myth, institutions, history, law, and particularly religion'. And he also questions the assumptions of some nationalist theorists (both Gellner and Elie Kedourie) that there actually exists a universal need to belong – which a common language satisfies.

> Human beings, after all, do very often feel a strong desire to return to some cosy security with a routine of habits and activities, when such a pattern has been suddenly overturned. But even here it would be rash to generalise. Some may actually feel liberated from the routine, others may fluctuate in their attitudes to it. . . . In other words, the question of individuals' needs, desires and habits requires

empirical investigation in each case. It cannot be settled from such a priori assumptions.[28]

So, if race and ethnicity, as well as language, no longer adequately serve to define Englishness as a discrete and separate identity, does culture (using the word in its broad sense, as meaning a way of life)? Is there a nationality of art, of science, of consumer goods and services? Is there such a thing as 'English science'? 'English art'? 'English consumer goods'? Certainly, there is science, art and goods which have originated in England. Yet, to fly in a jet aircraft (even though the jet engine was first developed in England) is not a particularly 'English experience'. Nor is there anything uniquely English about watching, or acting in, a play by Shakespeare (now performed throughout the world).

Also, in the modern mass-consumer society, food, clothes, cars and consumer durables are the great artefacts of globalism, the products of a transnational interlinked and interdependent economy. National distinctions – in terms of where a product was born or indeed is made – are increasingly meaningless. In this environment there are few consumer goods, even those made in England, which are in any sense uniquely 'English'. Although the mass-marketing industry still likes to differentiate products on the basis of country – the 'English' variety being leather goods, rural sports equipment and clothing, 'country house' and 'country cottage' furniture and fabrics, and foods such as marmalade, marmite and roast beef – these so-called 'English' products are now consumed and owned by millions of foreigners world-wide, making them part of the great cosmopolitan consumer market, hardly 'national' in any sense. And, often, the most 'English' of products not only possess a larger market abroad than at home, but are also made abroad. Crabtree & Evelyn is owned by an American multinational; even the popular melody 'English Country Garden' was composed by an Australian who lived in the United States.

The environment – including the built environment – remains something of an exception here. There remains such a thing as 'English architecture' – but only because of the large number of older buildings still standing, buildings which are products of their time, essentially monuments, on display in a global cultural era, to an earlier more separated 'national' age. By contrast, modern architecture, is, almost by definition, universal, extremely difficult to place in a national context. Also, urban scenery is becoming the same the world over (Hong Kong looks just like Manhattan or the City of London); and, although rural scenes still retain a certain national distinctiveness, the famed English rural landscape, although certainly distinguishable from the landscapes of, say, southern Europe or the southern part of the United States, may be difficult to tell apart from other temperate northern European landscapes.

BACKGROUND NOT COUNTRY

Many English people would, though, still rebel against the idea that 'being English' has little meaning, amounting to little more than a legal and geographic notion: living and working within the boundaries of England. For them 'being English' has real content and meaning, and represents a distinctive identity – separate from that of 'other' identities.

Yet, are the believed distinctions really *national* ones, or are they separated identities based upon different upbringings, backgrounds and familiarities? Certainly, the sights, sounds, smells and images of youth tend to breed separate familiarities, sensibilities and identities. French people, German people and Chinese people will all have separate youthful 'national' experiences which make them distinctive, and which may make them feel part of one particular identity ('we') which is thought to separate them from 'other' identities.

Indeed these youthful memories and sensibilities – memories and sensibilities shared with others of the same general background – may be at the core of the very idea and feeling of 'country'. Beyond the formal issues of laws and passports this shared background (or belief in a shared background) may be the very stuff of contemporary patriotism. Patriotism – or love of country – it is suggested is a perennial part of human life whereas nationalism is a product of recent times.

However, the sense of patriotism, the idea of love of country, may have little to do with 'country' or 'nationality'. It may, in fact, be little more than a love of background and familiarity – the familiar sights, sounds and smells of youth. Background and nationality may indeed overlap, particularly in countries small enough to foster a bond of common memories. Yet England has been so sharply divided by class and region (even locality) that shared 'national' memories – the sights and sounds and smells of youth – are rather few. What common memories would unite a working-class upbringing in Manchester with an upper middle-class 'compatriot' in a public school in rural Sussex?

Also, what common memories would unite differing backgrounds in the same region – say, an upbringing in urban Sheffield with that in the North Riding, or inner-city London with the rural rides of Sussex only a few miles away? Or, even, what common memories would unite same-class upbringings in different regions of England? Are an unemployed Cockney's memories and familiarities in any sense the same as those of an unemployed Geordie from Middlesbrough? And are any of these distinctive upbringings, or those of their respective ancestors in other centuries, productive of a 'common identity'?

During the industrial age, the spread of technology and mass information has, of course, brought certain 'national' events and images to England's diverse population, thus creating a degree of 'national' commonality and community. Almost every English person brought up during the 1950s would, thus, share in common certain formal or 'political' memories – the Festival of Britain, the coronation of Elizabeth II, the visit to Wembley Stadium of the victorious 1956 Hungarian football team, the first televised test matches. And most English people alive today would also have shared the films, television, radio programmes and newspapers – and all the cultural paraphernalia of the British state (and Americanised British mass-popular culture) in the postwar years.

The consciousness of 'being English' will not disappear altogether. Rather, for the English, a sense of Englishness will co-exist with other identities; though, in a world in which 'modern political identities are fractured and dispersed among a multiplicity of sites', Englishness will lose what was its uniquely powerful hold on the psychic identity of the people of England.[29]

5 A Federal Destiny

LIVING VICARIOUSLY

Not surprisingly, UK nationalism has not died quietly. The transition from a polity based upon the eighteenth-century nation-state to one more suited to a European role in the twenty-first century has been less than smooth. The history of the post-Second World War era has been one of illusions interspersed occasionally with bouts of realism. Even in the 1990s the illusion of British independence (and English exceptionalism) continues to infuse policy. As part of a dogged refusal to accept British absorption into the European Union some nationalists were still toying with the fanciful image of Britain as an independent off-shore global player: a northern hemisphere 'Asian Tiger' – like South Korea or Singapore. Yet, the story was not wholly one of delusions of grandeur, for at the same time as these continuing conceits, the realistic strain in the country had secured Britain's membership of the European Community in 1973 and had signed the Single European Act in 1987.

There were essentially two phases in the postwar national delusion of grandeur. The first ran from the end of the war up until the Suez crisis in 1956, and was based upon the illusion of Britain as a continuing world power, as a global player only somewhat less powerful than the United States and the Soviet Union. According to Ernest Bevin, Labour's foreign secretary in the postwar Attlee administration, the world had to understand that Britain was 'not just another European country'.[1] And later, Winston Churchill, at a State Department dinner in April, 1954, would argue that 'only the English-speaking peoples count: that together they can rule the world'.[2]

The Suez adventure of 1956 shattered this particular illusion. Britain's attempt at an 'independent' initiative (in collusion with the French and Israelis) in invading Egypt, an action considered commensurate with the presumed 'world power' role of the country, ended in humiliating failure – at the hands of the Americans. American terms for a resolution of the crisis, issued to its faithful 'special' ally, were clear: 'no financial or economic help unless and until there was a total withdrawal of British troops' from the Suez Canal area.[3] Britain complied in an atmosphere which was redolent with accusations of betrayal by

Washington; yet, amidst the recriminations, the reality of Britain's new status, and its obvious inability to play a world role, was becoming apparent.

Yet, the Suez crisis may indeed have been, in one interpretation of the double-edged words of Anthony Nutting, the Conservative minister who was the first to rebel against Anthony Eden, 'no end of a lesson'. For instead of putting British (and English) pretensions to rest, and clearing the way for a realistic appraisal of the country's position in the world – and perhaps too for a European future – the guardians of British nationhood and independence took the country down a new route. Eden's successor, Harold Macmillan, moved swiftly to repair the damage done to the Anglo-American alliance, and, particularly after the arrival of President John Kennedy, re-established a close British–American relationship. Behind this move by Macmillan was a new strategy to keep Britain afloat as an important, independent actor – this time through the good offices of a determinedly pro-American foreign and defence policy.

'Atlanticism' was to save Britain's honour, and that of the upper - class Englishmen who continued to run Britain. The idea was that through an association with American power Britain was to retain her world role. America, not a united Europe, was to become the ultimate enabler of Britain politically and Englishness culturally. By comparison, Europe offered Britain very little. Alan Milward presents evidence that large sections of Britain's foreign-policy elite simply refused to believe that the European project – then simply a Common Market – would get off the ground. The British ambassador in Washington represented the British elite view when he 'doubted very much whether, when the chips were down, the French would be prepared to make the internal adjustments which would be necessary for progress towards a common market'.[4] And, even should the European project develop then, by taking part in it, British sovereignty would be seriously compromised – evidently a fate avoided by the country's reliance upon the United States.

Thus, under the protection of the American 'special relationship', the British elite could continue to believe that their independence was secure, and that even a global role could continue to be contemplated. Thus, the idea of a 'special relationship' – as the beating heart of British foreign policy – was dusted off and given a new polishing. This 'special relationship' had been an English governing-class need ever since their more perceptive members first began to notice that their own base – in British power – was beginning to erode.

The idea of 'cousinhood', of the United States as an Anglo-Saxon country – even though by the end of the nineteenth century 'the proportion of English stock in the "white" American population had sunk to only one-third' – was fostered yet again.[5] Cultural kinship between Americans and English people (and between Americana and Englishness) was revived under the pro-American Macmillan (who also, like Churchill before him, was in part American) as he established a close personal relationship with President John F. Kennedy. Macmillan could have repeated with ease the words of an earlier scion of Englishness, Prime Minister Arthur Balfour, who declared in a 'classic statement of the pan-Anglo-Saxon myth to a Pilgrims' dinner': 'We both spring from the same root. . . . Are we not bound together for ever.'[6]

This fantasy was still enthralling the English half a century later, even after the Suez affair should have brought them down to earth. As Correlli Barnett has argued, even in the first few decades of the twentieth century 'the special relationship was a British fantasy. It was love in the perfect romantic style, unrequited and unencouraged, yet nonetheless pursued with a grovelling ardour.'[7]

Of course, the English elite who dominated the UK political establishment had not lost their innate sense of superiority, their imperial disdain for what they saw as the upstart 'colonists'. Part of them romanticised the American connection, yet another part treated the Americans as colonial inferiors. Anglo-American celebrations, like the Pilgrims' dinners – the regular transatlantic get-togethers – often hid the English elite's continuing disdain for America and Americans. 'In Washington, Lord Halifax once whispered to John Maynard Keynes . . . it's true they [the Americans] have all the money-bags but we have all the brains.'[8]

Whatever the fantasies of this beleaguered English elite, the Americans were far less certain that they possessed a 'special' relationship with the UK. The reality was of the UK as a client-state. This subordinate position was demonstrated most obviously during the Suez crisis. And since 1956 the UK has not engaged in any other genuinely independent foreign policy initiative. The UK gave full diplomatic support to the Americans in Vietnam; the country's entry into the European Community in 1975 was fully backed by the United States; and the Falklands War in 1982 was only successfully carried through after the United States government (particularly the Pentagon under the Anglophile leadership of Defence Secretary Caspar Weinberger) provided considerable material and intelligence assistance.[9] The one issue since Suez that caused a serious rift between the two countries – the American

invasion of Grenada in 1983 – saw the 'special' British left completely
in the dark whilst the United States (under the supposedly Anglophile
President Ronald Reagan) invaded the imperial sensibilities of Englishness by its incursion into a part of the Commonwealth where the
Queen had a representative in the form of the Governor-General.

From the American side the signals that the UK was no longer 'special'
had been emanating clearly, for all but the most infatuated to understand. Suez was an early signal. Increasingly, during the 1960's and
1970s, the US foreign-policy leadership saw the Federal Republic of
Germany – not only their 'front-line state' in the defence against the
Soviet Union, but also, increasingly, the most impressive military power
– as their principal ally in Europe, and were essentially at ease with
any European defence co-operation and integration. Washington always
received the British well, but the courtesy of the reception could hardly mask the American view of Britain's increasing geo-political
unimportance. This American view of Britain was clearly revealed by
the outgoing American ambassador to London, Raymond Seitz, who
upon leaving his post in 1993 went so far as to advise the British
government to fully integrate into the European Union in order to preserve what influence it retained in Washington.[10]

Yet, these signals were not, by and large, received. And very late in
the day, in the 1980s, British nationalism was yet again to be resur-
rected, this time by a kiss of life from a new President in the White
House: Ronald Wilson Reagan. The new American President was so
enthralled by Mrs Thatcher – not as a nationalist but rather as a free-
market purist – that he was willing to smile benignly upon the rather
florid rhetoric of nationalism which she evoked under the umbrella of
their 'special' personal relationship. She was his 'soul mate' he declared in his memoirs.[11] As befitted the realities of the Anglo-American relationship, his attitude was essentially paternalistic. He would
not change American policy one jot because of British pressure, but
when American policies differed from British he would accept a wig-
ging from Thatcher across the Atlantic phone like a proud uncle. After
one such ticking off he declared her to be 'great', and 'one hell of a
tough lady'.[12] Reagan could afford to be so relaxed; he represented a
superpower which used, rather than was used by, Britain. And America's long-term strategic need for an 'unsinkable aircraft carrier' off
the European coast – the real basis for the 'special relationship' –
came in very useful during the raid on Libya.

As the post-war decades rolled onwards the guardians of British
independent nationhood could no longer square the circle – or rather

the competing circles. Their room for independent manoeuvre was becoming smaller and smaller. On the one hand the 'special relationship' with the United States was increasingly one-sided. And, on the other, that alternative mechanism for maintaining some semblance of British independence and influence in the new world – Europe – was increasingly developing integrationist tendencies which would mean a formal, declared and open loss of sovereignty.

So British policy fluctuated, often violently, between the 'special relationship' and the new Europe. The premierships of Attlee, Churchill and Eden essentially steered clear of the early moves to European unity – Britain did not take part in the Schuman Plan (for a Coal and Steel Community), was more than hesitant about the Pleven Plan for European military unity, avoided and tried to sabotage the European Payments Union, and, crucially, withdrew from the Spaak Committee (after the Messina Conference, the progenitor of the EEC).[13] And during the 1950s British leaders displayed some remarkable bouts of wishful thinking about the potential of these fateful European conferences. The view that the 'mutual antagonism between France and Germany was so great that only Britain could play the honest-broker between them' was a standard view; and, later, the British ambassador to Paris, Gladwyn Jebb, had assured the Foreign Office that 'no very spectacular developments are to be expected as a result of the Messina conference'.[14] Yet, subsequently, under Harold Macmillan's and, later, Harold Wilson's premierships, Britain applied to join the EEC. The ruthlessly pro-European Edward Heath was followed by the more 'Atlanticist' Harold Wilson and the very pro-American Jim Callaghan. And this tortured British schizophrenia was even reflected in the premiership of Margaret Thatcher. For, even during her very pro-American tenure, she signed the Single European Act in 1987, at that point the single most impressive integrationist development in the recent history of Europe.

Increasingly boxed in, British policy-makers still resolutely refused to contemplate the loss of sovereignty – at least in public. So, even when some sections of the British leadership began to contemplate a European future, it was usually in terms of how to use the continent to continue to project British independence, and often even 'British greatness'. Ernest Bevin's dictum that Britain was not simply 'another European country', in other words it was a country with a world role, still resonated even amongst 'pro-Europeans'. Anthony Nutting, writing in 1960, argued that the British decision to refuse talks on the Schuman Plan was 'the most critical of the lost opportunities for Great Britain to *lead* Europe'. And the 'pro-European' MP Bob Boothby told the Commons in July 1956 that if the six European countries then contemplating a common market 'really see that we are prepared to come in and *take the lead* they will virtually allow us to write our own ticket'.[15] The economic historian Alan Milward has argued that these attitudes – which infused British policy-making throughout the early postwar decades – were based upon the belief that Britain 'was still in some sense a great power whose foreign policy should reflect that position', a view which 'reinforced its ignorance about its closest neighbours' and 'which strengthened both arrogance and myopic conservatism'.[16] And John Young, in his history of Britain's relations with European unity, has argued that much pro-European sentiment was not based upon a recognition of the end of sovereignty or on 'real idealism about Europe', but rather on 'a particular view of British interests, especially a desire to prevent a German-dominated European bloc'.[17]

The architect of Britain's eventual entry in 1975 into the EEC, Edward Heath, saw British entry in terms of improving Britain's economic performance, but also, according to one of his cabinet colleagues, 'saw Britain in Europe as the way back to being a Great Power'.[18] Some pro-European sentiments reached beyond the fanciful to the ludicrous: the Conservative Member of Parliament Norman St John Stevas (later to become Lord President of the Council in Mrs Thatcher's administration) offered the view that if Britain entered the European Community then the Queen would become 'Empress of Europe'.

The idea of Britain 'leading' Europe, and of Europe as representing a new platform for Britain to exercise a world role (incidentally, without losing its sovereignty), was perhaps the grandest post-imperial illusion of all, the high-point of the fever of self-importance which still gripped the British state's ruling class.

By comparison, and intriguingly, the 'Little England' arguments of some anti-marketeers (as those opposed to Britain's entry into the EEC were called) were less grandiose. Enoch Powell and Tony Benn, who based their hostility to Britain's membership of the EEC on differing aspects of the potential loss of sovereignty involved, were articulating old-fashioned notions of self-government, not delusions of national self-importance. Other anti-marketeers, however, displayed all the nationalist pretensions of some of their pro-market opponents. The anti-European 'world view' was based upon the proposition that the British nation-state was both a sovereign entity and a world player – a role ensured not only by the 'special relationship' but also by the Commonwealth of Nations. Even the normally progressive Labour leader Hugh Gaitskell, in his famous anti-market speech at Brighton in 1962, evoked this theme when he referred to the need to preserve 'a thousand years of history' as well as the imperial legacy (he argued that entry into the EEC would be tantamount to betraying the white dominions and the memory of the Australians lost during the battles of 'Vimy Ridge' and 'Gallipoli').

Yet, such was the reality of change – and of the increasing centrality of Europe for the British economic and trading system – that not only did Britain enter the European Community in 1973, but she also took part in all the later major integrationist measures. Britain signed the 1987 Single European Act and then, following the removal of Margaret Thatcher after her refusal to contemplate further European unity, finally signed the further bout of integration engineered by the Maastricht Treaty of 1992. No major political figure, with the exception of a former Chancellor of the Exchequer, was subsequently to call for Britain to pull out of the new European Union. The Conservative right based their strategy on a critique of the Union, not a rejection of it. For Britain's remaining nationalists, it became a case of complaining about reality, not of offering an alternative vision. They were being dragged, reluctantly, kicking and screaming into their new home.

UNCLE SAM'S DESERTED CHILD

The end of the cold war, and the bi-polar world which it brought into being, was a real blow to British nationalism and the state it supported. It was not so much the fall of the Berlin Wall, the emergence of democracy in Eastern Europe, and then the end of the Soviet Union, that mattered: rather, it was the political dynamic which these events unleashed which, uniquely amongst the Western powers, was to further dent Britain's already battered sense of importance and independence.

During the cold war Britain had something of a role. Whether it was the Americans' 'unsinkable aircraft carrier' or the intelligence partner of Washington or the political and cultural bridge between America and Europe in NATO and the Atlantic community, Britain at least possessed a niche, and, moreover, one which allowed its political class to retain a certain detachment from continental Europe. Now, though, the end of the cold war would inevitably mean serious American retrenchment, and, as a consequence, the loss of postwar Britain's geopolitical *raison d'être*. It would have no option but to make its peace with continental Europe, and fully join the new emerging European Union – and at the asking price.

Threats of American retrenchment were common even during the cold-war years. That the United States was shouldering too large a part of the defence responsibilities of NATO was a constant refrain out of Washington during the 1970s and 1980s. So were outbursts of traditional American isolationist sentiment.

The UK establishment simply misunderstood the depths of American unease – even during the height of anti-communist and anti-Russian sentiment – about its European, and hence its implicitly pro-British, role. Indeed, even the most rudimentary reading of American history should have persuaded the British foreign-policy leadership that its commitment to Europe was not normal, arguably a huge aberration. Ever since George Washington sounded the alarm, the Americans have been wary of 'foreign entanglements'. And John Quincy Adams summed up the mixture of international moralism and non-involvement which has been the underlying reality of American foreign policy for most of the country's life. 'She is the well wisher of the freedom and independence of all', he argued, but 'she is the champion and vindicator only of her own'. And, from Washington's and Adams's time right through to the 1941 declaration of war against Germany, American involvement in Europe was a fragile thing. The Senate refused to ratify the League of Nations. President Roosevelt's pro-British activity in the late 1930s very nearly got him impeached. And, just one day after VE Day, the Americans were already determined to bring the troops home. Indeed, mutinous demonstrations began breaking out amongst GIs in European bases, and President Truman, unable to withstand the tide of US public opinion in favour of US withdrawal, had demobilised the twelve-million-strong US army and navy by mid-1946.[19]

Senator Mansfield's famous amendment, which sought to lower the number of American troops in Europe at the height of American–Soviet tensions during the Vietnam War, was an omen. So, too, was the warning issued by Senate majority leader Howard Baker in 1980: 'Ive thought about taking up the cudgels, but the situation is too serious for that. When Mansfield was doing it there was virtually no support for that position in the Senate. Were I to do it, I'm afraid it would start a fire I could not put out.'[20] Yet, British foreign policy plodded forward, unmoved: the new British Prime Minister, Margaret Thatcher, was about to launch the country on a decade-long love affair with America, and, again, put off the necessary adjustments to Europe.

Ten years later, with the cold war coming to its swift and dramatic end, the retrenching theme was, ominously, being echoed on the Democratic side of politics, the traditional home of American internationalism. A not untypical view came from Democratic Congressman Pete Stark in 1991: 'For almost half a century', he suggested, 'the United States has played the world's policeman. With the end of the Cold War we don't need and can't afford to spend $200 billion on more than 300,000 troops overseas. Not when we're experiencing a severe recession, huge federal budget deficits and the prospect of closing military bases here at home.'[21]

And the conservatives were going even further. The American conservative Pat Buchanan articulated a strain in American thinking which was not too far from the minds of the incoming Clinton Presidency in 1993: 'Why', he asked, 'should kids from Idaho and West Virginia have to police a truce between Muslims, Croats and Serbs who have been killing one another since the crusades?'[22] He argued that America might indeed be the 'arsenal of democracy' but it was certainly not 'the western world's white knight on an endless quest to right every wrong or crush every tyrant'.

And so it was. By 1994 American troop levels in Europe had fallen dramatically – from over 300,000 during the last years of the cold war to about 100,000; and once the troops had been withdrawn, and the bases closed, it was unlikely that, except in a real emergency, and probably not even then, they would be restored. Potentially even more ominous for the remaining British supporters of the 'special relationship' – still gathering annually at their Pilgrims' dinners – were the political divisions opening up between Washington and Europe over a host of NATO and European issues, most notably the Bosnia crisis.

THE LOGIC OF EUROPE

A dynamic of European unity flowed inherently from the post-cold-war American attitude to Europe. It became clear that America was not umbilically linked to Europe for the duration of time – that, in fact, an enduring trans-Atlantic system had not been built during the cold war. Even had the cold war continued, increasing American economic interdependence with Asia, involvement in NAFTA (North American Free Trade Association), and frustration at inadequate burden-sharing with a continent as wealthy as itself, would have inevitably led to the 'agonising reappraisal' of American relations with Europe constantly threatened by Washington. And such a reappraisal, together with Germany's own desire to increase its geo-political influence (in league with the ever non-Atlanticist French), would have forged a more united Europe. Thus, as it was, when the Berlin Wall came down a further burst of European integration became unstoppable.

And the process of American retrenchment accelerated the long-time US goal – first articulated by President John F. Kennedy – of a united Europe as one of the 'twin pillars' of the West. Jonathan Eyal has suggested that the post-cold-war American leadership 'positively encourages the development of a distinct European identity as the only way to reduce America's outlays on European defence and spur the stabilisation of East European states'.[23] Ever since the early 1960s Washington had wanted to deal with one decision-making centre in Europe, a goal made more urgent by its post-cold-war desire to downgrade its interest in Europe and concentrate instead upon its domestic problems and its trade relations with Asia. In these circumstances Europeans would increasingly take more decisions for themselves, and, should they wish to have an influence over the geo-strategic future of Europe, would have to act in a more cohesive manner. The Presidency of Bill Clinton, and the Republican Congress elected in 1994, opened up serious divisions between the US and some of the leading countries in Europe about a range of issues – not least the Bosnian crisis – and thus presented the case for a unified European foreign and defence policy.

On top of the problems posed by American retrenchment, British nationalists also had to face the consequences of a more 'domestic' European geo-strategic change – German unification, and the emergence once again of what some European leaders saw as 'the German problem'. The collapse of the cold war, and the fall of the East German Communist regime, led directly to a unified Germany, and Western Europeans were now presented with a single polity comprising over 80 million Germans in central Europe. Europe's largest economy also became Europe's largest population centre: and potentially also an independent political centre of gravity for an entire continent stretching from the Atlantic to the Urals. It was this prospect which led the French political leadership (as well as the elites in some of the smaller Western European nations) towards a strategy which would further bind Germany into the structures of Western Europe – a process that found its expression in the 1992 Maastricht Treaty setting up the European Union and the proposals for a single European currency. And further impetus was given to this early 1990s burst of integration by the German political class's own desire to smother and restrict any potential German nationalism within the confines of a federal Europe.

For UK nationalists, fear of German nationalism (and Germany) was also very real. During the transition to unification Margaret Thatcher had held a somewhat condescending high-profile seminar on 'the German problem' at Chequers, and also bitterly annoyed much German opinion by not even turning up for the very historic (and emotionally charged) unification ceremonies. Yet, this fear on the part of some British led not to a strategy of inclusion (of Germany), but rather towards one of hostility to further integration. Britain's nationalists could not support the neutering of German nationalism lest such a process impinge upon its own 'sovereignty'. But, in the face of a determined Paris–Bonn consensus during the Maastricht negotiations in the early 1990s there was little UK nationalists could do to hinder a new burst of integration.

Yet, it was more than these geo-strategic changes that were propelling Europeans, including the British, towards European unity in the last decade of the twentieth century. The process of economic globalisation itself was also a major factor. Increasingly, the global economy was eroding the power of the traditional nation-states, particularly the smaller and medium-sized ones (such as the UK itself). And the biggest players in the global economy, the transnational corporations, were leading the way in making the world of sovereignties and nations redundant. Increasingly, the multinationals have improved their bargaining position against small and medium-sized nation-states: being able to play them off against each other in return for tax regimes, labour costs and practices, and regulatory environments which are acceptable to them.

The sheer size of the transnational corporation sector (unlinked to any sovereignty, owing loyalty to no nation-state) is impressive. According to UNCTAD (United Nations Conference on Trade and Development), about one third of all private productive assets in the world are under the 'common governance' of transnational corporations.[24] And individual transnationals can be gigantic. It has been calculated that in 1980 the sales of each of the top ten multinationals was over $28 billion, more than the GDP of 87 countries. Together, General Motors, Ford and IBM almost out-rank the UK in GDP (and, of course, in calculating the GDP of the UK the productivity of British-based multinationals is counted in!).[25]

These transnational commercial organisations, and the global market and global information networks in which they operate, may indeed have already essentially destroyed both the nation-state and the 'community of fate' which has sustained national identity. Yet, it has been the nation-states which, until now, have provided the political dimension of life, the structures not only of loyalty and authority, but of democracy too. And, as the nation-state withers, so too does the whole panoply of self-governing structures which protect and enhance the individual. Transnational corporations and global markets are certainly interested in individuals as consumers, but not as citizens. Corporations have nothing to say about democratic participation or elections; and free global markets are uninterested in rights. Indeed, left to itself – with nation-states essentially only shells of their former selves – the global marketplace would be unable to resurrect the liberal democratic practices which form such an integral part of the Western experience. Globalisation represents the triumph of economics over political authority, but it was politics (not only political structures like nations and cities, but the political habit of mind – which worried above all about the relations of individuals to authority) which produced and ensured the rights of individuals.

For Britons, as for other Europeans, these political functions, no longer able to be carried out by nation-states, will be progressively lost unless they reform themselves within new political authorities better equipped to exercise them in the global economy. And in Europe the only political organisation capable of exercising any kind of political authority over the market processes of globalisation is the European union. The Union – comprising 15 nations and over 300 million people – amounts to the political structure of a continental civilisation (in very much the same way as does the federal constitution of the United States). It is large and powerful enough to bargain effectively with the biggest transnational company and to regulate the portion of the global market which works its will in its territory. But, crucially, it is also able not only to proclaim but to enforce citizens' rights – not only against the state (a nation-state could do that!), but, more importantly, against concentrations of private power.

Hence, in this respect the European Union represents the renewal of politics, and, through the re-assertion of politics over economics, of the liberal democratic principles which form the very basis of Western civilisation. The problem for UK nationalists was that their nation-state (as was the case with other nation-states) was disabled in this utterly central democratic function. Unlike the Union, the nation-state (the United Kingdom of Great Britain and Northern Ireland) owns few weapons; it simply does not possess the power to properly regulate the transnational corporations or place limits upon the excesses of the global economy.

Thus, the irony: the assertion of UK nationhood and of the associated rhetoric of self-government – to the extent that it weakens the development of a continent-wide political union – ultimately serves to stand in the way of this democratic political imperative. By the end of the twentieth century the only way in which the UK nation-state could develop some real say over that part of the global economy which operated within its territory was to act against the multinational operators unilaterally, a course of action which would have little effect and would amount to establishing a siege economy by pulling out of the world economic system altogether – an Armageddon option with few supporters.

Yet, perhaps even more important than these political considerations is the incapacity of the nation-state in providing a much less tangible, but none the less very real, function: acting as an agency providing a sense of future to its peoples. As the twentieth century was coming to its end the old nation-states of Europe – no longer fulfilling the functions of government adequately in the new global system – were looking decidedly tired and increasingly anachronistic. There was a restlessness amongst their peoples, a 'crisis in the institutions'. Although the European Union presented serious problems of adjustment to the peoples of Europe, as well as the gnawing issue of its 'democratic deficit', it at least did provide a key new psycho-social ingredient – it introduced the peoples of Europe, including those of the British Isles, to a new and broader horizon, and thus a sense of hope, the idea (so important for the social development of the United States) that tomorrow could be an improvement upon today.

A FEDERAL DESTINY

By the mid 1990s it was clear that the UK nation-state had already been absorbed into a wider European polity. This new political reality did not involve a clear-cut substitution of one sovereignty for another (one nation-state for another), but, rather, amounted to a new world of eroded sovereignties, multi-loyalties and weaker boundaries. And within this changing Europe a new, though less total, political authority was emerging as the replacement for the nation-state.

For the British, as for the others, this historic change had been neither abrupt nor jolting, but had occurred incrementally over the decades. In strict legal (constitutional) terms the UK state had lost its sovereignty when Britain joined the European Community following the 1972 Act, which specifically designated European law as superior to UK law enacted by Parliament – the first formal limitation on the 'sovereign powers' of the Westminster state since the settlement of 1688 and the forging of the United Kingdom in 1707. The Single European Act of 1987, which saw the road cleared for a genuine single market in the Community, also saw, significantly, a real further inroad into national sovereignties by the extension of majority voting in the Council of Ministers (thus restricting Britain's power of veto). And the Maastricht Treaty of 1992 further weakened the nation-states by strengthening the power of the European Parliament, extending even further the use of majority voting and the competencies (policies) of the new Union – which, after Maastricht, the Community was to be known as. Intriguingly, too, the Maastricht Treaty introduced the very supra-nationalist (federalist) idea of a 'citizen of the Union', and although the rights of these new citizens (every person who was a national of an EU country) were limited, they could easily in future be extended. Thus in 1992, with the full support of the British government, and the later more grudging support of Parliament, did Britons, technically at least, slip free from their single loyalties and for the first time collectively become dual nationals.

Yet, at the heart of the Maastricht Treaty, representing its real significance, was the signed promise, if not the immediate reality, of federalism, of a so-called super-state. And the key instrument of federalism, the essential formula for dissolving the nation-state, was to be Economic and Monetary Union – the project of a single currency. Federalists believed that whatever happened – whether Britain exercised her 'opt-out' and stayed out of the single currency, or joined a core group going full steam ahead in 1997 or 1999 – Britain was so integrated in the economics of Europe that, whether or not it joined a single currency, its money – the pound sterling – was no longer independent. However, a single currency with a single European 'Federal Reserve' (independent of both nation-states and European politicians) would formalise the new monetary interdependence, and would mean that the European Union had, in legal and constitutional effect, essentially become a federated super-state.

The UK political establishment, surveying the damage done to their nationhood by Maastricht, were right to believe that a new supra-national political entity had already been created – even before the economic, monetary and political union promised in the treaty could come into effect. For the post-Maastricht European Union possessed all the hallmarks of a new political state. Its laws, covering more and more functions of government, were superior to those of domestic laws; its supreme court (the Court of Justice) was the ultimate arbiter of relations not just between Union institutions but, crucially, between the new Union and the nation-states; and in the Council of Ministers fewer and fewer decisions could be blocked by a national veto.

In these circumstances the debate intitiated by the UK political establishment – about whether the country should or should not retain its 'sovereignty' – became increasingly empty. In its place the real issue emerged: whether Britain was now part of a loose or tight, a centralised or decentralised, a confederal or federal, new continent-wide polity? The analogy with the birth of the federal system in the United States – when thirteen separate ex-colonies (and independent 'sovereign' states) came together and formed a 'more perfect union' – was, inevitably, a feature of the British debate. (Margaret Thatcher constantly warned against the construction of a 'United States of Europe' and the new Prime Minister, John Major, during the 1992 general election, argued that he was protecting British sovereignty against the threat of US-style 'federalism'.)

Indeed, the original Articles of Confederation of the United States – the rules governing the fledgling nation from 1781 until 1789 – bear a resemblance to the kind of polity which the de-centralisers were hoping was being constructed in Europe in the early 1990s. During the US confederacy each American state, like each European one at the time of Maastricht, was reassured of its '*sovereignty*, freedom and independence, and every power, jurisdiction and right, which is not by this confederation expressly delegated to the United States, in Congress assembled'.

Edward Countryman has sketched the character of this early US government in terms which show its ambiguity about centralisation: 'Congress had some of the qualities of a national government', he argues, 'but in other ways it was more like an alliance of sovereign republics. The articles gave it alone the power to make war and peace.... To that extent, the states were one nation, dealing with other nations as equals. But Congress had no power to tax, and no power to enforce its will. It might levy requisitions on the states, but they could pay or not pay as they chose. It might insist that its own decisions ... overrode state law, but state, not federal, courts, would decide whether that really was so. It took the votes of nine states to make major decisions of policy. It took the consent of the legislatures of all thirteen to change the Articles in any way.... To prevent congressmen from becoming a separate caste, no person could be a member for more than three years in a row.'[26] Also, 'the national government was thought of as an alliance of separate states, not a government "of the people".'[27]

The Maastricht Treaty was at the same time both *less* unifying and *more* unifying than the Articles of Confederation. Whereas the European union had no obvious power to declare war (although 'joint action' could in certain circumstances amount to the same thing), its law-making powers were greater than those secured by the American federal authorities in 1781, as were its law enforcing powers (through the European Court of Justice). And the European 'feds' were able to raise money more easily for its budget.

Indeed, Britain's Eurosceptics would have been right in pointing out that the European house under construction in the early 1990s was much more like the eventual US Federal Constitution than that of its confederal fore-runner. The similarities are indeed striking. First, the 'national supremacy clause' in Article VI of the US Constitution (which states that the laws of the United States shall be 'the supreme law of the land') is quite clear in asserting the supremacy of federal laws – as is the provision in the original Rome Treaty (reiterated by Maastricht) which ensures the supremacy of European over national law.

As in the Federal Constitution drawn up in Philadelphia, the Maastricht European Union lists the proper functions of the central (federal) authorities and, under the principle of subsidiarity (Article 3b), reserves everything not listed as a Union activity to the states (or in Europe's case the nation-states). Of course, the Philadelphia constitution placed a huge array of functions at the federal level – including questions of war and peace and the crucial ones of money coinage and regulation – whereas Maastricht secured a more limited list, although one which could be easily expanded.[28]

Maastricht was looser and more decentralising than Philadelphia over a range of constitutional issues. For instance, the European Union provided for no directly elected chief executive or President on the American model – although the President of the Council (the rotating position held for six months by the head of government of the presidency country) was certainly slowly emerging (alongside the President of the Commission) as Europe's representative figure. Also, whereas Philadelphia provided the 'feds' with direct taxing powers, Maastricht, probably prudentially, gave Brussels no ability to raise taxes from Europeans except through a levy on the member states (although, through the convergence criteria, the centre essentially set down the rules for nation-state budget deficits and borrowing requirements). And, whereas Philadelphia gave to Washington the very important foreign policy and war-making powers, Maastricht gave Brussels very uncertain powers in foreign relations (although, again, possessing a potential for federal action).

Yet, Maastricht was more centralising than Philadelphia in two crucial respects. First, unlike the Treaty of Maastricht, the original American Federal Constitution made no mention of a centralised monetary authority – the Federal Reserve Board was not set up until 1913, well over a hundred years into the new republic. And, secondly, Philadelphia set up a constitutional court, the Supreme Court, but provided it with indeterminate powers.

On the other hand, Maastricht was much more precise about the role and powers of the European Court of Justice (which was able to determine not only the relations between the separated Union authorities but, crucially, between the Union and the nation-states). Moreover, Maastricht provided a category of citizenship and some limited rights (which could be added to later), whereas the US Constitution, for all its powerful rhetoric of citizenship, omitted a Bill of Rights from the original document. (Of course, as it turned out, the Supreme Court, together with the Bill of Rights, became the great power-house for federalising (and arguably democratising) the American Republic. Yet, its ambiguous role in the original Constitution shows how constitutional courts can play a much larger role than the original intent of the founders and framers.)

The Treaty of Maastricht, like Philadelphia, was, though, only a piece of paper, a set of written rules. What counted, argued some commentators, was not the formal position: what mattered was the real world of European – power-broking in which the nation-states (or, rather, the leaders of the nation-states) played the dominant role. From this perspective the UK's national leadership class could have claimed to salvage something from the wreckage of nationalism. The new Union might indeed be developing into a federation, even one like the United States, but, unlike the American prototype, the member nations still shaped the Union. They did so through the Council of Ministers where all the key decisions were still taken, where the bargains were struck, and where the future direction of the Union was decided. Thus, Europe remained a 'Europe of the nations' proceeding by bargains between Kohl, Mitterrand, Major, Gonzales and the rest, and not according to the dictates of the supra-national institutions.

Nevertheless, this was also the way in which the new American Republic was forged. The Senators – representatives of the 'sovereign states' – were not heads of government, but they answered, as do the present members of the Council of Ministers, to an electorate back home, and the process was one of bargaining. The new Europe, even before the final phase of economic and monetary union, began to re-semble the structures of a federal union. The nation-states (as with the 'sovereign states' in the US model) were 'entrenched' and their powers were delineated as being any of those not allocated to the centre; the Council of Ministers, exercising more and more competencies and taking more and more votes by majority decisions, became what amounted to an upper house; the European Parliament (given major new powers of co-decision by the Maastricht Treaty) assumed the proportions of a lower house; the Commission developed as a kind of hybrid political executive and civil service (possessing the powers of initiative and execution of the American Presidency); and the European Court of Justice, provided with a more central place in the European Union than that originally reserved for the Supreme Court in the American union, became the constitutional court.

The residual British nationalism of the UK political establishment – heavy on traditional ideas of sovereignty, not only of the nation, but also of the 'Mother of Parliaments' – was obviously seriously threatened by these new European structures. Thus, increasingly, some sections of the UK establishment, despairing about ever being able to maintain an effectively independent role for 'the nation' (and themselves), were increasingly being forced into the extreme position of advocating the UK's *withdrawal* from the Union. Indeed, in late 1994, a former Con-servative Chancellor of the Exchequer became the very first senior politician in Britain to raise the possibility of the UK withdrawing from the Union – a sentiment increasingly shared by nationalists.[29]

However, for the majority of nationalists – both British and others – the option of 'working from the inside' still, in the mid-1990s, found favour. Amongst the UK political elite, nationalist resistance to the super-state hardly disappeared, indeed it grew; yet, in practice, it came down to a battle not for 'national independence', but rather for subsidiarity, for devolution within the union, and, ironically, for a deep-ening of the 'federal' structure of the Union (meaning an entrenched decentralised state, though a state none the less). Nationalists will want to locate devolved power in the nation-states, but may find that should serious devolution get under way within the Union then it may become entrenched regionally (or even locally) rather than nationally!

The UK political establishment has not been amongst history's great decentralisers, having inhabited one of the most centralised of the Western world's political entities. Yet, in the coming battle for decentralisation in Europe, UK nationalists will take a leading role, and are likely to be joined, though for different reasons, by many others, not least the generality of the peoples of the new Union – who also tend to be wary of centralised power. The first, most detailed poll on European attitudes to Europe in the post-Maastricht period was published in *The European* newspaper 13–19 May 1994. It was conducted in the 12 countries by MORI and 'associates of the International Research Institutes'. It revealed a widespread scepticism about a 'United States of Europe with a federal government'. In fact, Europe-wide, 49 per cent were against the idea and 32 per cent were in favour. Of the national responses, France, Germany and Britain displayed majorities against; and only in Spain, Italy, Greece and Belgium were there majorities in favour.[30]

'Public opinion' on the European issue, however, needs to be treated with some caution. It can often be contradictory. For instance, when, in the same poll, it came to estimating the popularity of a specific measure – that of the desirability of a single currency – which would do more to produce a 'United States of Europe' (and a federal state) than any other single development, public opinion reversed itself (58 per cent in favour to 32 per cent against).[31] In the same poll the European peoples also approved by 51 to 30 the creation of a central bank for the EU, even including the Germans (by 54 to 34). Also, 'public opinion' about the European Union is often largely a function of a more general dissatisfaction with all institutions: intriguingly, with the exceptions of Luxembourg, Greece and Italy the 1994 survey showed that every European Union member country's population was more dissatisfied with their national government than with the Union government.

British nationalists will find that generalised public opinion about the creation of a 'federal Europe' will tend to fluctuate – often in line with perceptions of economic prosperity – whereas elite opinion (which ultimately probably counts for more) tends to be both more stable and more federalist. In any event the outcome of how centralised Europe is to become is located outside of the writ of British domestic opinion: the key will lie in the relationship between the German political and commercial elite and their French counterparts. Should the leading French opinion-formers continue to believe in a strongly integrated union as a way of binding Germany into the Western European system, then, should the Germans themselves continue to support this strategy, it will certainly happen.

As part of its rearguard action against the developing federal character of the new union, the UK political establishment, as well as adopting the rhetoric of decentralisation, has also been critical of Brussels's 'democratic deficit'. 'Democratising Europe' has involved giving the centre and the executive less power and the nation-states and the national parliaments more.

Yet, 'democratising Europe' can also be a highly centralising process, and therefore a two-edged weapon for nationalists. Any serious proposals to bring the executive functions of the new Union under some form of democratic control inevitably involve a larger role for the European Parliament – which because it is elected directly, with no reference to national governments, is the most centralised of all Europe's institutions. A European Parliament with real power – the kind envisaged during the mid-1990s by influential Germans – would give to the central, federal, authorities a huge legitimacy, and pose the most deadly of threats to Europe's nation-state enthusiasts. A real European Parliament – sharing power with the Council and Commission, or even determining the executive – would effectively, and publicly, kill off the national parliaments.

KICKING AND SCREAMING

Whichever way the European Union develops – whether into a centralised federal union or a looser, confederal state – the process of British adjustment is unlikely to be smooth. The 'British problem' will continue to present itself – not least because large numbers of Britons simply cannot think themselves into being Europeans. Of all the countries polled in a 1992 survey, it was the British who displayed less 'European feeling' than any other member country of the Union. Whereas 60 per cent of Germans and 52 per cent of French 'feel European' 'often' or 'sometimes', only 28 per cent of British do.[32] The British were also last (out of the 12) in 'feeling a citizen of Europe'.[33]

Yet public attitudes can be fickle, and tend to rise and fall with prosperity and 'good feeling'. Elite attitudes to Europe are arguably more important and as hostile – not least because an *interest*, or interest group, is at stake. The dynamic of Europeanisation threatens not just a traditional culture, but rather a whole political class who have built

up, around the institutions of the UK state, a dense array of interests –
involving jobs and status.

The degree of threat posed by Europe to the UK political establishment is considerable. There are almost 2,000 legislators at Westminster
(in both houses), and as legislative power moves to Brussels – and
perhaps eventually down to the nations and regions – serious reduc-
tions of this London-based political class can be expected. For a nation
of 60 million in a wider federal union, 300 or so legislators would
seem more reasonable. The London-based civil service also faces severe
re-structuring (including relocation) as, increasingly, they become an
agency of 'the feds' rather than servants of the national state. And the
large London political media apparatus – which bases itself at Westminster and environs – also faces relocation as, increasingly, the stories
and sources for real politics emanate from the centre in Brussels and
the larger European cities (including London).

This UK political establishment can be expected to act like any other
interest-group and resist the force which threatens its existence. It can
be expected to both encourage and lead the conservative and traditional
forces which see Europeanisation as a threat to their identity, causing
serious problems of adjustment that may take decades, even centuries,
to overcome. In this sense late twentieth-century Britain resembles the
American South, the land of the old Confederacy ('Dixie'), as it attempted to adjust to the realities of life within the American federal
union in the 1950s and 1960s. Dixie then, like Britain in the 1990s,
was part of a wider political community from which it could not escape,
and its economic and political freedom of action was severely limited.
It was also, like Britain in the late twentieth century, having to face
profound changes caused by the dissolution of a traditional society.

Yet Dixie (again like Britain in the 1990s) was also proud of its
history, consumed with defending its identity and way of life, and strong
on old-fashioned ways of doing things. Like Britain, Dixie possessed
a landed aristocracy which retained significant political and cultural
power even well into the age of industry and democracy, and considered
itself to be socially and culturally superior to 'new' industrial and
commercial money.

Dixie's political culture – again, like the British – was also deeply
suspicious of 'abstract rights' and resistant to attempts to democratise
and open up traditional social structures. Consequently there was bitter
resentment of 'alien' influence (particularly that of outside judges in
the supreme court in the federal capital) and much talk of sovereignty.
Again, as in the British example, in 1950s Dixie adjustment to change

was most difficult among traditional elites – those who had done well out of the previous restrictive system and now had to compete for power, influence and resources – with 'foreigners' and 'foreign influences' – in their own domestic backyard.

Thus, in both the Britain of the 1990s and the American South of the 1950s, although the forces of renewal and development were certainly present (and were to surface in 'the new South' during the 1970s and 1980s), an unfortunate combination of attitudes seemed to congeal: a traditional class and culture which was bitterly resentful of its new circumstances in a wider union, was largely unwilling to contribute to, and look positively upon its future in, the union, but, significantly, was also frightened of withdrawing, of striking out on its own.

And Britain's difficulty in adjusting to its European future – represented in its often seemingly contrary and sullen negativism in the European councils – caused a reaction on the mainland of Europe. Increasingly the European partners were less willing to smooth the way and make allowances for Britain. Indeed, Britain quickly became the least 'trusted' and 'reliable' of partners. In answer to the question 'Which country do you think is your most reliable ally within the European Union?' Britain scored very heavily as 'the country least reliable' – highest marks for unreliability were awarded to Britain from the Dutch, Irish, Germans, French and Belgians, and highest too amongst all Europeans.[34] Nor, to its partners, was Britain a particularly attractive country. (The question 'If you could not live in your own country, which European Union country would you choose instead?' received the reply; France 19 per cent, Spain 10 per cent, Germany 9 per cent, Italy 7 per cent, Britain 5 per cent, Netherlands 5 per cent.[35] Thus, with an increasingly negative image amongst its partners, Britain's problems of transition were further compounded.

These cultural problems of adjustment were ultimately soluble. Over time the traditionalism and insularity of the British – as they travelled throughout the union, as they used the channel tunnel, as the domestic mass media brought images of continental Europe into more and more homes – could be expected to weaken. The instinct of separatism – of 'we' and 'they' – could thus also be expected to slowly dissolve.

Richard Kuisel has argued that national identity is primarily formed through negation – by establishing a counter-identity and constructing a 'we–them' dichotomy.[36] For the British under the influence of Ukania, continental Europeans, ever since the French Revolution, had become the most powerful of 'them'. Yet, although the category of 'them' is unlikely to be obliterated, the content of 'them' can change. For the

British, 'them' may increasingly cease to be mainland Europeans and become instead the Japanese, the South Asians, even the Americans or, for the English, the Scots, Welsh and Irish. And the 'we' could change as well. 'We' could increasingly be defined in national (English, Scottish, Welsh, Irish), regional or even local (or city) terms. And in the process 'they' or 'them', the 'other', could become erstwhile 'fellow' Ukanian people in other nations, regions and localities. Already, for many within England, the Northern Irish and the Scots are becoming 'they', as are the English in Scotland.

As the British adjust to the new realities of Europe there remains one very powerful source of separatist sentiment – particularly apparent amongst Ukania's political, social and literary establishment. The idea of England, Britain and the UK as an exceptional polity where liberty and individualism flourished dies hard. As does the complementary idea of an undifferentiated mainland continental Europe possessed of a weak liberal tradition, traditionally authoritarian and incipiently totalitarian.

British liberal exceptionalism has, of course, been fed by its impressive history of liberal development. Its early breach with feudalism, its republican experiment after the English Civil War, its nineteenth-century extension of the franchise and liberties – all these, along with its famous liberal political writers such as John Locke and John Stuart Mill, have induced an idea of Britain as a remarkably stable and hospitable environment for freedom and individuality.[37] And, by contrast, the slower overcoming of feudalism on the continent, the tyranny associated with the French Revolution, and most importantly of all – for modern generations – the two world wars (particularly the Second): all fed the notion of a continent ill at ease with freedoms.

This heavy-handed political stereotype takes little account of the fact that the history of Britain is not as liberal as it suggests, nor are the nations of mainland Europe as conservative. Britain, as well as possessing a liberal history, also owns a, perhaps more powerful, conservative tradition based upon its uninterrupted landed and aristocratic culture. And Britain's brand of conservatism – its ingrained Toryism – has not been a particularly robust friend of the individual. Indeed, British conservative thought – particularly in the nineteenth century – specifically rejected appeals to reason, and to the interests and rights of the individual. The High-Tory political philosopher Edmund Burke argued, in impeccable English conservative style, that 'individuals pass like shadows; but the commonwealth is fixed and stable'. And Britain's experience of class solidarities and loyalties before, during and after the industrial revolution has also limited the liberal appeal of individualism.

Although the idea has gained hold that individual rights and liberties are not firmly grounded on the continent, it is *Britain* that still possesses no entrenched Bill of Rights, one of the institutional symbols of a culture of individualism. And Larry Siedentop remains relatively sceptical about the more general robustness of individualism in Britain, linking its fragility to the historic weakness of the middle classes. He argues that

> the very openness of British society in the eighteenth and early nineteenth centuries led ... to the middle classes assuming quasi-aristocratic attitudes and accepting a more corporate conception of society.... There followed a partial collapse or failure of middle class values and ideology which is basic to an understanding of the condition of Britain today. It is the chief reason why the individualist movement here has been contained, if not reversed.

And, as Neil Ascherson has argued, 'Britain was scarcely touched by the great social–political conflicts of continental Europe ... out of which emerged republics based on the codified rights of the individual'.[38]

Yet, even so, the English nationalist writer Paul Johnson represents a strain of English thinking that not only sees Britain's experience as being uniquely both individualist and democratic but France's as being seriously illiberal. Representing a serious strain of English thought, for Johnson, France becomes a metaphor for the whole mainland continent when he argues that it 'has remained a bureaucratic oligarchy punctuated by popular reigns of terror'.[39] This all too familiar rebuke takes no account, though, of the utterly central contribution of the French Revolution and its republican tradition in the development of modern Western democracy – nor of the huge contemporary intellectual backing in France for ideas of liberty and freedom.

Italy has also been in the forefront of developing and sustaining the Western idea of individuality. The Italians of the Renaissance were no slouches when it came to establishing the notion of the autonomy – and the privacy – of the individual and of the individual's morality. And the Germans, too, have made a serious contribution to individualism. Thomas Mann argued that the uniqueness of German individualism was its compatibility with what he called 'the social principle' – the fusion of rights with collectivities, an aspect of the post war success of German companies and industrial organisation. Liberalism in

Germany, though, was always a tender plant, one that was pulled up by its roots during the 1930s.

The question now is whether the more organic and conservative (and obscurantist) traditional currents of German thought are now essentially irrelevant to an understanding of the depth of German commitment to respect for the individual. The Federal Republic, with its Basic Law and its entrenched rights for individuals imposed by the Americans in the 1940s, is thus the product, stable and seemingly enduring, of American democratic ideas. And the culture and society of postwar Germany has also been so infused with American forms that they have all but expunged traditionalist nativist impulses (a process more advanced than in many of the European nations, including Britain). In this sense at least, the much-feared Germany represents not only the engine of Europe's industrial and commercial might but also its stable democratic core.

6 Goodbye to All That

REVOLUTION

The decline of the nation-state of the United Kingdom, and of the national identity – 'Englishness' – which it sustained, is the single most profound force for radical political change in the islands since the English Civil War.

One by one the prized, indeed hallowed, institutions, icons and values of the kingdom (and Ukanian ideology) are being eroded. The loss of authority and legitimacy by familiar, mythologised, institutions such as the monarchy, the House of Lords, the House of Commons – the 'Mother of Parliaments' – is only the tip of the iceberg. The great fiefdoms of Whitehall, the Treasury, the Bank of England, the Home Office, the intelligence services, the Foreign Office – all are reduced in scale and importance. National totems heavy with symbolism – like the national money, the 'pound sterling'; or national justice, 'British justice'; and even 'all the king's men' in the military – are all shrunk in status and power as the nation-state they represent is both weakened by globalism and absorbed into a wider European framework. And with this erosion of the formal aspect of the life of the UK go the old social hierarchies, the seemingly entrenched class system which its very structures sustained. There are cultural implications too, for it was the nation-state itself, during the world-wide expansion of the kingdom in the imperial era, which helped foster the sense of Englishness – its exceptionalism, superiority and insularity.

The radicalising agency of globalism, and of Europe, has succeeded where domestic radicals have failed. By comparison, the country's various progressive and radical movements – from the radicals themselves, the Chartists, the Liberals and Radical-Liberals, and, in the twentieth century, the socialists in the Labour Party – were tame, incapable, and often unwilling, to centrally challenge the vitals of the UK state and its society. Of course, many of these movements and parties were in no real sense truly radical. Most had no wish to overhaul the stuctures of the system, only to reform it at the very edges. Some, like the mainstream of the twentieth-century Labour Party, sought to work wholly within it, indeed, during the high-point of 'Labourism' to evoke its power and glory. Left-wing socialists, even many of those 'red in tooth

150

and claw', saw their objective – a 'socialist transformation of society' as achievable 'the British way' – through the existing, virtually unreformed, structures of the UK state. Determined to overthrow 'capitalism', they largely ignored the democratisation of Britain. Thus, the vast extensions of public ownership after 1945 made little difference to the centralised, unaccountable structures of the kingdom – arguably, they even enhanced them.

Earlier radicals – the Chartists, the nineteenth-century Radical-Liberals and republicans – had been more searching in their critique of the UK state and establishment. And some of them targeted the very heart of the UK state's power – the unwritten, informal, nature of the constitution, the monarchy and the House of Lords and its relationship to the wider Parliament, and the egregiously restricted pattern of land ownership and the social and cultural power deriving therefrom. Yet, they too, achieved little. They were easily marginalised.

What sustained the kingdom and its establishment against these admittedly rather timid radicals was the power of nationalism and imperialism. Until well into the twentieth century even the most radical of politicians was forced to support the Empire – a process which induced that most *Ukanian* of party factions known as the Liberal imperialists! And, as imperialism waned, nationalism stood ready to take over. The problem for anyone seeking to challenge the very fundamentals of the kingdom – even those who argued from a democratic perspective – was that, in the age of nationalism, they stood condemned as anti-British – potentially or actually in league with foreign ideas if not foreigners. Only the erosion of nationalism, of the idea of the importance and centrality of the nation, would destroy this long (three centuries) inbuilt bias in favour of conservative, indeed reactionary, politics.

The defeat of the UK nation-state has therefore opened up the politics of Britain to a whole array of ideas effectively shut out during the era of nationalism, and, in the UK's case, during the era of triumphant imperialism. Tom Paine is both an exemplar and a metaphor of this process. His idea of rights based upon a republican system of government was the leitmotif of both the American and French revolutions. Yet, both he and these world-changing revolutions have been largely ignored in the domestic political debate – as political wisdom in the UK has continued to stress the crucial importance of organic growth and informal, unwritten and codified, political development.

Now that the UK state itself is losing its power and legitimacy, these democratic ideas and instincts – linking back to many currents operating in Britain during and before the Civil War – are now free again to challenge the very basis of the political order.

REPLACING OF 'THE *ANCIEN RÉGIME*'

The vacuum created by the loss of the power and legitimacy of the UK has already, by the mid-1990s, produced a shift of political power 'upwards' to the new European Union (and, over time, may also propel a shift 'downwards' to the nations and regions of the old kingdom). Yet, this new European political form, while it certainly absorbs the British islands and peoples, does not amount to an old-fashioned, straightforward transfer of sovereignty – a swap from one authority to another as often occurred following conquest or war. The whole European project takes place within a new historical context of less rigid 'sovereignties' and more negotiable politics than has ever been the case before. 'Sovereignty' in Europe may well 'become a sort of all-permeating medium, like water in a swamp, in which clumps and floating islands of self government will relate to one another in many different ways. The 21st century will be a period not only of fuzzy logic but of fuzzy democracy.'[1]

Nor does the absorption of the UK state into the European Union imply any transfer of loyalty and affection from British to European political forms. In any event, loyalties and affections are increasingly de-coupling from all political institutions, including nation-states (as can be testified to by public alienation from the late twentieth-century UK). Thus, in the new Europe the citizen will view the Union as the framework for laws, rules and economics, and less as a focus for emotions and identities. Identities are likely to remain fragmented throughout Europe – perhaps, with the rise of sub-state nationalisms, increasingly so – thus ruling out any serious development of a pan-European identity on the American model. The uniting symbolisms of a new European identity – the European flag with its circle of gold stars on a blue background, and the 'Ode to Joy' from Beethoven's ninth symphony – will take some considerable time to replace the old national symbols.

Yet the European Union will certainly become the new primary political reality – the main governmental environment for the British peoples of the old kingdom. It represents a new constitutional settlement as profound as that of the 'Glorious, Bloodless Revolution' of 1688 and the Act of Union of 1707 – the two political events which formed the basic structures of the United Kingdom, and have remained the constitutional template ever since.

More crucially, the new Union has become the unheralded and uncelebrated constitution of Britain and the British peoples (superseding that of the dying UK). And the Maastricht Treaty – and any subsequent treaties – have become the long-awaited written constitution, fundamental document or basic law of the peoples of Britain – one shared with the other peoples of the Union.

With this new constitution in operation – and with a more formal written constitution promised – the question remains: should reformers and revolutionaries abandon the search for constitutional change at home in Britain? Should they instead recognise Maastricht and its heirs as the basic law governing their lives, as the long-awaited written constitution?

It certainly possesses all the hallmarks of the kind of written constitution which radicals and democrats have been seeking for many decades. It is a written document. Like any modern constitution (but unlike the UK's) it sets out and separates the powers of the various political authorities both at the centre and as between the centre and the member states. It provides a Supreme Court to adjudicate upon disputes between the various authorities, and, as in the US, to protect individual rights, a function which could grow whether or not the post-Maastricht era sees the European Convention of Human Rights incorporated into the Union's laws. Above all, it has formally superseded, and made redundant, the *ancien régime* conception of 'the sovereignty of Parliament' under whose writ an overly-powerful executive, bolstered by a simple majority in the House of Commons, runs one of the Western world's most centralised, secretive and unaccountable state systems.

Many radicals and reformers have also campaigned for a republican system in which the hereditary elements of this *ancien régime* constitution – the monarchy and the House of Lords – would be replaced by elected officials. The constitution of the Union does just that. Reflecting the republican traditions of its founders in France and Germany the central institutions of the Union provide no role for hereditary qualifications for public offices. And even in the Council of Ministers – where the national governments hold sway – there is no room for the hereditary monarchs of Europe: for when the rotating Presidency of the Council falls to a country with a monarch it is the *elected* leader (the prime minister) who assumes the post. The Union constitution does not abolish the hereditary houses of Europe, but, by restricting their roles to their own countries only and refusing them a stake in the future, it diminishes them. In the twenty-first century, providing Britain does not become a republic first, then within the whole European scene the monarch of the UK, should it too continue to exist, might become as marginal a figure as Miss Clacton-on-Sea.

Of course, the European Union is itself a republic. Its joint Presidents – the rotating President of the Council and the President of the Commission – are elected and nominated, not hereditary. Thus, in this sense too, the European Union brings a republican system and republican virtues to those new 'citizens of the Union' who reside in the British Isles.

The monarchy's future is also threatened should the European Union ever incorporate into its body of law the European Convention of Human Rights, for an action against the monarchy could, at least theoretically, be brought by a citizen claiming that he or she was precluded from being considered for the post and thus discriminated against on account of 'social origin'. And the House of Lords is also weakened by the dynamics of Europe. Its one serious role – the Law Lords acting as the *ancien régime*'s highest court – will be severely reduced by the emerging European Court of Justice.

The reformers have also had their sights fixed upon the *ancien régime*'s all-powerful executive: Her Majesty's Government. Its control of Parliament through both the party system and the power of patronage, its ability to deflect overly-searching scrutiny, its secretiveness and its royal prerogative powers (to make treaties and even to declare war) – all have been primary targets for democratic reform and change. Yet, even as late as the 1990s, domestic campaigning had achieved little. However, the European Union succeeds where the domestic radicals failed. For the very first time in the 300 years or so of the UK state, an outside body can limit the constitutional authority of Parliament, and thus of the UK's imperious executive. A court, the European Court of Justice, has the right to declare its Parliament's and the executive's actions unconstitutional and to levy fines; Her Majesty's Government can be out-voted (with no veto power) on a range of policies which have a direct effect on the life of the British peoples.

Of all the historic demands of constitutional reformers and radicals perhaps the most insistent and important has been the campaign for a written constitution which would include – and thus entrench – a Bill of Rights. And here again the promise of the European Union is more impressive than the record of the British campaigners. As already argued, the Treaty on European Union – and subsequent amendments – can serve as the written constitution for the peoples of Britain. And should the European Convention on Human Rights be added to the treaty and incorporated into European law (as some Europeans were recommending during the mid-1990s), then Britain – like the Americans, who also added their Bill of Rights in the form of constitutional amendments – will finally, through the dynamics of Europe, possess this fundamental democratic safeguard for its peoples.[2]

As I suggest later, it may happen anyway – even without a formal change in the Maastricht Treaty. The new category of 'citizen of the Union', established in Article 8 of the Treaty of Maastricht, although giving few initial rights, is potentially of great significance. For not only are Britons, for the first time since the UK state came into being, considered citizens instead of subjects, but further and more serious rights can always be added to the initial Maastricht list later on.

Ultimately, this debate about rights is of great theoretical significance. The UK state's *ancien régime* rests upon the ultimate authority not of the people ('we the people' as goes the famous phrase at the beginning of the US Constitution) but of institutions – such as the Crown and 'the Crown in Parliament'. Yet, by creating entrenched rights – at least at the level of theory and symbolism – power is indeed passed to 'the people'. Rights attach to *people* not *institutions*, and are enforced in favour of individual people and against institutions.

Allowing the new European polity to write the first written constitution for the peoples of Britain has certain advantages. For there remains a large question mark over the ability of the domestic British political class – the UK establishment – to deliver a written constitution and the individual rights it would entrench. The written constitutions of other nation-states have derived from a revolutionary experience. The American written constitution was forged in the aftermath of the revolutionary war in the late eighteenth century, the German Basic Law was imposed after defeat in the Second World War, and the French Fifth Republic was enacted following the insurrection in Algeria.

Britain is not going to experience such a severe jolt, and such a need to write the rules for a new nation; so there will be no apparent urgent need to construct a new written document. Also, problems will arise about who should draw up the constitutional document, about how it will be ratified, about whether there will be agreement or consensus over the clauses? The Left will want certain social and economic rights added, and the Right, presumably, will want to stick simply to political rights. These potential pitfalls are surmountable, but they provide a powerful, almost compelling, reason for preferring a European solution to the British peoples' constitutional dilemma.

NATIONS AGAIN

Perhaps Europe's most profound challenge to the UK nation-state, however, lies in the threat it poses to the hold which the kingdom still exerts over the nations and regions of the British Isles. The importance to the UK political establishment of keeping the multi-national British Isles under one, centralised, nation-state structure was revealed when, at the height of the 1970s Scottish nationalist upsurge, no lesser a figure than the Queen spoke out on the question. In her only overt intervention in British politics during her reign she reminded her audience – in a speech in the Palace of Westminster in 1977 – that she was crowned as the monarch of the *United Kingdom of Great Britain and Northern Ireland* – a polity which included Scotland!

Yet, no matter the problems which an independent Scotland would produce for the monarchy, the dynamic of European integration continues to force the question of national and regional devolution and independence onto the political agenda. The sheer logic of Europe works to the advantage of sub-state nations and regions. The simple act of weakening the old nation-states creates a vacuum which lower levels of political organisation may, over time, fill. The principle of subsidiarity (that decisions should be taken as closely as possible to the people) – worked out in the early 1990s over three European Councils at Lisbon, Birmingham and Edinburgh – may also, although still interpreted somewhat ambiguously, act as a force for devolution, for pushing decision-making below and beyond the nation-state. Should power in Europe increasingly flow downwards as well as upwards then the union's 'ethnic nations' – the Basques in Spain and France, the Scots, the Welsh, the Bretons, the Catalans, other ethnic groupings with a quasi-tribal sense may well win 'self administration and can offer a stronger sense of community to the regional groups under their sponsorship. There may no longer be any reason for such ethnic groups to seek a nation-state, at least not in its pure form as a structure that weds citizens to an all-powerful state.'[3]

And to give some real political life to this possibility the European Union has, post-Maastricht, developed potential structures within which a 'Europe of the regions' could begin to flourish. The Union's Committee of the Regions – an advisory body, which can also give opinions on its own initiative – first met in Brussels on 9 March 1994. It had 189 members plus an equal number of alternates. Germany, France, Italy and Britain sent 24 members each. Membership ranges from the serious regional ministers (of the German Länder, some of whom have a greater budget than EU national members) to local councillors. Although an untested new institution in the politics of Europe, this Committee is pregnant with possibilities. At a minimum it can serve to increase regional–centre relationships. Alan Butt Philip argues that in time it may 'develop into a much more powerful body'.[4] And *The European* suggested in the spring of 1994 that as the Committee had just two years before its role was to be reviewed it possessed this time in 'which to demonstrate to its critics and supporters why it should be taken seriously'.[5]

For the peoples of the British Isles, though, a regional destiny may be a distant prospect. Unlike their German (and even their French) counterparts, the UK's political establishment has held the reins of centralised power very tightly. Thus, even during an era in which decentralisation and devolution had become a Western norm the most diverse of countries remained governed by the most centralised of structures. The kingdom remained a unitary state; and during the 1980s (with the abolition of the Greater London Council and other major 'regional' authorities) even enhanced the centralised nature of the state. Thus, post-Maastricht, Britain – with its distinctive regional life – did not possess the formal structures of regional government which even the erstwhile highly centralised French state had introduced in the early 1980s.

Thus, the general European dynamic in favour of devolution will not express itself, initially at least, in the creation of serious regional government. Rather, Europe will work its will in breaching the walls of the kingdom's unitary state in the first instance through the politics of Scotland. Scottish independence possesses a real attraction now that those who advocate it can place the future of an independent country within the broader European Union. Previously, Scottish separatists had to deal with popular fears that in the event of independence Scotland would be isolated and alone. Now, though, Scotland's nationalists can point to a new world in which Scotland not only possesses its own chief executive, or Prime Minister, but plays a role in Europe's political life – with a seat on the Council of Ministers and a Scottish Commissioner in Brussels. It can look forward to as big a role in Europe, perhaps bigger, than that already secured by the Irish Republic.[6]

With the European framework firmly in place, any number of events could trigger Scottish independence. Should Northern Ireland leave the UK state – either by being absorbed into an all-Ireland state, or through assuming statehood itself – then Scotland's independence would be irresistible. Also, Labour's devolution proposals (involving the creation of a Scottish Parliament) may not achieve the objectives of its authors. Instead of appeasing nationalist opinion, a Scottish Parliament, by focusing Scottish nationalism and creating a centre of Scottish political authority which could challenge Westminster, might easily become the forum for full independence. Alternatively, Scottish independence could be achieved by the electoral success of the Scottish National Party under its slogan 'An Independent Scotland in Europe'.

The break-up of the kingdom, however, poses serious problems for the European Union. Should Scotland leave the UK, then, under one reading, the UK itself would cease to exist. The United Kingdom was formed by the Act of Union (1706), a union between England and Wales on the one hand and Scotland on the other. Thus, the withdrawal of Scotland from the union might mean that, rather like a failed marriage, the union itself – the United Kingdom, with all the Westminster paraphernalia (monarchy, Lords, even Parliament) – would be redundant. And the remaining part of the old union, England and Wales, may not wish to become simply the rump of the old UK, but might make new constitutional arrangements too.

Yet, formally, it was the UK-state which joined the European Community in 1973 and the UK-state which signed the Treaty of Maastricht. And it is the UK-state which possesses the status of 'a member state' of the European Union. Thus, an independent Scotland seeking membership of the European Union would become, in Euro-parlance, a 'successor state'. (So, too, technically, would England and Wales!) The question of whether 'successor states', emerging out of the break-up of 'a member state' of the Union, can automatically assume all the rights of 'a member state' is still somewhat cloudy. The UK political establishment (particularly the Conservative governments of the early 1990s) have tended to argue that they would not.

The Scottish National Party, on the other hand, has argued that there is a precedent in the German example. The only variance of borders in the European Union's history so far occurred when, after the collapse of the Berlin Wall, the East German Länder joined the Federal Republic, thus adding some millions of people and some considerable territory to the Union. The SNP has argued that separate Scottish membership of the European Union, as it does not involve adding peoples and territory, would be a much less difficult arrangement. Also, the SNP has suggested that, upon assuming some of the largest oil and fishing rights in the whole European Union, the new state of Scotland would have the political and economic power to insist upon membership.[7]

Although, by the mid-1990s, the European Union has not formalised provisions for 'successor states', a newly-independent Scottish 'member state' would, presumably, assume all the obligations and rights which the old UK possessed in the Union. It would then be able to re-negotiate for itself the 'opt-outs' secured by the UK from Maastricht. It might seek to sign the Social Chapter and take part in the final stage of Economic and Monetary Union -- the single currency – although assessments would need to be made about how Scotland fitted into the economic 'convergence criteria'.

Scottish independence, by effectively repealing the 1706 Act of Union and breaking open the UK state, would open up the whole question of what should happen to the rest of the truncated state. Scotland could thus act as the first domino in a constitutional 'domino effect'. It would be inconceivable for Northern Ireland to remain in the UK-state should Scotland have left. Also, immediate questions would be raised about Welsh independence. And the English too might view themselves somewhat differently after almost half the landmass of the old UK had withdrawn from the UK Union.

The UK-state was essentially a product of Britain's world position and imperial role. Its structures, ethos and symbolisms fitted perfectly the needs of the ruling class of a far-flung empire. They are increasingly irrelevant to the English as well as to the Scots. The English peoples living south of the Scottish border have hardly ever had any interest in maintaining the broader union, and, indeed, the UK has cost them money – in the various subsidies (some hidden, some not) which have flowed from the south to the less economically fortunate Scots, Welsh and Irish. Nor have the English particularly identified with the UK-state. 'English', rather than 'British', and certainly not 'UKanian', is the preferred self-depiction of the peoples south of the border; and a Scottish withdrawal from the union might serve to beef up this sense of English separateness.

Yet, such a release from the UK-state might not ignite the fires of English nationalism; rather, it could just as easily light the touch-paper of English regionalism. As I argued earlier, regional identities are very real in England. And although an obvious public demand for regional government has been somewhat dormant for most of the postwar years, this may simply be a product of the fact that no party has placed it on the agenda. To some extent the politics of English regionalism may have been waiting upon events north of the border. In the event of Scottish independence, English regional political sensibility could arise fairly quickly.

Scotland, though, may never secure full independence. Instead, as

part of a process initiated by the UK political establishment to head
off the rupture of the UK, a general, across the board, devolution of
power might be engineered – one which would resemble the federal
structure of the German republic with its Länder system. In this scenario the old UK would yield up its unitary character, turning itself
into a federal state in which Scotland, Wales and England (or the English
regions) gained constitutionally entrenched powers. During the early
1990s the Liberal Democratic Party advocated a federal Britain. Such
a radical constitutional change – one which the majority of the UK's
political establishment bitterly resisted during the early 1990s – might,
should London's role over the affairs of the peripheries be seriously
devalued, be enough to satisfy enough Scottish nationalist sentiment.

In any event, should Europe be able to break asunder the rings of
steel which have bound the nations and regions of the British Isles
into a single UK governance, then the provinces of the old imperial
kingdom would be able to by-pass London and deal directly with Brussels.
Edinburgh, Cardiff, Newcastle, Manchester, Birmingham, Plymouth,
Bristol, Norwich and Nottingham would become political centres; and
the English regions' sense of being marginalised (which has grown
without relief since the height of industry and Empire) could begin to
be redressed.

London has little to lose from this emancipation from the UK state.
Although it would remain the political and financial hub of the south-
east region of England it would lose its role as the political and financial
capital of the UK. Yet London ceased to be dependent upon the UK
some time ago – as it assumed its world financial role. In the new
Europe, London is already amongst the Union's premier cities. Like
New York within the American union, London might be territorially
peripheral in Europe (in the sense that Paris, or Frankfurt are not), but
it remains a centre in every other way. It is the European Union's
largest and most cosmopolitan metropolis. It continues to be the financial
and commercial capital of Europe – which Frankfurt, even though it
hosts the European Monetary Institute, is unlikely to rival until well
into the twenty-first century. And it possesses the great advantage of
being the English-speaking capital of Europe and, thus, of linking Europe
to the wider English-speaking world. And with English dominating
the world not only of business but also of information, education and
the media, London – in Europe – stands poised to enhance its position. Indeed, the economic and financial role of London, the old UK's
great imperial capital, is one of the few examples of a successful British
transition from Empire to Europe.

NEW PARTIES

Britain's political parties, like other of the institutions of the *ancien régime*, are in trouble. They have been suffering throughout most of the 1970s and 1980s from a serious decline in membership, and also from the more general public disenchantment with all political institutions. Martin Jacques has argued that growing insecurity – about jobs, relationships, future prospects – caused by the 'flexible society' is at the root of the problem. 'The middle classes are cutting loose from their traditional political moorings' he argues, and 'as global competition intensifies with the rising challenge from East Asia, accompanied by growing pressure for flexibility . . . we are likely to see more Perots and Berlusconis'.[8]

Perhaps the most renewing of the consequences of the new Europe will be the inevitable re-definition of British political ideas, categories and parties. In the European republic of the twenty-first century the norms of political dialogue will change dramatically. 'British politics' will continue to exhibit the old divisions between 'left', 'right' and 'centre'. Yet these conflicts will produce much less heat, and be conducted at a much lower level of intensity as it becomes apparent that they can only be properly pursued within a broader European context. Similarly, the great technical economic dispute between Keynesians and monetarists, which has dominated British politics since the early 1970s, will continue, but will make sense only on a pan-European level – and economists, like businesses and other interests, will increasingly take their case, and their ideas, to the European politicians, bankers and financial regulators.

Of course, old-style party politics will still be needed in the British Isles, as in other member states, as it will be on a national basis that the ministers who are sent to the Union in Brussels are selected. Yet over time it is conceivable that so intense will be the interest in the political debate in the Council of Ministers or the European Parliament that interests, even parties, based in other parts of Europe – say in Germany – will help fund (maybe through bodies like the Friedrich Ebert Stiftung or the Konrad Adenauer Stiftung) and organise campaigns in the south-east of England or in the northern provinces of Italy. Thus, the British will find their 'national debate' (and television coverage) increasingly 'invaded' by Euro-politicians – from German chancellors and French presidents to a host of lesser functionaries.

Also, as public interest increasingly focuses on general European issues and the European Parliament grows in influence, then pan-

European parties, with pan-European agendas, perhaps even running pan-European candidates for Europe-wide public office (even eventually a directly-elected European President?) may gradually emerge as the main contestants for power. As in the USA, in the putative USE these continent-wide parties would stress domestic issues during domestic elections but would primarily exist to promote 'federal' agendas. The prototypes for these parties – clustered around the European Peoples Party (essentially the European Christian Democrats) and the Socialists (essentially the European Social Democrats) – already exist in the European Parliament.

Also, the great clashes of principle and ideas within British domestic politics are unlikely to remain solely about purely British issues. Instead they will tend to centre upon the European issue itself: between those who accept and those who resist the Europeanisation of British life. Lord Cobbold, in what may yet become a prescient letter to *The Times* in 1992, suggested that in Britain 'the political divide of the future is between Europeans and nationalists'. He went on to argue that the British prime minister should present the European issue to the House of Commons as a vote of confidence, after which 'those voting for and against would then reconstruct themselves as new political parties'.[9]

Of course, a resolution of Britain's European crisis might be attempted by another route, that of a referendum. Yet, so potentially resistant to Europe are some sections of British society that, whatever the result of a referendum, domestic politics might anyway divide up into anti- and pro-European parties. At the time of writing (early 1995), it certainly seemed a distinct possibility that the Conservative Party was transmuting itself into an anti-European party and Labour into a pro-European party. Any ultimate divide, though, would not be as clear and clean as this, with factions within each party re-aligning with majorities in the other.

RIGHTS AT LAST

The *ancien régime* gives Britons living in the UK-state no entrenched rights. Certainly the British live in a relatively free society. Yet these freedoms are dispensed at the whim of Parliament, they do not inhere to individuals simply by virtue of their citizenship. In effect, they are bestowed, granted, conceded by the authorities; and they can be taken away by them – essentially by a majority of one in the House of Commons, with the Lords and Queen concurring. As with most other aspects of the old kingdom's government it is all a question of the beneficence of an established political class. And, because in the old UK this established class works hand-in-hand with the executive (indeed, through the party system, sustains the executive), the UK system gives its executive immense power even in this most sensitive of areas. In Britain's *ancien régime* no court, basing its judgements on fundamental human rights, could over-rule this established political class.

The old kingdom developed a fetish about statute law. It was decreed that statutes would over-ride every other form of law – which in practice meant that, yet again, the executive (acting through its parliamentary majority) worked its will; and that statutes would over-ride the basic rights of individuals, should they conflict. Although Her Majesty's Government (the pompous term still used by the British executive at the century's end) had signed various international conventions of human rights, these were not incorporated into domestic law and thus did not supersede the kingdom's statutes. The kingdom allowed no court to side with an individual's human rights against the executive-driven Parliament – even when fundamental rights such as trial by jury were abandoned during the Northern Ireland emergency.

The Europeanisation of British justice changes all this. At the heart of the change is the European Court of Justice, which under the Maastricht Treaty is beginning to assume the role of an American-style Supreme Court for Europe – and, dramatically, for Britain too. The stark fact for nationalists is that the Law Lords (hitherto the *ancien régime*'s top court) are no longer the highest court in the land, *and* this European Court can strike down UK statutes as unlawful. An example of a British law which the European Court has effectively 'struck down', rather in the manner in which the US Supreme Court strikes down Congressional legislation, is the 1988 Merchant Shipping Act (for failing to comply with EC discrimination law).[10]

Article 177 of the Maastricht Treaty is crucial, for it is this article which ensures that national courts are in essence subservient to the European Court of Justice. One legal authority argues that 'it can therefore be concluded that the Court of Justice, although depending upon the cooperation of national courts, uses Article 177 as an effective means to guarantee the constitutionality of the laws of the Member States'.[11]

Yet perhaps one of the most important of all developments so far is that the *ancien régime*'s own national courts are taking their cue from the new powers of the European Court – and beginning to engage in judicial review on their own. For instance, the wider British public were suddenly informed by their newspapers – 'Women Gain Most from Lords Ruling' – in the spring of 1994 that the UK-state's highest court, their Law Lordships in the House of Lords, had taken the extraordinary decision to 'strike down' provisions of the Employment Protection Act of 1978.[12] This UK statute had provided weaker rights – over redundancy and unfair dismissal – to employees working fewer than 16 hours a week, and was in contravention of European law.

This important legal judgement also confirmed the right of the Equal Opportunities Commission to challenge British legislation as incompatible with European Union law, and eased the path to further claims for equality for part-timers on other fronts, including pensions and maternity rights. As one newspaper put it, 'Britain may now have, for the first time in history, a constitutional court.' This ruling, together with the revolutionary Factortame Case – where the Divisional Court suspended the operation of an Act of Parliament while the European Court of Justice (ECJ) ruled on the substantive question – effectively over-rules the well-nigh sacred Diceyan principle of parliamentary sovereignty. It was enough to cause an affronted outburst in the Letters column in *The Times* that '*anyone* will be able to challenge Acts of Parliament before the humblest court in the land'.[13]

The fact that Britain – either through the European Court or by its subsidiary court, the Law Lords in the House of Lords – now possesses a Supreme Court is a turning-point in history as fundamental as Magna Carta or the 1688 settlement. And how this new Supreme Court develops is one of Europe's – and Britain's – big political questions, one which had during the early 1990s effectively been hidden from public debate by the kingdom's political class.

There was no certainty about how the American Supreme Court would later develop. The extensive powers it now wields – reaching into all aspects of American life, from civil rights to abortion – were not set out in the original constitution. They developed over time. In France, too, the experience of a constitutional court is one in which its powers evolved. John Bell has shown how in 1958, at the outset of the constitution of the Fifth Republic, the French were hardly any better off than the British – possessing no serious regime of rights – but that since then the Conseil Constitutionnel has been extremely active and has basically added the declaration of rights of 1789 to the constitution.[14]

Our own new European Supreme Court may be able to evolve in the same manner. The progress it makes in establishing a regime of rights will be crucial. Nicholas Grief has argued that the ECJ will become, is becoming, a major factor in enforcing human rights in Britain: 'The Court of Justice has long made it clear that it will ensure respect for fundamental human rights in the context of the legal order of the European Community.'[15] He reports that in the Nold Case the court argued that whereas the main source of such rights was the 'constitutional traditions common to the Member States . . . international treaties for the protection of human rights on which the Member States have collaborated, or of which they are signatories, can supply guidelines which should be followed in the framework of Community law'.[16] And more importantly, in 1984 the European Court of Justice, in a fishing dispute, used the European Convention, Article 7 on the issue of retroactivity, as 'a constraint upon the United Kingdom'.[17] Also, in *Johnston* v. *Chief Constable of the RUC* (about the legality of not issuing firearms to female members of the Royal Ulster Constabulary), the European Court ruled in favour of 'equal treatment' as laid down in Articles 6 and 13 of the European Convention on Human Rights.

Even though the European Convention on Human Rights is not – as I write – incorporated into either European or British law, the European Court is none the less prepared to consider the fateful question of whether, over a range of issues, British national law is compatible with the European Convention – in much the same way as does the European Court of Human Rights. Should the European Court continue to assume this role as a kind of Supreme Court, then the peoples of the British Isles will finally possess a real Bill of Rights, and will be able to hold all the institutions of the UK-state accountable under it. There will be no more perfect test of the federal character of the European Union.

Another area of European law – that of its 'direct applicability' – will also become a sensible test of the extent of federalism. There is a theoretical distinction in this developing jurisprudence between 'directly effective' European law (where European law's writ runs automatically over the peoples of the Union) and the 'doctine of supremacy' whereby European law, although supreme, needs to be made effective – by, if necessary, a judicial decision of the European Court in the event of national courts not upholding it. Already, through the cases law – in van Gend and Loos, van Duyn, Simmenthal, Francovich, Factortame and Sevince – it seems as though European law may be becoming 'directly applicable'. And, through the legal mechanism known as 'copying out', more and more European directives are being absorbed into the body of English law *directly* – without translation into traditional *ancien régime* statutory language.

NEW ECONOMICS

By the 1980s the idea of a 'national UK economy' had about as much meaning as the idea of a 'sovereign' British government. And the Treasury and the Bank of England were as powerful as the 'Mother of Parliaments'.

The old-fashioned and crude model of the British 'national economy' implied a host of economic units, owned by Britons, which operated within the domestic territory and traded between each other within the domestic territory. It also implied that HMG (Her Majesty's Government) could, on its own, and determined by its own will, essentially guide the economic destiny of the inhabitants of its territory – rather as in the 'war economy' of the country during 1939–45.

The Europeanisation of the economy – let alone the global dimension – has made this image of 'a national economy', 'the British economy' utterly fanciful. Who is the 'we' 'we' talk of when 'we' talk of 'we'? When 'we' talk of 'our' exports do 'we' mean to include the exports of the Toyota plants or the Ford plants or other foreign-owned British-located companies? 'Britain's balance of payments' is now increasingly a measure of how well British-based *foreign* companies have done in the export market. And, with so many decisions affecting the British now being taken in the global market, and by people – private and public – outside of the shores of the British Isles, 'British economic policy' becomes a misnomer – as meaningful as Texan or Bavarian economic policy.

The economic future of the British people, unlike 'the British economy', is a real idea. And here, in the battle for jobs and prosperity, being part of 'the European economy' is much more important than being part of 'the British economy'. Being within the trading boundaries of the single market of the European Union remains the driving dynamic behind much of the foreign investment– the inward investment– located on British soil and in British waters. Had Britain been outside these European boundaries then not only the American and Japanese investment, but also the incoming intra-European (German and Dutch) investment might have gone elsewhere.

British economic life was becoming Europeanised some time before the single market got seriously under way. And not only by the test of ownership and investment. Trade patterns also told the tale. Between 1981 and 1989 trade between British-based goods and service industries and customers in European Union countries, and vice versa, went up dramatically – from 31 per cent of total trade in 1973 to 45 per cent in 1981 to 52 per cent in 1989.[18]

A properly functioning single market will further Europeanise the economy in the British Isles. And it is an economic dynamic with heavy political implications. Just as an earlier 'single market' – as it rolled over feudal, local and regional economic barriers – helped create the UK, so today's single market is eroding the barriers that the UK has constructed. A single market unified the UK during the eighteenth and nineteenth centuries; and, should it work without hindrance, it will unify Europe too.

Arguably, a single market ineluctably needs a single currency – the final act in the Europeanisation of the economy of the British Isles. In order to work, a single market cannot for long allow competing currencies. Such independent currencies allow countries, when they get into trouble, to devalue, and then the other non-devaluing countries will ultimately retaliate – probably by raising tariffs – thus destroying the single market.

Also, the single market sets up a dynamic which *anyway* will automatically lead to a single currency. A crucial – and under-reported – aspect of the Union's single market, the integration of capital markets including banking, will ultimately destroy the individual currencies of the old nation-states. Gavin Davies has explained the process in an exposition which needs to be set out at length:

> Potentially much more significant is the impact on national monetary policy of the integration of capital markets and banking services across the union. For the first time in recent European history, controls over the movement of money within the EU have not only been abolished, but have been permanently removed by international treaty. Firms and individuals can hold their money wherever they like and can (in theory) borrow from banks in any currency . . . irritating for the national central banks is the fact that the money stock of any individual economy will be subject to considerable disruption as people shift funds between different currencies to take advantage of small changes in interest rates and foreign exchange rates. This will mean that national monetary data will become devoid of importance as the private sector switches its money holdings between union members. . . . Recent studies have established clearly that the relationships between money growth and national income have broken down within many individual countries but have survived quite well for the EU as a whole. . . . It is for example conceivable that the recent [1993–4] strength of M3 growth in Germany may have occurred because the private sector across Europe has

switched into marks following the widening of the ERM bands last year. If so, it may be right for the Bundesbank to ignore at least part of the monetary overshoot. All this suggests that close integration of monetary policy, possibly even monetary union, may be a corollary of the single market in financial services. [Thus he argues] How ironic it would be if the Bundesbank found that it could in future implement its preferred methods of monetary control only in a European context.[19]

The European economic system which will cover the peoples of the British Isles via the single market and the single currency will also serve to more properly protect British-based industries and services from low-cost world-wide competition – particularly from the savagely competitive new Asian economic area.

The question of protecting European markets is still (at the time of writing, early 1995) a very sensitive one. Although 'managed trade' is a global economic reality, the strength of the idea of 'free trade' still precludes a reasoned debate on the possible European (and American and Japanese) responses to the competition from low-cost Asia.

Yet, in the great global trade game – played out between Europe, the United States, Japan and the rising economies of Asia – the old-fashioned medium-sized European nation-state (population around 50 million, GNP around $600 billion), of which the UK-state is a perfect example, is simply no longer able to negotiate from strength. Nor is it able to intervene successfully in the global market on its own. For instance, should the UK-state attempt to, say, restrict the movement of capital, it would pay an exorbitant price – including massive economic dislocation and the collapse of the City of London as a financial centre.

Yet, the question of long-term capital movements (job-creating investments) from Western Europe to rapidly developing low-cost third world nations (particularly in Asia) – where advantage can be taken of radically lower labour costs – is likely to become a major Europe-wide issue – as important as was the great 'free-trade versus protection' debate in Britain in the early part of the twentieth century. The 'managed trade' ideas of the financier and European MP Jimmy Goldsmith, outlined in *The Trap*, are an early shot in this coming great debate. He has suggested that attempting to compete with low-cost centres in the new burgeoning Asia (about to include China) is self-defeating. He argues that 'it must surely be a mistake to adopt an economic policy which makes you rich if you eliminate your national workforce and transfer production abroad, and which bankrupts you if you continue to employ your own people'.[20]

Should managed trade, both for capital and for goods and services, develop as a strategy for the survival, let alone the prosperity, of the peoples of Western Europe, then such a strategy can only properly be entertained in a continent-wide context. In the high-stakes global trade conflict the idea of 'Britain alone' is simply unsustainable.

NEW RELATIONS: THE GERMAN MODEL

The Europeanisation of British trade and economics will place serious pressures upon Britain to adapt to continental European (primarily German) economic culture – to continental ways of industry and industrial relations. The 'Social Market' capitalism of the northern European states, led by Germany, is very different from the American capitalist model which Britain has traditionally favoured. Because of this distinction – which separates a wide variety of British social and economic institutions from those of mainstream Europe, British traditions will need to adapt. Indeed, perhaps more than adapt. As Will Hutton, who has throughout the early 1990s been highly critical of Britain's economic culture, suggests, 'integration beyond today's level will demand little less than a *transformation* of British institutions'.[21]

At the heart of the distinction between British and Euro-German economic culture is the different role assigned to the individual. To liberals, one of the few attractive features of the 'gentleman culture' was its highly individualistic tone – based upon the economic power and the social confidence to be different. Yet this kind of individualism may simply not work in today's global capitalist environment. An individualist ethic helps entrepreneurialism. It provided the moral environment in which capitalism was born and grew – and it still remains crucial for entrepreneurship. Yet capitalism in the West is now mature and has entered its organisational phase. It needs less charismatic and more team leadership, less concern with immediate profitability and more long-term strategic sense.

The idea of 'social partnership' – a partnership between capital and labour, not the historically antagonistic system virtually built into British corporate structures – is the key ingredient of the social market system. Yet, in Britain, in their attitudes to workers, owners and management tend to reflect the British political establishment's more general inability to 'grant' its people serious, enforcible, rights. British company leadership still tends to be more interested in short-term profitability (without which they resort to lay-offs, and even the selling of the business) rather than long-term strategic development in which the workforce plays a crucial role. And in Britain, trade unions have resisted 'social partnership' as much as does management – as part of the general resistance to business unionism, a resistance which hardened during the militancy of the 1970s and early 1980s.

A more Europeanised system might produce, over time, not only a more highly-skilled workforce but also a highly-trained managerial structure no longer based upon class prejudices. Although some British-based businesses with workforces on the European continent are already adapting their labour-relations system to include workers based in their UK plants and offices, these changes can be expected to be resisted throughout much of the business sector.

Long-termism – or, rather, longer-termism than allowed for in the Anglo-American tradition – is another feature of the German model, the culture of which will need to be ingested should British-based businesses wish to compete with those on the continent. Longer-termism will involve a strategic sense or vision which looks at a wide range of 'bottom lines' (beyond immediate profit-maximisation) – particularly the gaining and holding of market share. It would view the higher social costs placed upon industry not as a cost which would eat into profits, but rather as an investment in a highly-skilled workforce. It would be prepared to sacrifice short-term profits for an increased market share. And it would also involve working in league with government to secure a larger share of foreign markets (as in the case of Airbus in its world-wide 'head to head' competition with the American Boeing corporation).

This model of corporate economics demands a long-term investment regime. German banks have a considerably larger long-term business than British banks (60 per cent of bank lending is overdraft type lending in the UK, 15 per cent in Germany), and they even lend long-term to (and take an interest in) the 'mittelstand' (German medium-sized family businesses). Yet their margins are lower; and should Britain adapt to the German model this will inevitably lead to lower bank profitability and less money for the 'Anglo-American' disease of take-overs and acquisitions.

Such long-term investment demands a low and stable inflation-rate. The key to German investment strategy is 'the mobilisation of huge flows of cheap, low margin, long-term bank finance to support the build-up of industrial capital', and for this strategy to be successful low inflation levels are essential, because as prices rise loans become less rewarding.[22] Ultimately, long-termism – more so than the policy of the Bundesbank or the legacy of Hitler – is what makes the modern German business community so concerned about inflation, and therefore interest-rate stability.

Mainstream European employment and social policy also reflects this 'partnership' concept. Although under the Social Chapter opt-out some key European employment practices are not binding upon British-based companies, they will none the less be implemented by those same companies with operations in other EU states. Alan Butt Philip argues that 'A more elegant and probably more effective answer to British concerns would have been for the UK to have agreed to the Social Chapter on condition that decisions taken under it should all be made unanimously.'[23] Being outside of the Social Chapter can mean that the British polity has no say in decisions which ultimately affect them. As Howard Davies, the Director-General of the CBI, has quipped, HMG was 'sent to mix the ouzos while this item was discussed' at the Corfu summit in June 1994.

As with employment policy, so too with social policy. In 'the German model' the social costs placed upon employers are generally seen not as a burden upon business, but, rather, as part of an upward spiral, a necessary key to winning consent, increasing security and thus productivity. The British conception – that social costs are ultimately uncompetitive in the global economy – has gained ground throughout Europe during the 1990s; yet the majority in Europe are likely to continue to argue that Europe cannot ever hope to compete on costs with low-cost South and South-East Asia, and thus that attempting to match these particular costs (as opposed to those in Japan and the USA) should not be a primary goal of European economic strategy for the next century.

European Union can be expected to gradually end Britain's special privileges gained by the opt-out from the Social Chapter. The majority in Europe will not enforce this new economic philosophy upon the British out of sheer ideological commitment; rather, the rationale for forcing the UK into line will be a perceived need by a majority in Europe to stop the UK 'cheating' (through its 'low-cost' policies') in the competitive game.

Because of these severe difficulties of transition from one economic culture to another, the UK political establishment will be in a constant state of tension with mainstream Europe. Although there are likely to be Europe-wide moves towards a more flexible labour market, and to lower social costs, the basic features of German-led European economic culture are likely to remain. Therefore, the UK political establishment will be tempted to run their 'Anglo-American' economic model (covering the British Isles) from within the European Union. There are two problems with this strategy. First, much of the evidence still shows that it is inherently less productive. And, crucially, in order to retain 'Anglo-American' economic and industrial practices they would need the freedom of a loose, non-federal system. This is unlikely. Existing, let alone further, integration is, inevitably, pushing the British-based companies into the European mould.

As Europe integrates, then the old UK-state and its establishment will inevitably be encouraged, induced, and sometimes directed, to follow the 'social market' route – a reversal amounting to a virtual up-ending of the Thatcherite project. The European majority have the tools at their disposal (regulations, directives, even the governing legal philosophy of the European Court) to achieve the transformation of the UK's traditional industrial, company and employment ethos – even should the UK-state remain outside the Social Chapter provisions of the Maastricht Treaty.

'The Opt-out may cut off one head of the beast, but others – many others – remain predatory . . .' was the comment of Philip Bassett on the ruling of the European Court (handed down on 8 June 1994) that British workers fired following privatisation might have compensation claims.[24] And *The Times* lamented that 'Europe now has a clear right to intervene, for instance, in the way in which a British council transfers a contract between one firm of dustmen and another.'

NEW MONEY

No area of British life has been more 'national' than money. The UK establishment – through the Treasury and the Bank of England – has viewed its control of money as one of its levers of power; and symbolical power too – for the Queen's head peers out of our money at her subjects – a prominent feature on all the coins and notes of the British.

Also, the pound sterling has been a nationalist virility symbol. 'The sterling area' was a source not only of pride, but of policy too, well into the post-Second World War era. And devaluations of sterling have been viewed as national humiliations. Harold Wilson's 1967 devaluation (from 2.80 dollars to the pound down to 2.40) robbed him of his political credibility, which was never to return; and Norman Lamont's 1992 devaluation, when Britain withdrew from the European Exchange

Rate Mechanism, was also viewed by many as a 'British defeat'.

Yet, like British sovereignty and the 'national economy', the king-dom's pound, like the Queen's shilling, is no longer what it used to be. The pound has not only been devalued over the decades; but, worse still from the perspective of nationalists, the value of the pound can no longer be determined by the will of the UK political establishment. By the late twentieth century the Queen's head might still adorn the notes, but in reality HMG and the Bank of England are increasingly marginal actors in determining the pound's value. The fact is that the tools of the monetary trade for the Treasury and the Bank of England – interest-rate policy, monetary targets and minimum reserve require-ments – are now dependent upon so many external factors that 'national monetary policy' has become a chimera. And by the late 1990s foremost amongst these 'external factors' was, inevitably, the monetary policy of Europe's most dynamic economy determined by the Bundesbank.

The UK's political establishment has attempted to break free from this impotence by a strategy of devaluation – otherwise known as a flexible exchange-rate policy. The staggering fact that in 1958 the pound bought over 11 Deutsche marks where as in 1995 it bought between 2.20 and 2.30 tells the sorry story. The UK-state's penchant for devaluing its currency (whether by Labour from a pegged rate or, during the Thatcher era, by 'floating down') has helped embed an inflationary psychology in the British. It is also an ingenious way of cheating the European system as it allows the devaluer to take advantage of the European single market whilst under-cutting the competition. Competitive devaluations – the withdrawal of sterling from the Exchange Rate Mechanism in 1992 was the latest example – may work for a while, but as a long-term solution to the problems of an uncompetitive econ-omy there are limits to their usefulness.

However, the devaluations of 1992 and 1993 which seemingly wrecked the ERM (and the move towards a single currency) proved to be a false dusk. The instability in the European money markets of 1992 and 1993 was caused by an unusual conjunction of events which some of the weaker European economies were unable to cope with. A deep recession combined with an extraordinarily harsh German interest-rate policy (caused in turn by the 'one-off' absorption of East Germany into the Federal Republic) placed severe strains on unemployment levels throughout the European Union.

Yet, within a year the humiliation of the near-collapse of the ERM had been forgotten, and most European currencies were floating back to their original parities. Indeed, rather than delaying monetary union some experts were beginning to believe that the collapse of the Exchange Rate Mechanism might, paradoxically, have accelerated the process by getting the European economies more synchronised. Central banks, as a result of the ERM crisis, 'have gone from an emphasis upon maintaining currency stability to a emphasis upon economic convergence'.[25] And many central bankers were reported to be convinced that the 1999 target date for a single currency, and even the earlier 1997 date, was achievable. A single currency was 'condemned to success'.[26]

By the late 1990s there appeared to be a growing inevitability about a Single European Currency. The idea is certainly attractive to some businesses because of the savings to be made on conversion costs and the stable currency environment which would allow the planning of investments with confidence. It is also attractive to governments, as the stability it ensures in currency exchange rates – by abolishing them – would reduce uncertainty and promote intra-European trade. It would also induce a competitive environment within the single market which the single currency covers. The United States 'with its single currency and absence of trade barriers is in many ways a blueprint for European integration'. And, to some, it was America's 'vast and highly competitive markets' which 'have helped Americans achieve a high standard of living'.[27]

Above all, the European single market will, through its own dynamics inevitably demand a single currency. A single market simply cannot work properly or competitively without a single currency (or a regime of permanently fixed rates, which amounts to the same thing) – because in a system of separate currencies some companies can opt out of the competition and gain an unfair advantage by getting their governments to devalue. And such cheating would, inevitably, be countered by the non-cheating governments (in order to protect their own trade), resulting in a European trade war which would destroy the single market. Thus, should the single currency 'wither on the vine', as some Eurosceptics hope, then so too will the single market.

Yet it is the *politics* of Europe, even more than the economics, which will insist upon a single currency. And in the developing political dynamic the UK-state and its establishment will take an unaccustomed back-seat. Essentially, everything will depend upon whether the convergence of interest between the French and German political leaderships continues to hold up. The French desire for a united money and the German for a united polity is the compact which drives further integration and the ultimate destiny of federalism.

France's geo-political aim has been to anchor Germany to Western Europe so that as Eastern Europe opens up, and Germany becomes more central in the geo-politics of the continent, it will not be able, let alone be tempted, to act independently. Former French Prime Minister Eduard Balladur put the French establishment's position clearly when he argued that unless Germany was bound by Maastricht it would 'act as it desires, without taking heed of its neighbours or its partners, without being constrained by any set of common European rules in its role as a military, economic, financial and monetary power in the centre of the continent'.[28] And, in order to secure this anchoring of Germany, the single currency becomes the most effective institutional mechanism. (It also, for the French, has the added advantage of abolishing the Bundesbank and giving French bankers some purchase upon Europe's future currency.)

However, the German political leadership (who in the early 1990s remained reluctant to give up its D-mark and its Bundesbank) would only embrace a single European currency should its own 'federal project'– political union – be advanced as a 'quid pro quo'. It wanted, and still wants, political union for its own reasons: that a more assertive German foreign policy – one that matches the relative strength of its economy – could be developed only within the European context.

But the German leadership also wanted, and wants, European political union for economic reasons – because political union would lessen the ability of the member states to use fiscal and welfare policies to pull in the opposite direction to monetary policy. This essential linkage between monetary and political union has become a contemporary theme of German diplomacy. A Bundesbank source has warned 'If you look at history, no monetary union has survived without political union. The fear is that concern about creating a single currency means people fail to look further. If the single currency fails that would be a disaster – it could endanger existing political institutions.'[29]

ADJUSTING TO A SINGLE CURRENCY

British adjustment to a single currency will not be easy. The transfer of monetary power away from London – from the Treasury and the Bank of England – will be total. The pound sterling (except perhaps as an image on a bank-note) will have ceased to exist. Changes in exchange rates would be out of the question. And, over time – or at once with a 'big bang' – the new currency would be introduced; it could either possess a European-wide design or continue, for a time, with a national British design, even including the Queen's head, on one side.

Such a drastic change-over to a new currency would bring home to millions of people the revolutionary character of the new economics of Europe. The UK government would no longer be able to use monetary policy as a stabilisation measure, or to react independently to shocks to the system such as a Gulf war or an oil price rise. Monetary policy for the British Isles – as for the rest of the European Union – would instead be determined by the European Central Bank (based in Frankfurt) which would be charged not only with fixing interest rates and money supply but also possibly, and crucially, with the rules of banking supervision.

Under a single-currency regime other things than money take the strain. In the British Isles – as in the states of the United States – wages, employment and fiscal policy will adjust rather than the currency. The American experience shows that in the single-currency area of the United States wages do tend to adjust to reflect the relative economic fortunes of different regions: 'between 1983 and 1989, wages rose by a total of 10 per cent more in the north-east than in the west, but the process is comparatively languid'.[30] There will also be a 'people adjustment' as less competitive areas lose jobs. Under a single-currency regime everything will depend upon the competitiveness of British-based companies. If they do well unemployment will fall (and unemployed labour from other parts of Europe may even gravitate to Britain); if they do badly it will rise – and Norman Tebbit's injunction to those seeking work to 'get on yer bike' (translating into 'get on yer jet' or 'yer cross-channel ferry') will assume a new importance, although these flows may be mitigated by the European Union's regional policy.

Yet, the process of global competition is already, irrespective of the single currency, affecting the less competitive regions of the UK-state (and other European regions too). In all federal systems (even in the USA) fiscal policy is one of the mechanisms for redistribution, for coming to the aid of those less competitive regions; and a pan-European fiscal policy can be expected to help those regions overcome economic shocks.

In the new single-currency regime Her Majesty's Government's one remaining reason for existence will be its ability to determine the level of tax and public expenditure for the British Isles. Yet even here, in the one remaining 'sovereign' function, the UK-state will be seriously constrained. Christopher Johnson has pointed out that fiscal constraints upon the UK-state are already 'explicit or implicit on the Single European Act' through the harmonization of indirect taxation. 'This', he argues, 'has led to general acceptance of a 15 per cent lower limit on the standard rate of VAT, and a 5 per cent lower limit on the lower rate.'[31] And the Maastricht 'convergence criteria' for budget deficits also act as another serious constraint upon independent nation-state activity.

The UK-state will not exactly be required (like most states of the US federal union) to balance its budget; but HMG can only run a high-public-expenditure regime if it also runs a high-tax regime (and because of harmonisation of indirect taxes this would need to be a high-income-tax regime). Yet, domestic British public opinion would tend to resist such a tax regime, thus leaving the UK Treasury with little fiscal room for manoeuvre.

The UK political authorities may be asked to adjust to this single currency very quickly. The Maastricht Treaty requires that a single currency be in operation at the latest by 1 January 1999.[32] There is also a remote chance that it could also happen before, during 1997, following a European Council meeting 'not later than 31st December 1996'.[33]

However , the fateful move to stage three of EMU – the single currency – is essentially a political decision to be taken by the summit of European heads of government. Although in 1995 Europe's member state economies looked increasingly 'convergent' there were still – as of writing, in the summer of 1995 – likely to be some states who do not meet the targets. Yet, as of mid-1995, Britain, contrary to much commentary (both domestically and amongst the country's critics in continental Europe), seemed well on target (more so than many Union founder-member states) to meet the convergence criteria at either the earlier or later Council meeting – thus not being in need of a 'derogation', or exemption, from the single currency.[34]

At the meeting when the fate of the single currency will be decided there will inevitably be 'strict constructionists' (hard-liners, probably led by the Germans supported by the Bundesbank) who will want the letter of the Maastricht Treaty's convergence criteria observed. And there will be doves (probably led by the French) who will want a more flexible approach. Alain Lamassoure, French Minister for European Affairs, and EU commissioner Henning Christopherson have already suggested that the Germans and the Bundestag may be unable to secure a 'hard-line' agreement. The French have suggested that the

ability of some countries to bring their ratio of national debt to gross
domestic product down to the aimed-for 60 per cent should, for instance, be seen as 'the desired result of EMU and not the precondition
to it'.[35] On the other hand, the German Parliament may block any
agreement if the convergence criteria are not met in full by the necessary eight member states.

However, should the doves prevail then the UK-state will certainly
qualify for the single currency – and providing that it revokes its 'opt-
out' by a decision of the UK House of Commons, re-enters the ERM,
and has freed the Bank of England from political control, it will enter
the system.

'ALL THE PRESIDENT'S MEN' – A EUROPEAN ARMY?

As in so many other areas of life under its remit, the old UK-state can
no longer provide the British people with a serious framework of security. Virtually all of the international problems which the rapidly changing
geo-politics of the world pose to the peoples of Britain find the old
UK-state (as well as the other nation-states of Europe) incapable of
acting alone. Whether the security problem is posed by population
movements (large-scale refugee influxes into Western Europe from East
Europe or the Mahgreb), by the Russian mafia (bringing with them
the problem of drug and nuclear smuggling), by nuclear blackmail by
unstable third world governments or indeed free-lance terrorists, or by
direct military threats (including ballistic missiles) to the West European continent from a future third world radical state (or, also, by a
hostile Russia), then the ability of the UK-state to deal with them alone
is extremely limited.

The idea that the UK-state could begin, on its own, to deal with all
the foreign and defence policy questions arising from the changing
political climate surrounding the borders of the European Union – not
only in Eastern Europe but also in the Middle East and north Africa –
is more than fanciful. Hardly any of these challenges can be seriously
addressed without a single European decision-making centre – even
though the decision may in the first instance involve all the separate
views of the national states. A united European security policy can
bring to bear a scale of operations – police, intelligence, diplomatic,
economic, military – which a separate UK-state simply cannot command. And retaining an independent UK foreign policy (or a French

or German one too) within the Union could easily lead to an invitation to under-cut a European policy by 'playing off' one country against another.

A European Union security policy is also needed as a mechanism for finally eradicating the omnipresent potential for old nation-state rivalries and antagonisms to flare up into tension and conflict. Thus, one of the compelling forces (particularly for the generation brought up during or just after the war) driving a united European security is the perceived guarantee it provides for a stable European peace. For one of the leading contemporary architects of the new federal union, Chancellor Helmut Kohl of Germany, this is in fact the major imperative: 'For me, there is no question that European unification is the most effective insurance against a new flare up of nationalism, chauvinism, and political rivalries in the western part of our continent. The success of European unification efforts is, in the end, a question of war and peace in the twenty-first century.'[36]

Thus, British security can no longer be understood in strictly British terms – indeed attempts to resolve security issues by a unilateral and independent UK policy, by inhibiting collective action, could threaten the security of the peoples of the British Isles. This assessment, although often unappreciated amongst the British public and pundits, is increasingly understood in the Whitehall security community. Ever since the dawn of the nuclear age – and East–West nuclear rivalry – UK security policy (and the posture of the UK-state's military) has been formulated upon one central objective: to work as a junior partner in tandem with the US administration's global security strategy – particularly as it concerns 'the European theatre'.

However, although the UK security establishment, during the NATO years, understood the value of a multi-lateral approach, it has been slower to understand that with the end of the cold war the UK now needs to change principal partners – from the USA (and NATO) to the European Union (and a European security umbrella). For some years following the collapse of communism, the UK's security and political establishment continued to gear their whole posture to the 'special relationship' with Washington, fearing that too strong a Euro-centric security policy would frighten off the USA from even its residual involvement in Europe.

The UK establishment also continued to believe that Europe had a limited ability to construct a coherent foreign policy, an argument also held amongst some in the Washington foreign-policy elite. American columnist William Pfaff set out the case:

A European Union in economic and social matters is possible because its members have common economic and social interests, as
well as a consciousness of themselves as a historical and cultural
community. But the members of the European Union do not have a
common view of their foreign policy interests, or any geo-political
conception of a world role for Europe. There is a common interest
in collective security against external aggression, an interest in peace,
a concern to defend the values of Western political civilisation. This
does not add up to a foreign policy.[37]

Yet, this European inadequacy obtained during a period of heavy US
involvement, and, crucially, during an era when the US and Western
Europe had virtually identical interests. In the very first post-cold war
European crisis – in the ex-Yugoslavia – American and European perceptions of interest differed radically. Such a collapse of the old verities was
one of the huge incentives to create a united European security policy.

And – deadly news for the old-UK's world view – even parts of the
Washington security community were acting as cheerleaders for British involvement in a united European foreign policy. The UK establishment was told at the annual Pilgrims' Dinner by no less a pilgrim
than the out-going US ambassador that even the road to Washington
would in future run through Brussels:

> While Britain's role in the Union is indisputably complicating . . .
> our relationship to it is also indispensable to the relationship [with
> Britain]. . . . America's transatlantic policy is European in scope.
> It is not a series of individual or compartmentalised bilateral
> policies, and never has been. It is the policy of one continent to
> another. There is a simple observation that if Britain's voice is less
> influential in Paris or Bonn, it is likely to be less influential in
> Washington.[38]

The UK-state's scepticism about the potential for a European security policy was given some life by the lack of any serious will on the
continent to construct one. Although the skeletal form of what the Brussels
mandarins call 'European Political Co-operation' has been around for
some time, its development into anything resembling a European security
policy has been hesitant and ambiguous.

By the mid-1990s, though, a European security structure, if not a
security policy, was beginning to take shape. The structures of its operation were set out at Maastricht and woven into the fabric of the

Union: it would work its will through 'common positions' and 'joint actions' – a formula which basically meant 'deciding unanimously to decide by majority vote'.[39] And it would also work through the revived Western European Union organisation – which would develop beyond its erstwhile NATO function into becoming the 'defence arm' of the European Union.

There were (and are) three ways forward. One, preferred by the UK political establishment of the early 1990s, is via the co-ordination of the foreign policies of the old nations, achieved by consensus. Under this model all the old national establishments would have to agree upon a course of action, or no collective European action would take place. Even some Euro-enthusiasts supported this approach – in the expectation that once the more immediate economic and currency integration had taken place then the security integration – including the UK-state – would follow quite naturally.

Alternatively, the co-ordination of national foreign and defence policies could be made effective by a strategy of majority voting with no national vetoes. The problem here would be that those nations who were out-voted would feel a resentment and take part in the policy – or the action – in a half-hearted way. Of course, as with American foreign policy and the security policy of other federal states, support for a policy is often contingent upon its success or failure. 'Nothing succeeds like success' and should a future European initiative – including a high profile military action- meet with success then even a sceptical UK administration would feel inclined to associate itself with the policy. Indeed, a European security policy based upon majority voting would not be that dissimilar to the politics of security in the United States (which, in all essentials, needs a *majority* in the US Senate to be effectively prosecuted). Integration, rather then co-ordination (the preferred option of Euro-federalist enthusiasts), would make the political command structure of security somewhat clearer but would not, of itself, make much of a difference to the potential effectiveness of security policy.

It is often argued that a key element will be the degree to which the apparatus of the Community – the Commission – is able to involve itself in security issues. The European Commission has considerable experience of international politics through its trade function, and already directly runs over 100 missions world-wide. Should the Brussels Commission take a central role in security policy it would certainly completely under-cut the 'national' role, including that of the Foreign Office in London.

Yet, even should the more realistic option prevail – and the inter-governmental Council of Ministers continue to take the lead in foreign and defence policy – then, as long as majority voting increasingly replaces the veto, a coherent European foreign and security policy fit for a new super-state and super-power will still emerge. Indeed, the inter-governmentalism of the Council of Ministers might serve to give the new security policy its necessary initial support throughout the Union.

However, whether the favoured approach to European security policy is co-ordination or integration, these structural questions ultimately matter only marginally. Much more important is the political will amongst the leading national players in Europe – including the British. UK Eurosceptics have continued to believe (and to hope) that the UK-state would be saved from absorption into a European security policy not by the structural questions, but rather by the will – or lack of it – of Europe's leaders. The supposition is that Europe's national leaders will simply never agree upon a systematic or specific security policy, and, even should they agree, will not share an intensity of feeling over the issue. The gut instinct is that, faced with a serious foreign and security challenge, Europe will not create a coherent response and, without America, will fall on its face.

But the 1990s were early days. America's disengagement, together with the force of world events and the converging security interests of the national member states, will, ultimately, either induce the emergence of a common foreign and security policy or, alternatively, leave the European Union completely anarchic and defenceless. There was no middle way.

As a common European security begins to cohere then so too, as a necessary complement, will a common European diplomatic policy. In the old UK-state the image of diplomacy and diplomats has been both an evocation of, and a preserve of, Englishness – the late nineteenth-century public-school ethos infused with the flavour of the old Empire. For the UK-state and its establishment the future of Her Britannic Majesty's diplomats remains a culturally sensitive issue. Yet, ultimately, the diplomats of the UK-state – the famed Foreign Office mandarins evoked so successfully in Hollywood movies – will no longer represent the peoples of the British Isles when they travel abroad, nor will they represent them to third countries.

As a European foreign policy gets under way then the need for separate national diplomacy becomes redundant – as does the expensive operation of separate European embassies in third countries. A sign of times to come was outlined for European foreign ministers in Lisbon in February 1992, by the Portuguese foreign minister, João des dues Pinheiro, who had examined the options for the future of Europe's separate diplomats. He argued that they 'ranged from sharing facilities, such as buildings and vehicles, to setting up single EU missions with multi-national staff in which the chief diplomatic posts would rotate amongst the twelve. However, the latter option was ruled out as too ambitious.'[40] (Also, by the mid-1990s the European Commission already has a diplomatic network 'more extensive than that of many member states, several of whom have been seeking ways of reducing at least the costs and in some ways the size of their diplomatic services'.)[41]

Such an ambitious and imaginitive projection would meet, initially at least, considerable national opposition. In the early 1990s a French court ruled against joint missions on the grounds that only a French citizen could represent the French president. Similar objections about 'the Queen being represented by a foreigner' can be expected.

Just as culturally – and psychologically – sensitive for the UK establishment is the issue of 'a European army', the full integration of the Union's member-state armed forces into one centralised military force. The idea of a 'European army' has a long pedigree, going back to the early 1950s when a European Defence Force was mooted, and subsequently scuppered by the French and the British. So soon after the Second World War, the British establishment was in no mood to see its military wing absorbed into a European force. 'Her Majesty's armed forces' were still a serious military operation with troops deployed world-wide, with an esprit de corps and a central role in the cultural and ceremonial paraphernalia of the sovereign UK.

Since then, though, a slow but perceptible post-imperial ethos has been established. 'Options for Change', the Conservative government's new defence policy issued in the early 1990s, set a more realistic level of defence expenditure. And the UK defence establishment even began to contemplate the erstwhile unthinkable: some kind of pooling – with the French – of the last great totem of national independence, the British bomb, the Polaris and Poseidon nuclear weapons in the submarines.

Europe's army (and navy and airforce) can develop in one of two ways, or both at the same time. It can possess a joint command structure, as does NATO now – with every individual nation's armed forces retaining their national command but being placed under an over-all multi-national command and commander. This was the structure under which the British armed forces fought during the Second World War when an American, General Dwight Eisenhower, assumed over-all command.

Eisenhower, however, spoke English, and was considered a 'country cousin' by the British. Britain's still relatively culturally chauvinist military personnel might, though, find the idea of serving under a German or French commander-in-chief somewhat more disconcerting than serving under an American. However, in the joint-command model, with the British military retaining their own commanders right up to 'army level', the cultural problems are likely to remain minimal.

The same will not be true should, ultimately, Britain's armed forces be integrated into the 'Eurocorps' system. Created on 5 November 1993, the 'Eurocorps' is the prototype for the armed forces of a new super-state. Headquartered in Strasbourg, the corps integrates the various national soldiers right down to the unit level. At full strength it will be 50,000 troops. It is headed by a German – Lt-Gen. Helmut Willman. The inner corps is the Franco-German brigade, made up of 4,200 French, German and Belgian troops. The founders of the corps, Chancellor Helmut Kohl and President Mitterrand, insisted that it assume a customer relationship with the varying Western political authorities – for instance, it could be assigned to NATO or to the WEU, although ultimately the hope of the federalists is that it will become the basis for Europe's army.

The UK-state will surrender its control over its military only at the very last minute, and only as the final step on the road to a united Europe. Thus, even should a federal European state have become a reality (after full monetary union had been secured with the UK-state as a full partner), then the control of military forces would still, for a time, remain in the hands of the UK-state (and other member states). The European militaries remain amongst the most traditional (thus 'nationally' minded) social organisations in Western Europe; and national political leaders still see control over their 'own' militaries as one of the few, albeit increasingly symbolic, roles for national governments. The inability to use these forces unilaterally does not detract from this perception.

Thus, certainly for the UK-state's establishment, should a genuinely federal European military emerge, the preferred command structure would remain that of the wartime Alliance: same objective, joint command, possibly even a foreign commander-in-chief, but *national* units up to army level.

Yet, this reticence towards military *integration* may not spill over into hostility to joint European operations. Indeed, the UK-state's history of military prowess places it in a strong position in the European Union – far stronger than its economic ranking or political influence. The UK possesses one of the two independent nuclear deterrents in Europe (although its reliance upon American satellite support makes it less 'independent' than the French) as well as one of the most professionally capable armed forces. British forces also play a prominent role in NATO's Rapid Reaction Force and in its Multi-National Airmobile Division – which comprises Dutch, German and Belgian heliborne brigades as well as British. And being able to play such a leading role may cause the UK political establishment to look much more favourably upon the common security policy than upon the common monetary policy.

A NEW IDENTITY: RE-INVENTING THE BRITISH

As the structures of the UK-state melt down, and the peoples of the British Isles begin to inhabit the broader and looser European political institutions, then the constrictions imposed by the straitjacket of UKanian nationality – its old national perceptions and identities – will also be swept away.

Yet, this end of nationality is not a kind of zero-sum game in which an existing sense of nationality is expunged in favour of a new one. Rather, existing identities will be refined and, crucially, added to. Thus, the peoples of the British Isles can be expected, over time, to develop a new view of their relationship to Europe. Twenty-first-century Britons will see the British Isles as being a part of Europe, not separate from it. And in this process of integration perceptions will expand, as for Britons English becomes a European language, London, Cardiff and Edinburgh become European cities, Wembley Stadium becomes a European football ground, and the BBC becomes a European television company.

Similarly, British sensibility will expand to encompass continental European history as part of its own. The nationalism of the UK-state has devalued the contributions which continental European philosophy and political thought (particularly that deriving from the epoch-making French Revolution) has – together with continental art, science and technology – made to the development of life within the British Isles.

And as the British acknowledge the wider streams from which their own life is drawn – and the wider European civilisation of which they are a part – then the country's horizons will widen too.

The possibility of wider horizons – the sense of belonging, not to a cramped and constricted nation-state, but rather to a continent-wide civilisation (that sense possessed by Americans) – is a sense which nation-state nationalism denies to the people within its borders. Yet, such an opening to new possibilities and frontiers (even if only in the mind and imagination) could provide the somewhat forlorn peoples of the British Isles some confidence in the future.

The ideology and culture of Englishness – the official culture of the UK-state – was never able to provide a vision for the average Briton. There never was a 'British dream' to match 'the American dream'. British absorption in Europe – with its bounty of wider horizons and new frontiers – provides just such a possibility.

From this perspective the UK-less British in Europe become not a tragic people robbed of their freedom (as much of the late twentieth-century UK establishment would have it), but rather, 'the lucky country' with the good fortune – in an increasingly competitive and unstable world – to be a part of a seriously going concern.

There may be a certain irony in the British end-game: a people which in the twentieth century went through the traumas of a lost empire, the loss of millions of its people in two world wars, a seemingly unstoppable economic decline, and the slow implosion of their state, none the less do not end up inhabiting an isolated poverty-stricken off-shore island, but rather, are rescued from such a fate by a continent they have, by turns, disdained, feared and devalued. Such a fate, rather than being bemoaned, could be envied.

Notes

Notes to the Introduction

1. Ian Ousby, *The Englishman's England: Taste, Travel and the Rise of Tourism* (Cambridge, 1990).
2. Jane Mackay and Pat Thane, 'The Englishwoman', in Robert Colls and Philip Dodd (eds), *Englishness: Politics and Culture* (Beckenham, Kent, 1986).
3. From Sebastian Faulks, 'A Quick Word', *Guardian*, 30 April 1994.
4. Richard Kuisel, *Seducing the French* (London, 1993) p. 233.
5. Quote from *The Washington Post*, 12 August 1994.
6. Mathew Horsman and Andrew Marshall, *After the Nation-State* (London, 1994) p. xvii.
7. Ambassador Raymond Seitz's address to the Pilgrims' Society, reprinted in edited form by *The Times*, 20 April 1994.

Notes to Chapter 1: The Making of Englishness

1. This account is given in Beram Saklatvala, *The Origins of the English People* (New York, 1969).
2. Ibid., p. 14.
3. See the great protagonist of this view: J. H. Round, *Feudal England* (1895) and R. Allen Brown, *The Normans and the Norman Conquest* (1969).
4. All quotes from Geoffrey Elton, *The English* (Oxford, 1992). The quote from Bede can be found on p. 2.
5. Elton, ibid., p. 28 and p. 27.
6. Ibid., p. 14.
7. Quoted in Robert McCrum, William Cran and Robert McNeil, *The Story of English* (New York, 1986) p. 77.
8. Robert Claiborne, *The Life and Times of the English Language* (London, 1990) p. 123. The numbers of warriors are estimates made by Claiborne.
9. Georges Bourcier, *An Introduction to the History of the English Language* (London, 1981).
10. Claiborne, op. cit., p. 100.
11. Poem quoted in McCrum *et al.*, op. cit., p. 77. The survival of English under the Normans is set out in R. W. Chambers, 'On the Continuity of English Prose', introduction to *The Life of Sir Thomas More* (London, 1932).
12. McCrum *et al.*, op. cit.
13. Gerald Newman, *The Rise of English Nationalism, 1740–1830* (New York, 1987) p. 4.
14. Ibid., p. 127.

15. See Linda Colley, *Britons: Forging the Nation, 1707–1837* (London, 1992).
16. Elton, op. cit., p. 182.
17. Colley, op, cit., p. 162 and p. 164.
18. Ibid., Chap. 4.
19. Ibid.
20. Quote from Newman, op. cit., p. 116. Bull's quote from Herbert Atherton, *Political Prints in the Age of Hogarth: A Study of the Ideographic Representation of Politics* (Oxford, 1974) p. 216.
21. Elton, op. cit., p. 70; my italics.
22. See Ian Gilmour, *Inside Right: A Study of Conservatism* (London, 1977).
23. Keith Thomas, *The New York Review of Books*, 19 November 1992.
24. Peter Fordudo, 'National Pride in Seventeenth-Century England', in Raphael Samuel (ed.), *Patriotism: The Making and Unmaking of British National Identity*, vol. 1 (London, 1989).
25. Colley, op. cit., p. 286.
26. See Jeannie Surel, 'John Bull'; Madge Dresser, 'Britannia', in Samuel (ed.), op. cit.
27. Newman, op. cit., p. 124.
28. Ibid., p. 127.
29. Peter Scott, *Knowledge and Nation* (Edinburgh, 1990), p. 168.
30. For a systematic analysis of this cross-fertilisation of English and Scottish, Welsh and Irish, see Colley, op. cit., pp. 155ff.
31. Thomas, *The New York Review of Books*, 19 November 1992.
32. From a column in *The North Briton*, 26 June 1763, quoted in Colley, op. cit., p. 116.
33. For a discussion of how this mix of land and finance – and information – in a relatively few hands has continued into contemporary Britain see James Bellini, *Rule Britannia* (London, 1981).
34. Michael Hechter, *Internal Colonialism* (London, 1975) p. 59.
35. See Correlli Barnett, *The Pride and the Fall* (New York, 1986); my italics.
36. For data regarding Scottish imperial influence see T. C. Smout, *A History of the Scottish People, 1560–1830* (1970, 2nd edn).
37. Colley, op. cit., p. 293.
38. Ibid., p. 293.
39. Ibid., p. 111.
40. See, for instance, T. H. B. Oldfield, *The Representative History of Great Britain and Ireland* (1816); and 'The Norman Yoke', in *The True Levellers' Standard Advanced* (1649). These, and other examples of radical thinking about an ancient constitution of liberty, are supplied in the extremely useful and erudite *Democracy in Britain: A Reader* (Oxford, 1994), edited by Jack Lively and Adam Lively.
41. In *The True Levellers' Standard Advanced* (1649), quoted in Lively and Lively (eds), op. cit., p. 23.
42. Burke's quote from 'Reflections on the Revolution in France', quoted in Lively and Lively, op. cit., p. 20. Also, see Sir David Lindsay Keir, *The Constitutional History of Modern Britain since 1945* (London, 1964).
43. See Ferdinand Mount, *The British Constitution Now: Recovery or Decline* (London, 1992).

44. Edward Countryman, *The American Revolution* (New York, 1985) p. 16.
45. Ibid., p. 111.
46. See R. A. Cage (ed.), *The Scots Abroad: Labour, Capital, Enterprise, 1750–1914* (London, 1985).
47. See Ian Gilmour, *Inside Right: A Study of Conservativism* (London, 1977) p. 87.
48. Frank Reeves, *British Racial Discourse: A Study of British Political Discourse about Race and Race-related Matters* (Cambridge, 1983) p. 114.
49. Robert Colls and Philip Dodd (eds), *Englishness* (Beckenham, Kent, 1986), p. 45.
50. Andrew Roberts, *Eminent Churchillians* (London, 1994) pp. 213–14.
51. Quoted in Alan S. Milward, *The European Rescue of the Nation-State* (London, 1992) p. 432.
52. First quotation from Lady Selina Hastings, in Phyllis Hatfield, *Pencil Me In: A Memoir of Stanley Olson* (London, 1994) p. 94. Second quotation from an American observer of the English and Englishness scene (ibid., p. 95).
53. Katherine Tidrick, *Empire and the English Character* (London, 1992) p. 3.
54. Ernest Barker, *National Character and the Factors in its Formation* (London, 1928) p. 42.
55. Both quotations from Correlli Barnett, *The Collapse of British Power* (London, 1972), p. 25. A general description of the education of Victorian public-school children also appears in the same chapter.
56. Colls and Dodd, op. cit., p. 4.
57. Quotation from Cornelli Barnett, *The Collapse of British Power* (London, 1972) p. 36.
58. Ibid.
59. Luigi Barzini, 'The Imperturbable British', in *The Europeans* (London, 1983), pp. 52–53.
60. Tidrick, op. cit., p. 280.
61. Philip Dodd, 'Englishness and the National Culture', in Robert Colls and Philip Dodd (eds), *Englishness: Politics and Culture* (Beckenham, Kent, 1986).
62. McCrum, op. cit., p. 24. For a survey of the emergence of standardised English see Raymond Williams, *The Long Revolution* (London, 1961).
63. Dodd, op. cit., p. 16.
64. See Williams, op. cit.
65. See ibid., pp. 54–62, for a fuller analysis.
66. See Alistair Service, *London 1900* (Granada, 1979).
67. Thomas Burke, *London in My Time* (London, 1934), about the recognisable types of girls seen on London streets around 1900, p. 65.
68. Cited in Hugh Cunningham, 'The Conservative Party and Patriotism', in Colls (ed.), op. cit., p. 286; my italics.
69. Ibid., p. 298.
70. Cited in Theo Aronson, *Victoria and Disraeli* (London, 1977) p. 194.
71. Colls, op. cit., p. 36.
72. Neil Ascherson, *Games with Shadows* (London, 1988) p. 151.
73. See Barrington Moore, *Social Origins of Dictatorship and Democracy* (Harmondsworth, 1966) p. 16.

74. Tidrick, op. cit., p. 279.
75. Ibid., p. 3.
76. Charles M. Hampden-Turner, *Gentlemen and Tradesmen* (London, 1983) p. 3.
77. Quotation cited in Cunningham, op. cit., p. 298.
78. Intriguingly, Ernest Barker, in his 1927 book *National Character*, does not, even fleetingly, have anything to say about the influence of Empire on national character and culture.
79. Cited in Lively and Lively (eds), op. cit., p. 238, from George Lamming's *In the Castle of My Skin*.
80. *The War Speeches of Winston Churchill* (London, date not supplied) compiled by Charles Eade, vol. 3, p. 512
81. Elizabeth Young, 'Canon Law', *Guardian Magazine*, 4 February 1994, p. 20.
82. Stephanie Lewis, *The Times*, 'Shopping' section, 23 April 1994.
83. See *Country Life*, 11 November 1993. One such 'hero of the country-side' is Lady Aldington, *Country Life*, 12 May 1994, who founded the Jacob Sheep Society in 1969: 'In the Aldington house-hold, everything stops at three. But not for tea. This is the appointed hour when the Jacob sheep which roam the nearby fields are fed.... Lady Aldington is the first to admit she is rather obsessed by her distinctive horned, piebald sheep ...'.
84. 'Yellow Socks and Coronets', by James Knox, entitled 'How a Gentleman should dress: A Duke advises', *Country Life*, 19 August 1993.
85. 'Whatever the Weather', by June Marsh, *Country Life*, 23 June 1994.
86. *Country Life*, 23 June 1994.
87. *Country Life*, 30 June 1994.
88. Phyllis Hatfield, *Pencil Me In: A Memoir of Stanley Olson* (London, 1994) pp. 3–4.
89. Ibid., p. 52.
90. *Country Life*, 19 May 1994, 7 July 1994, 30 June, 11 November 1993.
91. David Edelsten, 'Leather on Rural Willow', *Country Life*, 12 May 1994.
92. Paul Addison, 'The Day the Dream Began to Die', *Independent*, 6 June 1994.
93. The depiction of J. B. Priestley was by Paul Taylor, 'Bennett and the Betrayal of Englishness', *Independent*, 23 May 1994. The depiction of George Orwell was by Bernard Crick, *George Orwell: A Life* (London, 1980).
94. Described as such in Paul Taylor, op. cit.
95. From 'The Lion and the Unicorn: Socialism and the English Genius', in *The Collected Essays, Journalism and Letters of George Orwell*, vol. 2 (London, 1968).
96. Paul Johnson, *Wake Up Britain* (London, 1994).
97. Quoted from David Starkey, 'Freedom and Responsibility', *LSE Magazine*, Spring 1994, p. 24; my italics.
98. Beram Saklatvala, *The Origins of the English People* (New York 1969), p. 28.
99. Cited in Robert McCrum, *et al.*, op. cit.

Notes to Chapter 2: An Audit of Englishness

1. See Paul Kennedy, *The Rise and Fall of the Great Powers* (New York, 1987). He sets out the figures clearly in three tables, on pages 171, 243 and 436.
2. Dodd, in Colls and Dodd (eds), op. cit., p. 22.
3. Ibid.
4. Reported in *The Times*, 6 April 1994.
5. On 5 April 1954, cited in Milward, op. cit., p. 432.
6. Prime Minister's address to conference of Conservative women, 2 December 1994, quoted in Joe Rogaly, 'A Dangerous Battleground', *Financial Times*, 6 December 1994. The comment is from Rogaly, in the same article.
7. 9 May 1945, cited in Correlli Barnett, *The Audit of War* (London, 1986) p. 3.
8. Quotation from Bevin is cited in Milward, op. cit., p. 354, n. 14.
9. *The Times Higher Educational Supplement*, editorial, 24 June 1988.
10. Cited in Stephen Haseler, *The Battle for Britain* (London, 1989) p. 150.
11. Cited in Ian Gilmour, *Inside Right: A Study of Conservatism* (London, 1977) pp. 87 and 92.
12. Katherine Tidrick, *Empire and the English Character* (London, 1992) p. 275.
13. Elton, op. cit., p. 235.
14. Ibid., p. 70.
15. Quoted in Jack Lively and Adam Lively (eds), *Democracy in Britain* (Oxford, 1994) p. 15.
16. Cited in Keith Thomas, *Times Literary Supplement*, 19 November 1992.
17. Anthony Smith, *Varieties of Nationalism* (2nd edn) (1983) p. 231.
18. Ziauddin Sardar, in *Independent*, 3 March 1994, following a dispute between sections of the British press and the government of Malaysia (over alleged corruption in the financing of a dam).
19. Lively and Lively (eds), op. cit., p. 275.
20. Quoted in ibid., p. 285.
21. Orwell, *Collected Works*, vol. 2, p. 69.
22. E. P. Thompson, *The Making of the English Working Class* (London, 1974) p. 486.
23. Barnett, *Audit of War*, p. 189.
24. Description by Professor Robert Cowan in Cmnd 6153, pp. 53–4, cited in Barnett, *Audit of War*, p. 195.
25. Report of the Endowed Schools (Schools Enquiry) Royal Commission, C. 3966 (1867–8), vol. 1, part 1, p. 72.
26. Quoted in R. H. Heindel, *The American Impact on Great Britain 1898–1914* (New York, 1968) p. 153 and cited in Barnett, *Audit of War*, p. 205.
27. See R. T. Mckenzie and A. Silver, *Angels in Marble: Working-class Conservatism in Urban England* (London, 1968), for an account of the politics of deference in early post-Second World War Britain.
28. Martin Weiner, *English Culture and the Decline of the Industrial Spirit, 1850–1980* (New York, 1987) preface.
29. David Coates, *The Question of UK Decline: The Economy, State and Society* (Hemel Hempstead, 1994) p. 145.

30. See M. Mathieson and G. Bernbaum, 'The British Disease: A British Tradition', *British Journal of Educational Studies*, 26 (2) (1988) pp. 158–9.
31. See Joan Thirsk, 'The Field Systems of England', in J. Thirsk (ed.), *The Agrarian History of England and Wales*, vol. VI: *1500–1640* (Cambridge, 1967).
32. Newman, op. cit., p. 205.
33. Quoted in Ousby, op. cit., p. 159.
34. See Ken Worpole, 'Village School or Blackboard Jungle?', in Raphael Samuel (ed.), *Patriotism: The Making and Unmaking of British National Identity*, vol. III (London, 1989).
35. Alex Potts, 'Constable Country Between the Wars', in ibid., vol. III, p. 174.
36. Ibid., p. 168.
37. Ibid., pp. 160.
38. Jonathan Raban, *Soft City* (London, 1974) p. 59.
39. Correlli Barnett, *The Collapse of British Power* (London, 1972) p. 100.
40. Quoted in Barnett, *Audit of War*, p. 216.
41. Quoted in Sanderson, *The Universities in the Nineteenth Century* (London, 1975) pp. 123–4.
42. Ibid. p. 127.
43. See Barnett, *Audit of War*, pp. 217–18, for a short survey of nineteenth-century literary attitudes towards liberal education.
44. Charles Hampden-Turner and Fons Trompenaars, *The Seven Cultures of Capitalism* (New York, 1993).

Notes to Chapter 3: Identity Crisis

1. Quotations from Nick Crafts, 'Managing Decline? 1870–1990', *History Today*, vol. 44 (5) (June 1994) p. 38 and p. 39.
2. Figures from Crafts, op. cit., and for iron and steel production from Paul Kennedy, *The Rise and Fall of the Great Powers* (New York, 1987) p. 200.
3. Correlli Barnett, *The Collapse of British Power* (London, 1972) p. 12.
4. Ibid., pp. 14–15.
5. Barnett, *The Audit of War*, p. 160. The military data is also drawn from Barnett, *The Audit of War*, ch. 9.
6. Both quotes from Barnett, *Audit of War*, pp. 144 and 145.
7. For a description of British politics during the Korean War see Callum MacDonald, *Britain and the Korean War* (Oxford, 1990).
8. See David Carlton, *Britain and the Suez Crisis* (Oxford, 1988) pp. 87–91.
9. Ibid., pp. 332–3. The quote from Eisenhower appears in David Carlton, *Anthony Eden: A Biography* (London, 1981) p. 460.
10. The ability of the British forces to use US basing facilities and intelligence reports, as well as military material support, was a central factor in the outcome of the conflict.
11. See Andrew Roberts, *Holy Fox: A Biography of Lord Halifax* (London, 1991) p. 297.
12. Kennedy, op. cit., p. 425. The economic data is also cited in Kennedy, op. cit., p. 425.

13. The quotes are from David Starkey, 'Freedom and Responsibility', an abridged version of an article first published in *Daily Telegraph*, LSE magazine, Spring 1994.
14. 'Overlong, Overdone and Over Here', *Sunday Times*, 8 May 1994.
15. Ibid., p. 92.
16. Ibid.
17. Quoted in Arthur Marwick, *Culture in Britain since 1945* (Oxford, 1991), from Charlie Gillett, *The Sound of the City*, rev. edn (London, 1983).
18. Marwick, op. cit., p. 34.
19. *Sunday Times*, 8 May 1994.
20. Marwick, op. cit., pp. 56–7.
21. See McCrum, chapter 7. Also, for the influence of Yiddish on British-English see Leo Rosten, *The Joys of Yiddish* (London, 1971).
22. Kuisel, op. cit., p. 233.
23. F. H. Hinsley, *Sovereignty* (Cambridge, 1986) p. 142.
24. J. C. D. Clarke, *The Language of Liberty 1660–1832* (Cambridge, 1994), quoted in Jack P. Greene, 'Why Did they Rebel?', *Times Literary Supplement*, 10 June 1994.
25. Quotation from Hinsley, op. cit., p. 208–9.
26. Harold Laski, *The Grammar of Politics* (1941), cited in Hinsley, op. cit., p. 216.
27. Mathew Horsman and Andrew Marshall, *After the Nation-state: Citizens, Tribalism and the New World Disorder* (London, 1994) p. 49.
28. Anthony Sampson, 'A Worthless World of Money', *Independent*, 16 November 1994.
29. Neil Ascherson, 5th Sovereignty Lecture, 'Local Government and the Myth of Sovereignty', given to Charter 88 on 25 February 1994, and reprinted in *New Statesman*, 11 March 1994.
30. Joseph A. Camilleri and Jim Falk, *The End of Sovereignty* (Aldershot, 1992).
31. The dissolution of the state may never amount to a formal act, but could effectively occur over several decades.
32. S. Mulhall and A. Swift, *Liberals and Communitarians* (Oxford, 1992) p. 67.
33. Alan S. Milward, *The European Rescue of the Nation-State* (London, 1992).
34. Colley, op. cit., p. 291.
35. This view is outlined in *English in Use*, by Gabrielle Stein and Randolph Quirk (London, 1993).
36. Quoted from John Plamenatz, 'Two Types of Nationalism', in *Nationalism: The Nature and Evolution of an Idea*, ed. Eugene Kamenka (Canberra, 1973) p. 23.
37. Kenneth Minogue, *Nationalism* (London, 1969) pp. 23–4.
38. Ernest Gellner, *Nations and Nationalism* (London, 1983).
39. Newman, op. cit., p. 199.
40. Ibid., p. 87.
41. Quoted in ibid., p. 110.
42. Horsman, op. cit., p. 253.
43. Quoted in Newman, op. cit., p. 53.

44. Quoted in W. H. Greenleaf, *The British Political Tradition* (London, 1983) p. 257.
45. This definition of identity appears in *The Oxford English Dictionary*, 7th edn (1982).
46. Quoted in Newman, op. cit., p. 49.
47. Quoted in Sampson, *Independent*, 16 November 1994.
48. Quoted in Colley, op. cit., p. 291, from J. R. Dinwiddy, 'Parliamentary Reform as an Issue in English Politics, 1800–1810' (London University Ph.D. dissertation, 1971).
49. Neil Ascherson, op. cit.

Notes to Chapter 4: True Brits, Real England

1. Martin Weiner, *English Culture and the Decline of the Industrial Spirit, 1850–1980* (New York, 1987) preface.
2. Richard Crossman, *Planning for Freedom* (London, 1965) pp. 3–4.
3. *Commentary* magazine, New York, August 1991.
4. See Justin Champion, *The Pillars of Priestcraft Shaken* (Cambridge, 1992).
5. Joel Kotkin, *Tribes* (London, 1992) p. 80.
6. Quoted in ibid., p. 80.
7. Ibid., p. 71.
8. John Morley, *The Life of Richard Cobden*, vol. II (1981) pp. 481–2.
9. Jack Lively and Adam Lively, Introduction, *Democracy in Britain* (Oxford, 1994).
10. For a comprehensive modern constitutional text-book, which approaches the British polity from this conservative viewpoint, see Philip Norton, *The Constitution in Flux* (Oxford, 1982) p. 27.
11. For a discussion of this view see Arthur F. Midwinter et al., *Politics and Public Policy in Scotland* (London, 1991).
12. See H. M. Drucker and Gordon Brown, *The Politics of Nationalism and Devolution* (London, 1980); and Richard Rose, *Understanding the United Kingdom* (London 1981). The Central Statistical Office's *Regional Trends*, 23 (HMSO, 1988) reveals that Scotland possessed £5,725 per head, the South-West of England £5,699, the North-West £5,621, the South-East £7,183, the West Midlands £5,550, East Anglia £6,048, and Wales £4,989.
13. See Hechter, op. cit.
14. Source: Census, Office of Population Statistics.
15. Rodney Hilton, in Samuel (ed.), vol. 1, p. 39.
16. Source: *Social Trends*, Central Statistical Office, 1994.
17. *Social Trends*, 1994, p. 145, revealed that the UK's active church membership as a percentage of the total population was amongst the lowest in Europe.
18. The BBC broadcast a survey of unpublicised mass violence in Britain in its 'Forbidden Britain' series, 17 November 1994, BBC2.
19. Kotkin, op. cit., p. 79.
20. McCrum et al., op. cit., p. 24.
21. See McCrum, op. cit., pp. 271–83.
22. Figures from *Social Trends*, 24, 1994, p. 79, figure 5.26, Central Statis-

tical Office. They refer to Gross Domestic Product per head in current
prices at factor cost.
23. *Social Trends*, 24, 1994, based upon figures from the Inland Revenue.
    This assessment is based upon marketable wealth less value of dwell-
    ings, and is a United Kingdom figure. Figures for England only are not
    available.
24. Thomas Sowell, *Race and Culture: A World View* (New York, 1994).
25. Quotation from Professor Randolph Quirk, 'Nation Speaking unto Nation',
    The Culture Essay, *Sunday Times*, 17 April 1994.
26. Ibid.
27. Kotkin, op. cit., p. 75.
28. Anthony D. Smith, *Theories of Nationalism*, 2nd edn (London, 1983) p. 144.
29. Quotation is from R. B. J. Walker, 'State Sovereignty and the Articulation
    of Political Space/Time', in *Millennium*, vol. 20, no. 3 (Winter 1991) p. 445.

Notes to Chapter 5: Federal Destiny

1. Cited in Milward, op. cit., p. 354. n. 14.
2. Cited in ibid., p. 432.
3. John Dickie, *Special No More: Anglo-American Relations: Rhetoric and
   Reality* (London, 1994) p. 95.
4. Cited in Milward, op. cit., p. 426.
5. Quotation from Barnett, *Collapse of British Power*, p. 258.
6. Ibid., p. 263.
7. Ibid., p. 262.
8. A report by a British Embassy official in Washington during the loan
   negotiations, December 1945, cited in Andrew Roberts, *The Holy Fox: A
   Biography of Lord Halifax*, p. 297.
9. For a detailed description of American help to Britain during the Falklands War see Dickie, op. cit., chapter 1.
10. Annual Pilgrims' dinner, London 1993.
11. Ronald Reagan, *An American Life* (New York, 1990), cited in Dickie,
    op. cit., p. 172.
12. Dickie, op. cit., p. 182.
13. When the Schuman proposals were made Britain had nationalised its coal
    industry and had plans to nationalise its steel industry too. Thus, the
    British government was reluctant to hand over its new-found control to a
    European authority – the Coal and Steel Authority.
14. Both quotations from John W. Young, *Britain and European Unity, 1945–
    1992* (London, 1993); the first, p. 29; the second, p. 44.
15. Both quotations, from ibid; in first quote, my italics.
16. Milward, op. cit., p. 395.
17. J. W. Young, op. cit., p. 53.
18. Quoted in P. Whitehead, *The Writing on the Wall* (London, 1985).
19. From an account by Pat Buchanan. 'Wise Up Europe, the Yanks Aren't
    Coming, *The European*, 27 May–2 June 1994.
20. Cited in Stephen Haseler and Werner Kaltefleiter, 'NATO and Neutral-
    ism', The Heritage Foundation (Washington, 1981).

21. Cited in Dickie, op. cit., p. 234.
22. Buchanan, op. cit.
23. *Independent*, 3 March 1994.
24. Cited in Horsman, op. cit., p. 201.
25. Based upon a Conference Board of New York report in 1992, cited in Horsman, op. cit., p. 201.
26. Edward Countryman, *The American Revolution* (New York, 1985).
27. Dye and Zeigler, *The Irony of Democracy*, 4th edn (Belmont, California, 1978) p. 26.
28. The Tenth Amendment to the US Constitution reassured the states that 'the powers not delegated to the United States ... are reserved to the states respectively, or to the people'. Thus, the states generally retain control over property and contract law, criminal law, marriage and divorce, the provision of education, highways, and social welfare activities, the control over the organization and powers of their own local governments. Finally, the states, like the federal government, retain the power to tax and spend for the general welfare.
29. Norman Lamont, at the Conservative Party Conference, Brighton, October 1994.
30. Answers to the question: 'On balance, do you support or oppose a United States of Europe with a federal government?'
    Belgium Yes 58% No 33%
    Denmark Yes 11% No 74%
    France Yes 33% No 45%
    Germany Yes 25% No 67%
    Greece Yes 50% No 31%
    Ireland Yes 33% No 56%
    Italy Yes 46% No 26%
    Luxembourg Yes 39% No 45%
    Netherlands Yes 21% No 73%
    Portugal Yes 18% No 40%
    Spain Yes 34% No 33%
    UK Yes 17% No 68%
    TOTAL Yes 32% No 49%.
31. Voting on the question of a single currency was published in the following week. Answers to the question 'On balance do you support or oppose a single currency?'
    Belgium Yes 74% No 25%
    Denmark Yes 29% No 61%
    France Yes 65% No 25%
    Germany Yes 45% No 50%
    Greece Yes 67% No 21%
    Ireland Yes 74% No 22%
    Italy Yes 73% No 12%
    Luxembourg Yes 64% No 28%
    Netherlands Yes 64% No 28%
    Portugal Yes 37% No 31%
    Spain Yes 68% No 21%
    UK Yes 40% No 55%
    TOTAL Yes 58% No 32%

32. *Eurobarometer*, Public Opinion in the European Community, Commission of the European Communities, no. 37 (June 1992) p. 48.
33. Ibid.
34. *The European*, 19–25 May 1994.
35. Ibid.
36. See Richard Kuisel, *Seducing the French, The Dilemma of Americanization* (London, 1993).
37. See Jack and Adam Lively (eds), *Democracy in Britain*, for a useful and stimulating account of Britain's contribution to the democratic experience.
38. Larry Siedentop, 'The Strange Life of a Liberal England', *Times Literary Supplement*, September 1985; and Neil Ascherson, *Games and Shadows* (London, 1988) p. 150.
39. Paul Johnson, *Wake Up Britain: A Latter-Day Pamphlet* (London, 1994) p. 175.

Notes to Chapter 6: Goodbye to All That

1. Quotation from Neil Ascherson, 5th Sovereignty Lecture, op. cit.
2. 'The European Movement of the UK', in *Reform of the European Union: Proposals for British Policy towards the Intergovernmental Conference of 1996* (1995) p. 7, suggests such an incorporation.
3. Horsman, op. cit., p. 83.
4. Alan Butt Philip, 'Old Policies and New Competences', in *Maastricht and Beyond*, eds Andrew Duff, John Pinder and Roy Price (London, 1994).
5. *The European*, 4 March 1994.
6. See Andrew Marr, *Battle for Scotland* (London, 1992); and Andrew Gamble, 'Territorial Politics', in *Developments in British Politics* (London, 1993) for some excellent analyses of contemporary developments in the Scottish National question.
7. In an interview with the Leader of the SNP, Alex Salmond, by Brian Walden on the eve of the 1992 general election, Salmond made the point that economic and political considerations, primarily Scottish oil, more than the strict legal position, would tend to govern the negotiations between a newly-independent Scotland and the European Union.
8. *Sunday Times*, 12 June 1994.
9. *The Times*, 5 October 1992.
10. See *The Times*, 15 November 1993.
11. J. Rinze, *Public Law* (London, 1993) p. 443.
12. Reported in the *Guardian*, 4 March 1994.
13. See Letters Page, *The Times*, 11 March 1994, letter by Walter Cairns.
14. See John Bell, *French Constitutional Law* (Oxford, 1994).
15. *Public Law*, Winter 1991.
16. Case 4/73, *Nold* v. *Commission European Court*, Reports 491 at 507, para 13.
17. The case was *R.* v. *Kirk*, Case 63/83 ECR 2689.
18. Source: Dept of Trade and Industry, EC Commission; cited in Michael Franklin, *Britain's Future in Europe* (London, 1990).
19. Gavin Davies, *Independent*, 31 May 1994.
20. James Goldsmith, *The Trap* (London, 1994) p. 18.

21. Will Hutton, *Guardian*, Monday, 20 March 1994.
22. Will Hutton, *Guardian*, Monday, 16 January 1995.
23. Alan Butt Philip, 'Old Policies and New Competences', op. cit., p. 131.
24. Reported in *The Times*, 9 June 1994.
25. Glenn Whitney, 'EU's wide bands for currencies seem to work well', *Wall Street Journal*, 1 August 1994.
26. Victor Smart, in *The European*, 4 March 1994.
27. Robert Minikin, *The ERM Explained* (London, 1993).
28. Quoted in David Marsh, 'EMU Strain Begins to Show', *Financial Times*, 17 January 1995.
29. Smart, op. cit.
30. Minikin, op. cit., p. 92.
31. Christopher Johnson, 'Fiscal and Monetary Policy in EMU', in Duff *et al.* (eds), op. cit., p. 78.
32. The Treaty on European Union, Maastricht, Article 109j, section 4.
33. Ibid., section 3.
34. Article 109k, section 2, of the Treaty on European Union, Maastricht, allows the nation-states which receive a 'derogation' to join later when their economies meet the convergence criteria.
35. Allan Saunderson, *The European*, 22–28 April 1994.
36. Quoted in *Suddeutsche Zeitung*, from *European Press Survey*, vol. 1, no. 11, 29 June 1994.
37. *International Herald Tribune*, 10 February 1994.
38. US Ambassador Raymond Seitz's address to the Pilgrims' Society, reprinted in edited form by *The Times*, 20 April 1994.
39. See Article B of the Treaty on European Union, Maastricht.
40. *The European*, 6–12 May 1994.
41. Geoffrey Edwards and Simon Nuttall, 'Common Foreign and Security Policy', in Duff *et al.* (eds), op. cit., p. 95.

Index